ALEX MACKAY'S COOKBOOK FOR
EVERYBODY
EVERYDAY

ALEX MACKAY'S COOKBOOK FOR
EVERYBODY
EVERYDAY

Photography by Peter Knab

BLOOMSBURY
LONDON · BERLIN · NEW YORK · SYDNEY

CONTENTS

ADVENTURES WITH INGREDIENTS   36

Six 'heroic' ingredients, and six super ways to serve each one

THE MAGIC FRIDGE   124

Six saucy standbys, and six tricks to turn each one into dinner

SLOW COOK SORCERY   224

Six fantastic feasts, and six wizardly ways to transform their leftovers

HOW I COOK

Take me to your kitchen. Let me show you how to make everyday food delicious and delicious food every day. No starters, no sweets, just three practical ways to help you cook your meals and vary them easily. First, I'll take you on a series of adventures where I'll show you how to cook six easy-to-find ingredients and serve them six different ways. Next, I'll reveal how to add magic to your food with six ways to use six saucy standbys. After that, I'll show you six ways to transform the leftovers created from six slow-cooked meals.

The seed of the idea for this book was sown fifteen years ago when Raymond Blanc put me in charge of his cookery school, and I realised that I had to show people what they could cook rather than just show off! I then moved to my own cookery school in Provence, where I answered questions from morning to midnight. My transformation from restaurant chef to home cook became complete after a decade of teaching regularly with Delia Smith and meeting thousands of people who love, and rely upon, her meticulously tested recipes.

Raymond taught me to taste, Delia taught me to test, but it was the questions from home cooks that taught me to think carefully about everything I do in the kitchen.

The most important ingredient

I've written most of the recipes for two, so they're easily halved or multiplied. Each recipe is opposite a picture of the finished dish, because that's how I put my food in front of you. My recipes are practical, sometimes exciting, other times comforting, often economical and they will make you more confident as you learn. But a recipe book has to be about taste above anything else, and every recipe here kicks and screams with flavour. My recipes don't rely on expensive or hard-to-find ingredients. That's not what I'm here for; I just want to help you cook. The most important ingredient in your kitchen is your desire to be there.

Before you start cooking, I'll ask you to read a short introductory section. First, there's How to Use this Book (pages 10–15). Then, because I'm obsessed with the subject, there's How I Season (pages 16–19). After that, there are ABCs of Ingredients Prep & Tips (pages 20–25), Cooking Terms & Techniques (pages 26–29) and Equipment (pages 30–35). Through these I hope to show you that the more comfortable you feel in your kitchen, the more you will enjoy cooking, and the more pleasure your food will give.

Good cooking is not about making something completely different every day; it's about cooking something good. It's easier to cook something good if the process feels familiar, and it's hard to cook a recipe for the first time. But cooking is like anything – if you practise, you get better at it. You don't want to eat the same thing every day, though, so I'll show you how to change meals just a little to make them taste entirely new. I'd like to show you that repetition can bring variety and excitement. Once repetition makes you as confident at baking a piece of salmon or chicken as you are toasting bread it's just as easy to change the topping to make it taste completely different. I've cooked and eaten every meal in this book countless times with my wife Jess and sons Jake and James. I'll continue to do so; these recipes are a joyful part of our everyday lives.

Your smile will always make its way into your food. This smile comes from the confidence that is gained through practice, and learning to decide what you're going to do before you do it. Start with a tidy kitchen, get everything you need in one place before you begin, rely on thermometers and a timer, learn to use your senses to help you, and your food will taste all the better for it.

Feeding young kids

If you get your kids interested in cooking and eating, they will have a gift for life. There is no such thing as kids' food. Don't make separate meals for adults and kids; make one meal and adjust it slightly. Put in less of an ingredient that they might be unsure of, leave it out entirely or cut it differently, then serve their food before you season yours. (No salt is the best starting place for kids; they don't know it and they don't need it.) When our kids were tiny, they ate earlier than we did; we still ate the same food, but they would eat it the next day. We'd chop or purée their portions in a mini-processor or blender, and freeze any leftovers in flexible ice-cube trays for times when we had no time. I'll give you suggestions for this in the introduction to each recipe. A microwave is the best way to heat these up; how I've come to love this little oven.

I've learnt that it is most often texture, not taste, that stops kids trying new foods. Don't be afraid to give kids new tastes. Flavours like cinnamon, curry, Chinese five spice, basil and mint are enticing for kids if you introduce them in small quantities. While I'll certainly never force my kids to eat anything, I'll never stop trying to feed them good things. (Though I've learnt not to give them other food between meals if they don't eat what's on the table.) I try not to let mealtimes get associated with stress.

The best way to get kids interested in eating is to get them interested in cooking. A kitchen is a playground for kids' curiosity. Cooking teaches kids about their senses. Cooking encapsulates reading, maths, geography, social studies, languages, sharing, safety and glorious manual skills. If you don't have much time, cooking is the best way to combine play and practicality, as you can be with your kids, and have dinner ready at the end of it. It might take a little longer, but only a little, and it's time you get together, so each minute is its own reward.

Ask your kids to help choose the ingredients while you shop, and encourage them to handle and smell the different fruit and vegetables as you go along. At home there are endless everyday activities in the kitchen for kids. Show them how to measure with spoons and scales, spread butter on toast, pick herbs off plants, bang garlic, sprinkle cheese, grind pepper, stir, whisk, spin salad, squeeze citrus and set the table. You'll start them on an adventure that will last a lifetime of meals. For more about cooking with kids, and notes on the individual recipes, visit www.everybodyeveryday.co.

Taste, taste, taste

We'll go a long way and pay a lot of money for a delightful scent or a delicious taste. But these are things you can experience every day in your kitchen if you engage your senses. Tasting, constantly, is the best thing that you can do. I'll give you everything I can to help you, but the only person who knows how much to season your food is you, and the only 'right' way for you to eat it is the way you like it best.

I've said enough, now come and cook with me. Bring your spoon, your smile and the tip of your tongue. Take me to your kitchen.

HOW TO USE THIS BOOK

By nature I am the messiest, most chaotic, finger-licking, sauce-smearing, every-spoon-in-the-house-using, tea-towel-singeing tornado of a cook. But when I demonstrate recipes I'm pretty tidy, and I'm often told I make things look easy. It only looks easy because everything is ready before I start, and all I need to think about is cooking my ingredients and using my utensils, not searching for either. To test the recipes for this book I confined myself to the 90cm long worktop next to my cooker in my galley kitchen, and I worked as I do when I demonstrate. I had a great time doing it, and what I learnt during the process is distilled in the next few pages.

Before you start...

Choose your recipe and read it through The key to getting a recipe right is to know what you are going to do before you do it, and to be sure that your ingredients and equipment are ready. However good a cook you are, when you prepare a recipe for the first time it won't feel easy. I find cooking someone else's recipe hard for the first few times, and I've cooked professionally for over twenty years. No matter how few ingredients or steps a recipe has, it is only 'simple' once you are familiar with it.

I have, however, tried to keep the shopping simple from the start. My recipes only use ingredients that should be easy to find at any reasonably sized supermarket. The three exceptions to this are mince, belly pork and lamb shoulder, which I buy from my butcher. Choose the freshest and best ingredients in your price range and cook them wonderfully.

Decide how many you are serving I've written most of these recipes to serve two, because it is the easiest number to divide for one serving, or multiply to serve four, six, eight or more. Scale the recipes according to the number you are cooking for, and while you do, consider cooking extra to give yourself the base for another meal (see page 15). On the whole my portions are on the large side. If you scale the recipes up or down, take into account the size of saucepans and frying pans, as a lot more or less food will need different size pans, which may change cooking times a bit.

Decide on any side dishes Many of the recipes are complete meals, so consider what, if anything, you'd like to serve with your meal. I've indicated where I think there is a need for something. I've also given options 'for bulk', in case you're really hungry, or you want to stretch the meal further, say to make two portions of chicken serve three. Sometimes I've given suggestions where I think an accompaniment would be nice, but is not essential. Have a look through Side Dishes (pages 320–43), choose something you like and see how it fits in with the timing of your main recipe, as you may need to start the side dish first.

Give yourself enough time I have given you **prep ahead** suggestions where applicable in case you want to get ahead, but you don't have to.

The **prep/cooking** time indicates how long to allow overall. I appreciate that I probably chop faster than you do, and I've no way of knowing how long it takes you to find things in your cupboards or fridge, so the prep allocation is the time I've taken to do it, plus a bit extra. The first few times will always take you longer.

The **active time** is the amount of time you can expect to spend actually doing something rather than waiting for things to cook; this includes anything you need to stand in front of while it cooks rather than just set a timer and leave.

Start with a clear worktop If you start in a mess you will finish in a bigger mess. Get rid of anything on your work surface that doesn't get used all the time, ie everything except your kettle, microwave and chopping board. Clear yourself a space to prepare your ingredients and cook. Make sure your dishwasher is empty or, if you don't have a dishwasher, have a washing up bowl full of hot water that you can put dirty dishes into, leaving your sink free to drain or rinse ingredients.

Preheat your oven I will tell you which shelf position you'll need at the start of each recipe; adjust it before you turn on your oven, so you don't burn your hands doing it when the shelves are hot. To check that your oven gets to the right temperature, use an oven thermometer. If your oven is not hot enough, or too hot, your recipe may not work.

Get your workspace ready Work next to your cooker so that you can see what is happening with a glance. Make your chopping board your base and put a wet cloth underneath it to stop it slipping. Have a plastic or metal tray, about 40 x 30cm, between your chopping board and the wall. Call this your prep tray. Put all of the ingredients for your recipe on the tray before you start, to save jumping about from fridge to cupboard to search for elusive ingredients while others boil and fry. Put bottles at the back of the tray so you don't knock them over getting to other things.

Stand two tall metal or plastic tubs, about 16–18cm in diameter, on or next to the tray, half-filling one of them with water (to stop it tipping over). Get the utensils you need for the recipe and put them into the half-filled tub. After you've used a utensil, rinse and then put it back into the tub, so you have it to hand when you need it next. Put your whisk in handle downwards, otherwise it will pull everything else out when you grab it. Put your rubbish and peelings directly into the second tub to keep your board clear.

If you need a bowl to drain fat into, a rack to rest meat on and/or a colander in your sink, get these ready now too. Boil your kettle.

Follow your recipe...

The ingredients list If I've indicated that something needs to be peeled or chopped or weighed in the ingredients list, do this before you start cooking. The exceptions to this are the small spoon measures. Just keep your set of measuring spoons and ingredients to measure in spoonfuls on your tray. If you're using powdered stock, make this up now too. Now, put away anything that you no longer need. The ingredients are listed in the order in which they are used in the recipe. Line them up in that order and you won't leave anything out. Also, if you need to add something to a pan quickly, you'll be able to grab it instantly. Once you get to know a recipe, you can work out what preparation you can do comfortably while other things cook.

Measure your ingredients accurately All spoons are level unless I've said otherwise. Apart from where I ask you to slice or dice an ingredient as thinly or finely you can, I've given measurements, as everyone has a different idea of 'finely chopped', 'thickly sliced' etc. The size of something you cook is just as important as the weight – a 4cm slice of carrot will take longer to cook than a 1cm slice. Use a ruler to give you a good starting point.

The method I have written the recipe instructions in short 'single task' sentences so you can concentrate on one job at a time. Confidence comes from the feeling of being in control. Don't waste one hand holding a tray, pan or bowl that could rest on the worktop or hob, so that you have two hands to work with. Don't panic if things aren't going quite to plan. Keep an eye on things as they cook. The best bet if something is happening too fast in a pan is to take it off the heat. Use your timer, and using a thermometer with a probe to check the interior temperature of your chicken, pork or burger will teach you exactly how the meat feels and looks when it is cooked.

Variations in the size and initial temperature, the way your hob and oven perform and many other factors will affect how a recipe works, so it is most important to keep testing, touching and tasting.

Heat your plates. Hot plates give you more time to serve up your food without it getting cold.

Preparing to serve...

Before you dish up, run through this checklist:

- Make sure that you have your cutlery and drinks on the table so that once you are ready with the food you can sit and eat.
- If a cold sauce, cream, salad or bread is served on the side or at the end, put it on your table, so you don't forget it and you've got less to put on the plate in your kitchen.
- Make sure you have a clear space on your worktop next to the food on (or in) your cooker, and check you've got the utensils you need.

- Put a rack on your worktop or have a space on your hob for hot pans.
- Boil your kettle again, as you may need to add boiling water to a sauce or put a pan to soak before you sit down.
- Have an oven glove or dry tea towel handy so that you don't burn your hands on hot pans or trays.
- Make sure everything is cooked before you start dishing up. If everything is not ready at the same time, none of the hot food in this book (except fried eggs) will be ruined if you keep it warm for a few minutes in your oven at 50°C with the door slightly ajar.
- Check you've got any food out of the oven and microwave. I'm always forgetting things at the last minute.

Once you are ready to dish up...

Take a minute to do the things that make a nice meal delicious. Taste and season everything to make sure it is as good as it can be. Make your meat glossy with its cooking juices. Stir a knob of butter through your peas and season them with salt and pepper. Add a spoonful of boiling water to your pasta so that it's slippery and loose...

Presenting your meal...

I like food to look lovely and I like it to look tempting. Making everyday food look good is more about good cooking and getting everything ready before you start to serve than it is fancy fiddling. If green vegetables are cooked carefully so they stay bright green, a sliced tomato shines with seasoned dressing, fried potatoes are golden, lamb glistens with gravy, pasta flows irresistibly, the milky residue is brushed off salmon, a cheese topping is bubbling brown, and soft herbs are vibrant because you've added them at the last minute, then your food presents itself for you.

Some recipes are best served in their cooking vessel. I love passing food around in pots and spooning hot sauces onto food directly from saucepans; it's inviting, sociable and your food stays hot for longer. I avoid intermediate serving dishes that I have to wash up and find extra space for. Whether you serve your food in pots or on plates, try to make best use of the ingredients' natural beauty and contrasting colours. Brush your food with its cooking juices, sauce, or dressing – an intensely flavoured sheen makes your mouth water and your meal leap towards you. If your food sits and starts to look dull, then freshen it up with another brush at the last minute.

Beyond that, making food look good is about dishing up with confidence. It is vital to put things down and make both your hands available. If you're dishing up on plates, pull them close to you so that you don't have to lean over them. Put one item on all of your plates before you start with the next one, decide where you're going to put it before you position it and leave it there.

If you move the food you'll smear your plates. Spoon sauces and dressings onto your food at the table. Clear as you go, putting small things onto your prep tray and pans in a pile on your rack or cooker to keep your worktop clear.

Good cooking makes food look good. Having everything ready and close to you makes presenting it fun.

After your meal...

Cooking extra I'll show you later how you can double up some recipes and freeze half for another meal, and how others are good to make into sandwiches, salads or wraps for a portable lunch the next day. As a general suggestion, you will need to season cooked food more generously if you are going to eat it cold.

Sometimes you need a little glue to hold a filling together, particularly for wraps: in place of mayonnaise, try chickpea purée (page 341), yoghurt, quark, tomato compote (page 177), basil pesto (page 129), tapenade (page 145) or soft, sweet, sticky onions (page 161). As well as sandwiches and wraps, I've discovered a number of pre-cooked grains that I now use as the base for salads with my leftovers; they provide tasty bulk in much the same way as bread and give you more variety.

Cooking extra gives you varied and exciting lunch boxes, and saves you time and money.

Leftovers If you don't know when you're going to use leftovers, put them in a container, let them cool completely and then cover, label and freeze them, rather than put things back into the fridge to be forgotten and go off. If you reheat something from the freezer rather than the fridge it only takes a few minutes longer in the microwave. Freeze your leftovers in portions and they become homemade ready meals that you can just heat and eat.

Freezing I've always had better luck freezing cooked food than raw. Everything cooked changes slightly when you freeze it, but very little in most cases. And in the case of your homemade ready meals, they'll often taste even better because they are there when you need them most, with very little effort and even less washing up. I've kept cooked meals in airtight containers in my freezer for months. Plastic takeaway containers with tight-fitting lids are ideal – they fit a single portion and they stack easily.

Clearing up Wipe your oven when it cools every night, at the same time as you wash up or load the dishwasher. It'll only take you a minute, keep the oven clean and if any fat has dripped onto the bottom it won't burn the next time you turn the oven on. If you're roasting, put an oven tray with slightly raised sides on the bottom shelf of the oven to catch any fat and prevent it burning on the oven floor.

HOW I SEASON

Taste. Season a little. Taste again. Season again if you need to. Good cooking is about little things that make a difference, and seasoning is the simplest way to make the most impact on your everyday cooking. It can be the difference between a recipe that is nice and one that is fantastic. I love the French word *relever*, to pick up, to lift and to liven flavours. My seasonings are my liveners, my pick-me-ups.

I season with salt, dry and fresh spices, curry powder, sugar, citrus zest, citrus juice, honey, olives, herbs, vinegars, bacon fat, fruit juice and dried fruit. I use small quantities of these to enhance other ingredients without overpowering them. In my Adventures with Ingredients chapter (pages 36–123) I'll show you how to transform ingredients with different seasonings.

Instead of pepper

We're locked into pepper, we reach for it after salt when we hear 'season' because we've always done so. Pepper goes with most things, but so does curry powder, fresh ginger, paprika, ras-el-hanout or chilli. Get to know the spices you like. If you feel comfortable with just three or four more than pepper, you can vary what you eat a great deal. The idea is to stop automatically reaching for your pepper grinder and to ask yourself where you would like your spices to take you today.

Throughout the book, I've suggested a choice of spices instead of pepper where they suit an individual recipe. It'll just be a pinch unless I'm asking you to make the food spicy; you can always add more or less to suit your personal taste. When I say season to taste and I don't specify, I mean that you should use the salt/spice/sugar in the ingredients list.

How to season

Add salt first I add salt to bring flavours out, not to make things taste salty. Salt strengthens a spice or citrus juice's flavour, so add it to a sauce, salad or anything else first, taste, and then add your other seasonings. Cold food often needs more help than hot; season food at the temperature that you will eat it at.

Balance/over-seasoning To balance salt, sweet, acid and spice you need to add a little seasoning at a time and keep tasting. You can always add more, even at the table if you want to, but you can't take it out. If a sauce or dressing is too sweet, add a touch of lemon or vinegar. If it is too acidic, add a touch of sugar. If it is too rich or cloying, add a touch of lemon juice, vinegar or spice. If it is too salty, the only rescue is to add more liquid. You will avoid over-salting by tasting but if it does happen, make another recipe of the sauce or dressing without salt, mix the two together, then keep or freeze half for another time.

Season both sides from a height Take your time. Make sure your chicken breast, salmon fillet or halved aubergine, for example, lie flat rather than overlap and sprinkle your salt and spices from 20cm above them. Sprinkling from higher up distributes the seasoning more evenly and all of the ingredient will have a little, rather than some too much and some none at all. Once you've seasoned one side, turn it over and season the other side; it will be twice as tasty. When I use a fine powder like paprika, I sprinkle it on, then brush it into the ingredient for maximum impact.

Season all elements as equals Taste and season your vegetables, salad, sauce and anything else separately, with the same amount of care, and your meals will be much better for it. When I don't want contrasting flavours, I often use the same spice to season more than one element of a meal, a salmon fillet and its sauce for example. The spice joins the elements together and makes them into a dish that flows from one mouthful to the next. In these cases I season each element quite sparingly so that the whole meal gently hums with spice rather than having one part that overpowers the others.

Everyday seasonings

Fine salt I use fine table salt to season most ingredients because it covers and sticks to them more evenly. It also dissolves quickly and completely in sauces and liquids so that you can taste and tell almost instantly if you've added enough or you need to add more.

Salt flakes and coarse salt I love salt flakes as a luxury. I sprinkle them onto everything from steaks to sliced tomatoes as a finishing touch. I like the crunch, either on its own or mixed with spices, thyme, rosemary or citrus zest. Salt flakes are very different to coarse or rock salt, which is not really intended for sprinkling as it is hard rather than crunchy. Coarse salt is best used in grinders and for curing or marinating.

Pepper Unless I specify black or white pepper, you can use either, preferably, but not strictly, freshly ground. If I use pepper along with another spice, the pepper is there for gentle heat and aggression and the second seasoning, nutmeg for example, is there for fragrance.

Cayenne pepper/chilli I use cayenne pepper frequently with tomatoes, peppers and many other ingredients, almost never enough to make a meal spicy, but to add a gentle bite. Chilli powder will do the same job.

Sugar Like salt, sugar brings out flavours that are already there. I add it to savoury food to enhance the natural sweetness – of cooked tomatoes and peppers, for example. Sugar is vital to balance and improve dressings made with lemon or vinegar, or any sauce made with red wine. You never need much, just enough to calm down the acidity and in the case of red wine, the tannins. Unless I say otherwise, all sugar is caster or granulated.

Citrus juice Lemon and lime juice are very strong. I'll ask you to use citrus juice in specific spoonfuls to ensure that it doesn't overpower your other ingredients. You can always add more if you want to, just keep tasting and balance the juice with sugar if necessary. When I use orange juice I generally boil and reduce it first so that it has a more concentrated impact. Roll all citrus fruit between your palm and your worktop before you squeeze them; this softens the fruit so that it is easier to squeeze and yields more juice.

Citrus zest Citrus fruit's fresh-tasting, brightly coloured, thin outer skin is an excellent seasoning, but the white pith directly under it tastes bitter and needs to be avoided.

I grate the zest finely when I only want the taste. I use a zester when I want longer strips for texture or presentation as for the chicken, jerk spice and sticky onion recipe (on page 164), but that's just an old Alex habit; you can grate your zest for all of the recipes. Grate zest directly into your bowl or onto your food so you don't lose the spray that comes off the zest with each movement; this spray adds almost as much flavour as the zest itself. Once you grate the zest from a section of a citrus fruit, don't grate that part again as you'll hit the pith; turn the fruit to a section that still has zest on it.

Dried orange zest This is an incredible seasoning that enlivens stews and tomato-based sauces. Make a batch with 5 oranges. Use a vegetable peeler to remove the zest, but not the white pith, in long strips. Line a baking sheet with greaseproof paper. Scatter the zest over the top in a single layer. Dry the zest in the oven at 110°C/lowest Gas for 2–3 hours until brittle but not brown. Leave to cool. Stored in a sealed jar in a cool dark place, it will keep for months.

Spices I've used pre-mixed curry powder and spice mixtures to make the recipes as accessible as possible. I buy my spices in sealable foil bags or I cover clear glass bottles with foil and store them in a cool dark place. Their flavour and colour fades in the light and heat.

Liquid seasonings Use raw vinegars for a little bite; boil and reduce them for a deeper taste. Balsamic syrup, soy sauce, brown sauce and Worcestershire sauce add a lot of their own flavour, but sometimes this is exactly what a meal and your mood needs.

None of this information is any use if you don't taste your food as you cook. When I say 'season to taste' in my recipes I mean season to your taste and give the vital touch that turns a meal from good to glorious.

Taste, season a little, taste again. Season again if you need to.

ABC OF INGREDIENTS
PREP & TIPS

These are the tips that relate to more than one of my recipes. If you can, buy your vegetables, meat and fish loose so you get exactly what you need. Where I use a packet or tin, it is almost always all or half of it, so you're not left with odds and ends. If I ask you to use half a tin or packet, I'll give you a suggestion for the remainder, either alongside the recipe or in Side Dishes (pages 320–43).

Aubergines I don't salt aubergines for the recipes in this book, because it isn't necessary. Today's aubergines do not have bitter juices to degorge and salting aubergines ruins their soft and creamy texture.

Breadcrumbs I use up old bread and crusts to make coarse breadcrumbs (like the ones I use for the cassoulet topping on page 252). They need to be completely dried out in a low oven before I blend them. Fresh bread will only blend into crumbs if you cut the crusts off first. In either case, make extra breadcrumbs and freeze them in an airtight container so you've got some whenever you need them.

Chestnuts I use vacuum-packed peeled, roasted chestnuts, which are always stuck together inside their bags. To make them easy to separate, simmer the bags of chestnuts in a pan of hot water for 5 minutes before you open them. You can freeze any leftovers.

Chillies The easily available, large mild chillies are the ones I generally use in recipes, for their colour and gentle bite – more for seasoning and appeal to the eye than to make the food very spicy. Don't touch your eyes or skin as you prepare them and wash your hands immediately afterwards.

Coconut milk In some recipes I use this in small quantities. Freeze the rest of your tin in little tubs in recipe-sized quantities.

Cream and crème fraîche Whipping cream, double cream, full- and half-fat crème fraîche can all be used to make cream sauces. Your sauce will only separate if you boil it too long and reduce it too far. Watch over the sauce as it thickens and take the pan off the heat as soon as it just coats the back of a spoon. If it does start to separate, take it off the heat and whisk in 1–3 tbsp of hot water. As a side dish, soured cream, yoghurt and half- or full-fat crème fraîche are interchangeable in my recipes.

Cream cheese/mascarpone/quark You can interchange these, though quark has little fat and a more tangy taste. They don't freeze well, so if you have any left over, mix it with icing or caster sugar and vanilla or orange zest for a flavoured 'cream' to serve with berries or roast fruit.

Filo pastry Keep filo pastry in the fridge until you need it. Only take out what you need. Keep it covered with cling film or a very lightly dampened J-cloth while it's out and work fairly quickly. Freeze the remainder in multiples of 2 or 4 sheets, wrapped in cling film, supported by a bit of cardboard from the box so it doesn't snap in the freezer. If your filo pastry does dry and crack, you can scatter the scraps over the top of a shepherd's pie, or stewed fruit, dab the pastry with melted butter (and sprinkle with icing sugar for fruit) and it will crisp up wonderfully.

Fish Join Hugh Fearnley-Whittingstall's fish fight (go to fishfight.net) to learn more about sustainable fish.

Fruit juice I use a lot of fruit juice in savoury recipes: as a seasoning, in dressings, instead of stock, and instead of wine. If you replace wine with fruit juice, your sauce will be sweeter, but you can balance this with vinegar.

Garlic Bulbs or 'heads' vary in size. In my recipes one garlic clove is an average clove from an average-sized head, which is the size of a golf ball, weighs about 35g and has about 12 cloves. If you have very large cloves, halve the amount; if they are very small, double the amount. I like a lot of garlic but none of the recipes taste strongly of garlic. If you are less keen, then halve the quantity.

To peel a large quantity of garlic, put the cloves in a bowl and cover them with boiling water. Leave the cloves until they are just cool enough to handle, then peel them. The skin will have softened and come away from the inner clove, which makes them easier to peel. If you're just using a few cloves, smack them with the heel of your hand to make the skin easier to peel.

I often slice rather than chop garlic, simply because it is quicker. You might prefer to chop your garlic in a mini-chopper. I don't like garlic presses; if you do, remember that you lose quite a bit in the press.

Gravy, pan This comes from the caramelised juices in a pan after you've fried a burger, steak or chop. While your meat rests, vigorously stir a few spoonfuls of water into the pan juices off the heat, boil it and then add a knob of butter. Tip in the juices from the resting plate. Brush and coat the meat with the glistening juices – they make the difference between good and great.

Gravy, roast I love roast gravy and I make sure my recipes have plenty of it. Soaking up gravy with bread, mash, grains or leaves is one of the most exciting things that can happen on a plate. The true flavour comes from the roasting juices in the tray. Any extra small bones or chicken wings that you can add to your tray will make your gravy taste more of the roast. I make gravy with stock rather than water so that I get a more intense flavour and don't need to reduce it down as much. I often add dark soy sauce to gravy to deepen the colour.

If you like a thicker gravy, you can thicken it with more cornflour than I suggest. Mix 1 part cornflour with 3 parts water until smooth. Bring your gravy to the boil and whisk in a little of the diluted cornflour. If your gravy is still not thick enough, add a little more. Boil your gravy for 10 seconds to cook out the taste of the cornflour.

Don't keep gravy warm for long, or it will lose the flavour of the main ingredient and taste stewed. Once your gravy is ready, take the pan off the heat. When you're ready to serve your gravy, heat it up quickly. If you have gravy left over, freeze it.

Herbs Keep pots of herbs on your windowsill so that you have them as fresh as possible and you don't need to buy a whole bunch each time you need a few leaves. If you can only buy bunches, cut 2cm off the stalks, wrap the herbs in damp kitchen paper and submerge the ends of the stalks in a mug of water in the fridge; they will keep for 4–5 days (change the water twice).

As a general rule, add soft herbs (basil, chives, coriander, mint, parsley etc) to recipes at the last minute; add hard herbs (rosemary, sage, thyme etc) early on to slow-cooked recipes. But many 'hard' herbs are now grown indoors and are softer, so I'm also happy to add them – thyme, in particular – to recipes at the last minute.

As the size of bunches and leaves varies so much, I've given herb quantities in spoonfuls. Pick the leaves and pack them into measuring spoons (gently in the case of basil): 1 very heaped spoonful of leaves will equal 1 level spoonful once you've sliced them, so you'll get the right amount with no waste. Having said this, soft herbs are a seasoning, which is a personal thing, so feel free to adjust the amount to suit your taste. You can also change the herb if you like, using mint instead of basil for example. An exception to this is tarragon, which is very pungent and best used sparingly.

Only wash herbs before you cut them if you really need to, and dry them well afterwards. If the leaves are wet you will end up with mush rather than sliced herbs that you can scatter. Stack soft herbs and slice them through with a sharp knife or snip with scissors. I slice mine about 5mm thick so you can taste them but they don't overpower the other ingredients. There's no need to chop them finely. Only cut herbs in a chopper/processor if you prepare a lot for pesto; a small amount will catch in the blades and get bruised rather than cut. I cut rosemary and sage very finely, otherwise they are unpleasant to chew.

Honey I use this in some recipes, but if you don't like the flavour replace it with fine-cut or rindless marmalade. Honey can harden or crystallise in the jar; it is still fine to use and will become liquid if you warm it.

Mussels These need to be bought live. Make sure your fishmonger doesn't seal them in a foil bag, or they will quickly die. When you get your mussels home, wrap them in a wet tea towel and store them in a bowl in the fridge. It's best to eat mussels within a day and prepare them just before steaming. If a mussel is open, tap it on your worktop. It should close or at least try to;

if it doesn't, it's dead and must be thrown away. Most mussels have a hairy 'beard' attached to the join in their shell. Pull it lengthways from the thin pointed end of the mussel down to the thick end to remove it easily. Rinse the mussels under cold running water and they're ready to cook; you don't need to scrape the shells.

Make sure that the water is boiling before you add your mussels; I rarely add wine as I prefer to maximise the mussel taste. Cover the pan tightly and steam them open as quickly as possible, over your highest possible heat. Any mussel that doesn't open enough for you to see the flesh inside must be thrown away. From an average 1kg bag, I'll discard 3–5 mussels before or after cooking.

Oil When I ask you to use vegetable oil, you can use sunflower or any other non-scented oil in its place. In most cases I use oil to help stop ingredients from sticking to a pan, or to keep them moist during baking. (You only need a thin film in the bottom of the pan, so feel free to use an oil spray; it does the job and you'll use less oil.) Fritters, however, need more to crisp the edges.

Olive oil Light and heat can ruin the flavour of extra virgin olive and other cold-pressed oils. If you can, buy extra virgin olive oil in dark bottles and store it somewhere cool and dark. It is best to buy smaller bottles because, once you open it, olive oil tends to deteriorate within about 6 weeks, even when it is stored carefully. It is a waste to use extra virgin or cold-pressed nut oils for frying because these oils burn at a lower temperature than vegetable oils and their flavour is ruined by high heat, but I'm happy to sweat vegetables in extra virgin olive oil at a low temperature.

Olives I mostly use black olives cured à la grecque or little Niçoise olives in olive oil for my recipes. See tapenade (page 145) for further notes.

Onions The size can make a big difference to a recipe, so where necessary I'll give you the weight. In other cases, I'll suggest small or medium onions. As a guide, 1 small onion weighs 80–120g and 1 medium onion weighs 130–160g.

When you peel onions, only cut off the very end of the root, as the rest holds the layers together and makes it easier to slice. Cut the onion in half first, then lay it cut side down on your board and slice it.

Parmesan An easy way to grate Parmesan is to cut it into chunks and grind it in a mini food processor; I also prefer the texture when it's prepared this way.

Prawns If you get the chance, buy raw prawns with their shells on and use the shells to make a quick stock (see page 108), which you can freeze.

Puff pastry Shop-bought, ready-rolled puff pastry is convenient to use. Packets of pre-rolled pastry aren't all the same weight or size, so please look at the final measurements you need for the recipe. Freeze any you have left over, in pieces cut to the size that you are most likely to use. You will find that it is easier to cut puff pastry cleanly when it is cold and hard; if the pastry is not cold, you will squash the layers together and they won't rise as well.

Soy sauce Use dark rather than light soy sauce for my recipes, except vegetarian curry paste.

Stock I realise that you won't always have fresh stock to hand so I set out to cook all of these recipes using powdered rather than fresh stock. My effort was rewarded because I've come up with ways to use 'instant' stock as a base for sauces and gravies without overpowering the more natural flavours. In some cases I decided water was ok, in others I've used fruit juice, and for bangers and mash I decided that the powder's taste was just right.

If I say 'stock or water' in the ingredient list, I mean that stock will give you a stronger taste but water will work too; you'll just have to season it a bit more. If I'm using bouillon powder or a stock cube, I use three-quarters of the amount suggested on the packet or tub to the amount of liquid, to get a less overpowering flavour.

Make stock with leftover chicken or duck bones (from the recipes on pages 229 and 277 respectively). Put the bones into a large pot. To deglaze the roasting tray, add water, boil and then scrape. Add the liquid and any caramelised bits to the pot. Cover with water and bring to the boil. Skim the surface. Add two chopped onions and two garlic cloves. Simmer for 3 hours. Strain into a clean pan. Bring to the boil and reduce by three-quarters. Freeze the stock in ice-cube trays. Transfer the frozen cubes to a plastic container to store in the freezer. When you need stock, use one cube and three times its volume in water.

Tinned pulses Most tins I use are 400g. If they need to be drained, I'll say so in the ingredients list. If I don't then you'll be using their liquor as well.

Tinned tomatoes The mid-priced range of tinned tomatoes is fine for my recipes. To boost the flavour of a cheap tin, add 1 tbsp tomato purée. If you need only half a tin, freeze the rest of the tomatoes in a sealed container.

Wine for cooking 'The better the wine, the better the dish' is simply not true for any recipe where it will be cooked for a long time or reduced. What you do need is gutsy wine with body and, if it's red, a deep colour. I'd suggest Cabernet Sauvignon or Shiraz for red, Chardonnay for white.

Vinegar I'll ask you to boil the vinegar until it is almost dry in some recipes. This is so that you get a concentrated and more balanced acidity rather than the overwhelming taste of raw vinegar in your sauce.

Yoghurt I find the lower fat the yoghurt, the more acidic it is; this can be nice as a seasoning, but keep it in mind.

ABC OF COOKING
TERMS & TECHNIQUES

These are the cooking terms and techniques that I use in this book.

Baste I baste food with gravy, oil and dressings to flavour and moisten the exterior. I use a brush rather than a spoon to get a full and even coating.

Boil Water is boiling when it is bubbling furiously in the pan on your highest heat. The quickest way to boil water is to use your kettle. So when you need a pan of boiling water, boil your kettle. At the same time, fill your pan one-third full with water and bring to the boil. When the kettle boils, fill the pan just over two-thirds full (or as much as you need to). It takes a short while for water to come back to the boil once you've added an ingredient to it, so it's important that you start your cooking time once it's bubbling furiously again.

Braise To cook meat or fish on top of, but not totally submerged in, a liquid, sauce or vegetables. Flavours are exchanged, the liquid reduces as it cooks, and the taste gets more concentrated. If I cover the cooking dish, instead of a tight-fitting lid, I use greaseproof paper to let steam escape rather than dilute the flavours. Braising is best done in the oven rather than on the hob, as the heat is more even and the food is less likely to catch on the bottom of the pan.

Brush I use a pastry brush to brush rather than drizzle or sprinkle seasonings and oil onto ingredients, to coat them evenly and completely.

Caramelise This doesn't just apply to heating sugar. It describes frying or roasting onions, meat or other ingredients to a golden caramel colour.

Carve I carve meat in large pieces or thick slices. It's quicker and easier, the meat stays hotter and I prefer the texture. It's worth keeping a razor-sharp knife just for carving. Like wood, meat has a grain and you need to carve across the meat's fibres, not in the same direction. This presses the fibres together to give you smooth slices and makes the meat more tender to chew.

Chop Learn to chop well and it will make your life much easier in the kitchen. Cut large and cumbersome round ingredients like potatoes or onions in half before you chop them and put them flat side down on your board so that they don't roll around as you slice and chop. Feel free to use a food processor.

Coating consistency When I ask you to boil a liquid until it is 'thick enough to coat the back of a spoon', run your finger down the back of the spoon and it should leave a channel. Take your pan off the heat while you check this. If a liquid needs to be 'thick enough to lightly coat the back of a spoon', it will cling to the back of the spoon and you'll be able to see the spoon through the liquid.

Cover with water When I ask you to 'just cover with water', this is the minimum needed for cooking – the water should barely touch the top of the food. The water is often used afterwards, either as it is or reduced to a glaze.

Deglaze This technique uses those lovely browned bits of concentrated flavour left in the pan after you've fried meat, fish or vegetables. Just add a little water, boil it and scrape the bits off the bottom of the pan with a wooden spoon. You then have a flavourful base for a glaze, gravy, sauce or dressing.

Drain When I say 'drained well' as opposed to just 'drained' I mean to get the ingredient as dry as you possibly can, usually because it will be fried afterwards. The dryer the ingredient is, the better it will fry. The easiest way to drain the fat from a frying pan or roasting tray is to transfer the ingredient to a plate next to the cooker, drain off the fat and then return the ingredient to the pan.

Egg wash I brush pastry with egg wash to give it a golden glaze. Use an egg yolk mixed with 1–2 tsp of milk for a smooth and easy to apply egg wash.

Emulsify To mix two liquids, such as oil and vinegar, or gravy and butter, to create a thicker liquid or sauce. The result is an emulsion.

Fry/Pan-fry To get a crisp, golden surface your pan needs to be very hot. If it's not hot enough most ingredients will stew rather than fry, and potatoes will stick. If you don't get a loud sizzle when you add your ingredient to the pan, take it out and let the pan get hotter. In some cases I use both oil and butter, but not at the same time. I start with the oil, as it can get really hot without burning, and fry over a fairly high heat until the food is golden brown. Then I pour off the oil, lower the heat and add the butter. The butter needs to brown but not burn, so if the pan is getting too hot, take it off the heat for a bit. When you pan-fry rather than sauté, don't shake or lift the pan as this takes heat out of it. For the same reason, don't turn things more than once. Instead, spoon the hot fat on top of the food and baste it with a heatproof brush.

Glaze I brush oil, gravy or dressing over meat or fish to glaze it, and coat vegetables with their reduced cooking liquor and butter to make them glossy. I'll often brush part of a glaze onto an ingredient before I cook it and add more just before serving, to get both the cooked-in and freshly added flavour.

Reduce To thicken and concentrate a liquid by boiling it. If you reduce stock, juice or wine by half, you get twice the flavour in half the amount of liquid. Reducing sauces gives them a more concentrated flavour and a better texture. Liquids will reduce more quickly in a wide, shallow pan. If you are not sure if a liquid has reduced enough, pour it into a measuring jug to check.

Refresh To immerse boiled vegetables in cold water after cooking to stop them cooking immediately and preserve their colour and texture. I also use the term to describe adding an ingredient near the end of cooking that I have already used at the beginning – like ginger or green curry paste – to refresh the flavour and make it fresher, more instant, more fragrant.

Reheat Most things reheat better in the microwave. Use a low setting for soft food like braised meat and lentils in sauce so that they heat through evenly and you don't break them up by stirring. Use a high heat for green vegetables so they don't overcook and go brown. To reheat and glaze vegetables at the same time, cover just the bottom of a shallow pan with water, add 5g butter per portion and bring to the boil. Add the vegetables, bring back to the boil and boil furiously until the water has evaporated and the vegetables are glazed.

Resting Meat needs to be rested after it's cooked to let the heat penetrate evenly from the outside to the centre. I rest fish, pasta and pulses for the same reason. Depending on its size, roast chicken or pork belly will be 3–6°C hotter in the middle 10 minutes after you remove it from the oven than the moment you took it out. While it rests, meat relaxes, becomes more tender and the juices settle into the flesh. Don't cover your meat tightly, or it will continue to cook as it rests. Use a warming oven if you have one, or the oven you've just used, but turned off with the door ajar. If there is something in the oven, then rest your meat at the back of your cooker, or close to it.

Sauté To shake the pan around while you fry. I'll ask you to do this when the ingredients need to be tossed as they cook. Otherwise I'll say fry.

Score To cut through the skin of meat or fish. I don't score duck or fish, but I do score the fatty part of pork chops (see page 83) as the fat browns better, and belly pork (see page 263) to make it easier to slice.

Segment To segment citrus fruit, use a sharp knife to cut the top and bottom off the fruit so that it sits flat on your chopping board. Cut away the peel in strips, removing all the white pith. Holding the fruit over a bowl, cut out each segment between the white membranes. Once you've cut out all the segments, squeeze the juice from the membranes over them.

Simmer After bringing a liquid back to the boil, turn the heat down or shift the pan to a smaller burner so that the ingredients cook more gently in the simmering liquid. When I ask you to simmer gently, I mean to have the occasional bubble break the surface. When I say to simmer rapidly, I mean to have bubbles continually breaking the surface but to stop short of a rolling boil; this is best achieved on a medium burner at its medium setting.

Storing meat You will get a better, more golden crust, skin or crackling if the surface of your meat or poultry is very dry. Store meat and poultry uncovered in the fridge for at least a day before cooking to help dry their surface.

Sweat To cook vegetables in a covered pan with butter, oil or a little water to soften them without browning. For chopped or sliced onions and garlic, allow 7–10 minutes in a covered pan over a medium heat.

ABC OF EQUIPMENT

Like clothes that fit, the right equipment for you is the equipment you find comfortable, that's the right size for what you cook and the number of people you cook for most often. You don't need a lot. Don't be tempted to buy sets, which give you more tools, pans and bowls than you need. The more equipment you have, the harder it is to find the things you need to use; the more you use, the more you need to wash up and put away. Have a place for everything. In my little galley kitchen I have most of my equipment hanging on my walls. This is the equipment I use.

Appliances

Dishwasher This saves you time and clutter. If you haven't already got a dishwasher in your kitchen and you can get one, check that it's got a fast cycle. If you can't, buy a large plastic tub to put your dirty dishes in as you work to keep your worktop and sink clear.

Grill Always watch anything under your grill carefully and adjust my recipes if necessary. Grills differ in terms of their size, heat level and position of the grill tray from the heat. I've specified two settings in the recipes: medium and hot. If your grill has only one, position the grill pan close to the heat source for hot and move it further away for a medium heat.

Hob I prefer to cook on a gas hob, as the burners respond instantly when you adjust the heat, but I've tested and written the recipes for electric too. I say 'take the pan off the heat', rather than 'turn off the heat' because an electric hob stays hot for a while when you turn it off and could burn what's on it if you don't move it. If you buy an induction hob, make sure it will work with the pans you have or be prepared to replace them all.

As a guide to the most accurate heat settings, this is what I used when I cooked the recipes on my gas cooker:

Very low heat The smallest burner at its lowest setting
Low heat The medium burner at its lowest setting
Low to medium heat The medium burner between low and medium
Medium heat The medium burner at its medium setting
Medium to high heat The medium burner between medium and high
High heat The medium burner at its highest setting
Very high heat The largest burner at its highest setting

With electric hobs you can just set the numbers. You need to heat the burners before you start, like an oven, and you often need to adjust the heat as you go, so be prepared to move pans to different burners, particularly if you have an electric hob that takes a while to heat up or cool down. Set one burner at a lower temperature than the one you're using so that you can transfer your pan instantly to a lower heat in the same way as gas.

Microwave I rarely cook from scratch in the microwave, but I've learnt that it's the best way to reheat most food because you can do it very slowly and evenly, or quickly if you need to. A short burst on a high setting is best for green vegetables to get them hot without overcooking them.

Ovens Don't trust the temperature of your oven. Ovens vary enormously; there is an accepted variance of 10–15 per cent either way from the actual setting. Use an oven thermometer and a meat thermometer, then you will know for sure how hot your oven is and when your meat and fish are cooked.

There is rarely an exact middle shelf position in an oven; it's usually a little above or below. If I say middle shelf in a recipe it's the one that's slightly higher. If I say upper middle shelf it's the one above that. I don't use the top shelf.

Don't open your oven door during cooking more often than you need to, and close it as quickly as possible when you do, because the temperature drops dramatically, by as much as 20°C, in a matter of seconds.

A fan oven accelerates the cooking process, so if you are using one you will need to set the oven 15–20°C lower than the setting given in the recipe.

If you are considering a new cooker, buy one with a double oven. I have a standard oven with a little oven over the top (that has an integral grill), which is perfect for heating plates, resting meat, keeping food warm and grilling while you use the main oven.

Processors and blenders A hand-held stick blender with a mini chopper/processor attachment is the ideal machine to do the small quantities of blending called for in this book.

An advantage of having a free-standing blender/liquidiser as well is that it makes the smoothest purées. Because a tall blender throws the mixture up and gravity brings it back down onto the blades, herb leaves seem to bruise less and make a brighter green pesto or curry paste than they do in a food processor, which throws and bashes the mixture away from the blades. When you purée pesto, curry paste or other thicker mixtures in a blender, the blades may turn but not blend the mixture. In this case, lift the blender off its base, tap it to release the trapped air at the bottom, scrape down the sides with a spatula and carry on. If this doesn't work, add the liquid or oil you're using, 1 tbsp at a time, until the mixture moves freely.

Cooking equipment

Baking trays and sheets A baking tray is shallow with a lip. A baking sheet is flat, or has a tiny lip. I use a baking tray when food might release liquid or fat, to stop it dripping onto the oven floor. I use a baking sheet when I want to be able to slide something off it. Use the size best suited to what you are cooking. Also, buy some reusable non-stick mats to fit your trays; it's so much easier to get food like sticky baked tarts and aubergines on and off trays if you use these.

Ovenproof dishes I cook a lot of meals in these. There are two typical sizes: oval or rectangular 24 x 18cm, 6cm deep, for 2–3 servings; and 28 x 20cm, 6cm deep, for 4 servings; you can also get individual pie or gratin dishes if you like. I use glass, porcelain or metal dishes; they all have similar dimensions. An ovenproof 20cm frying or sauté pan works well as an ovenproof dish for all the recipes that use a baking dish in this book.

Pans Good sturdy pans with thick bases and sides make a huge difference to your cooking. Food will burn on the bottom and sides of thin pans much more quickly. Use ovenproof pans if possible; this saves you transferring food from a hot pan to a cold oven tray, which lowers the heat, makes things take longer and gives you more washing up.

Pans with glass lids are ideal for keeping a close eye on what's happening. If you don't have a lid for your frying pan, you may find that the lid for your largest cooking pot will do.

Use the right size pan for the job. You don't need endless pans, you just need pans that suit the amount of food that you cook.

These are standard-sized pans (base measurement):
- Small saucepan, 16–18cm
- Small frying pan, 16–18cm
- Medium saucepan, 20cm
- Medium frying pan, 20cm (preferably ovenproof)
- Medium-large frying pan, 24–26cm
- Large frying pan, 30cm
- Large sauté pan, 24–30cm
- Large deep cooking pot, 24cm for all green vegetables and long pasta (20cm is ok if you're cooking for 1 or 2 people but 24cm is still better)
- A good non-stick frying pan of the size that suits you, kept solely for frying food that will otherwise stick

The number and size of pans you need depends on how many you cook for most often. If you cook for two people, most recipes in this book could be done with a 20cm ovenproof frying pan, a deep 24cm pot, two smaller saucepans, a baking tray and a roasting tray. If you cook for four, add a large frying pan to the list. There is a bit of leeway, but if you use much smaller or larger pans than I suggest, it will change the cooking times. For example, liquids will reduce faster in a wide, shallow pan because the liquid can evaporate more quickly.

If you use a pan that's not non-stick for a non-stick job it will probably ruin what you are cooking. If you use pans that are too large for what you fry you are more likely to burn the cooking juices/oil/butter around the outside. Pans for frying burgers and chops do not need, or really want, to be non-stick, as you want their essence and juices to stick to make your pan gravy with.

I like sauté pans – shallow pans with straight, raised sides – because you can use them as a frying pan and they're ideal for poaching, braising, reducing and sweating too. But in most cases frying and sauté pans are interchangeable. If I ask you to get a shallow pan in a recipe, you can use either.

Roasting trays This is an excellent example of how the right equipment can improve a recipe. My 38 x 35cm roasting tray, which is 5cm deep, has sides that taper out. For the roast chicken (on page 229) it works much better than my deeper tray with straight sides, which hide the bird's thighs from the heat. A 30cm ovenproof frying pan also works for the pork, duck and chicken. You will need a wire rack for resting meat; a roasting tray may come with one.

Preparation equipment

Chopping boards I like a wooden chopping board because it feels good to cut on. Choose one that you can lift easily, with a handle if possible, so that you can easily transfer what you've chopped into saucepans and bowls. I keep a plastic board to prepare meat or fish on, because it can go straight in the dishwasher after I've dealt with them. Replace your chopping board if it starts to warp, as the warp makes a gap between your knife and the board and makes chopping harder. For carving, a board with channels around the outside is good to catch the meat juices to add to your gravy.

Knives These need to be sharp and feel comfortable in your hand. All you need is a chopping knife of the size that best suits you, a bread knife, a small, serrated paring knife and a speed (Y-shaped) peeler. Keep a very sharp knife solely for carving too. Either get lessons on how to sharpen your knives or get them sharpened professionally; this will save you time, stress and money. Speed peelers will go blunt and need to be replaced from time to time.

Mixing bowls Use your serving bowls if you don't have much storage space for these. Use shallow bowls or baking dishes for tossing salads; you'll coat them more evenly with their dressing and leaves are less likely to be bruised than in a deep bowl. One deep bowl is useful to mix liquids in.

Prep tray and tub Have a plastic or metal tray to put ingredients on while you cook, and a tub to put your utensils in (see page 12).

Sieves and colanders Get a stainless steel colander that can go in the oven (you'll see why on page 174) and a large, sturdy stainless steel sieve.

Measuring equipment

Measuring tools Get a set of measuring spoons and a measuring jug, preferably a thick plastic one, that's the right size for you – check that the graduations start at 100ml or less, otherwise it will be unhelpful in a lot of cases. Use a ruler or a measuring tape for size, as you use scales for weight.

Oven thermometer Get an oven thermometer and use it whenever you use the oven.

Timer/probe thermometer I've saved myself a fortune in burnt food since I started using a timer and have become much more relaxed since I started using an electronic meat probe. I now have a gadget that does both and it only cost £24. The meat probe has a cable so that you can either probe the meat as you cook it on the hob, or put it into your meat in the oven and set the final temperature you want – the alarm will go off when your meat is ready. The suggested final interior temperatures are chicken, 74°C; fish, 60°C (I prefer 55°C); pork, 63°C (71°C for well done); beef, duck breast and lamb, rare 49–52°C, medium-rare 55–57°C, medium 60–63°C, well done 69–71°C.

Weighing scales I like electronic scales. You can weigh an ingredient directly into the pan or bowl you're using, press zero, then add the next ingredient.

Small utensils

Buy good-quality, sturdy utensils that don't bend or buckle and, if your pans are non-stick, make sure you get utensils that won't scratch them. These are the utensils I use in this book:

- Fish slice: a wide, long, sturdy, non-flexible fish slice (and a heat-resistant one, which might be slightly flexible, to use in non-stick pans)
- Grater: choose one with at least two grating options. You need a coarse grater for cheese and carrots, and a finer version of this for citrus zest (avoid fine graters with very raised cutting holes, as the zest gets stuck)
- Kitchen serving spoons: two large ones
- Lemon squeezer: ideally a plastic one with a detachable base
- Pastry brushes: two heat-resistant ones, for seasoning and basting (silicone brushes are ideal and dishwasher-proof)
- Potato masher (one that definitely doesn't bend) or a ricer if you prefer
- Roasting fork: handy but not absolutely necessary
- Rubber spatula, heatproof: to get every last bit of sauce out of your pans
- Tin opener: pay a bit more and get a good one, these can be a nightmare
- Tongs: buy sturdy ones that won't bend easily
- Whisk: get one that will fit in your smallest saucepan
- Wire skimmer: a skimmer with large gaps is more effective than a slotted spoon or slotted skimmer for draining things as you lift them out of water
- Wooden spoons: you only need a couple. Buy one with a flat top to get to the bottom of your pans
- Zester

You will also need rolls of cling film, greaseproof and/or non-stick baking paper, and aluminium foil – buy the wide rolls of thick foil.

1/
Adventures with Ingredients

Six 'heroic' ingredients, and six super ways to serve each one

Join me on my Adventures with Ingredients, and I'll show you how to cook six easy-to-find ingredients, then give you six everyday ways to serve each one. The best way to learn how to cook an ingredient is to cook it again and again. Repetition makes cooking intuitive and helps your confidence grow. It's a lovely way to cook, especially as the taste never need be repetitive.

I know that 'simple' has become a complicated word for home cooks. Often recipes start with the perfect scenario of the perfect ingredients. As much as I love great ingredients, I know that a complete focus on ideal ingredients shifts responsibility away from a recipe and limits the number of people who can cook it successfully. So in this chapter, and all the way through this book, my focus is on how to cook a good dinner with everyday ingredients.

For each adventure, I've given a detailed 'hero' recipe for how to cook the main ingredient at the start, then an abbreviated and slightly different version for each of the subsidiary recipes, so you don't have to turn back to the main recipe – although you can if you want a fuller explanation or need more help. I hope that each time you go off on one of my adventures it will encourage you to take off on another one, giving you more and more confidence until you are ready to have adventures on your own. These adventures are all about good food – food that happens to be quick, pretty, easy to find and easy to adapt.

The recipes in this chapter are so varied that the same main ingredient can easily be made to taste fresh and new each time you cook it. As I tested and wrote the recipes at home, we often ate our way through an entire adventure in succession, and it never felt as though we were eating the same thing twice.

I've chosen ingredients that need the least possible preparation before you cook them. The portions are clear: a chicken breast, a salmon fillet, half an aubergine, a pork chop, 100g of pasta or 150g of mince. This makes the recipes simple to scale up to serve more, or scale down for one person, with the minimum possible waste and leftover ingredients. Along the way, where it suits, I've suggested cooking extra portions of the main ingredient or entire recipe for the next day's lunch.

First I'll show you how to cook each 'heroic' ingredient well. Next you pick a sauce, salsa or salad that catches your fancy. Once you are confident cooking the main ingredient then your adventures are all about delicious details. I'll ask you to coat your chicken with a sticky glaze, drench your aubergine with dressing before and after you roast it, turn your mince steak and pork chop to a meaty gloss in their cooking juices, and add hot water to your pasta to make it saucier. These little touches make the best of what you have and are the difference between a nice dinner and a delicious one.

Once you are comfortable with the six basic cooking techniques, you have six starts to a meal that you can serve simply and superbly cooked, with potatoes or other carbs, vegetables or a salad. As well as the six subsidiary recipes that I offer for each 'hero' recipe, I've given you ideas for seasonings instead of pepper. (I know I go on about this, but it is vital to season the ingredients evenly all over.) If you want to find further ways to flavour your adventures, look for some tricks in The Magic Fridge (pages 124–223).

Smell, touch and taste your way through the recipes. Once you become confident cooking an ingredient because you've become familiar with it, you'll know when it's ready, you'll know how long it can sit, and your confidence will give you the freedom to relax, to play around in the kitchen, to adapt and to make my recipes yours.

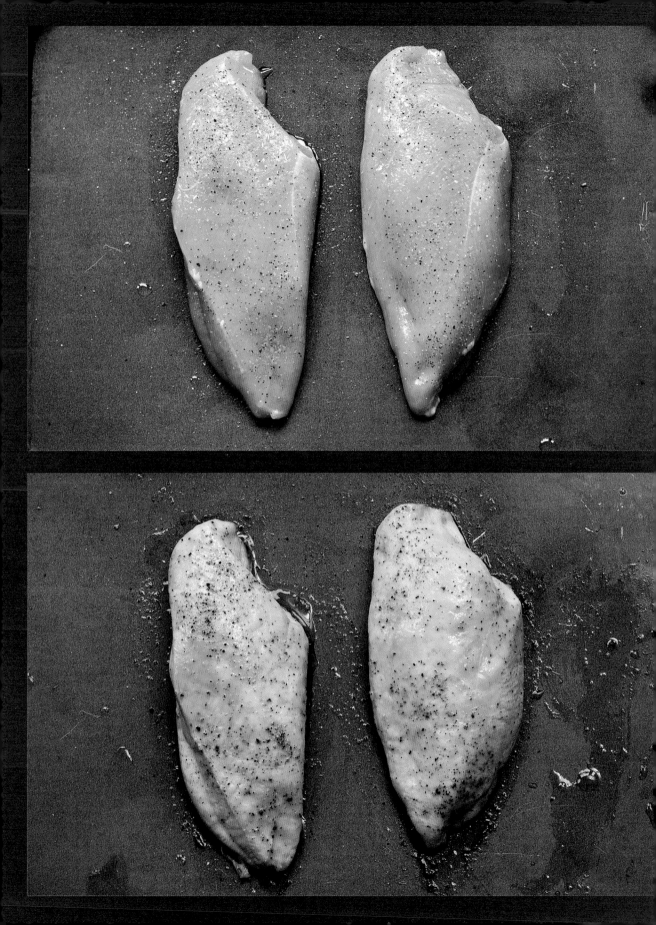

BAKED CHICKEN BREASTS

A baked chicken breast is a blank canvas that cries out to be revived by other flavours. I like to get it excited, to brush it with chilli or lemon, glaze it with honey or soy sauce, or macerate it in mustard or porcini cream. The chicken is always better for the experience.

Baking is the best and easiest way to cook skinless, boneless chicken breasts. The trick is not to bake them for too long and always to let them rest afterwards. This gives you very juicy flesh and none of the dry and chewy exterior you cannot avoid if you fry them.

Tender and mild in flavour, chicken breasts are useful for kids. They're easily mixed with vegetables, pasta or grains, and a good means of introducing new tastes alongside something they are comfortable with. For babies and toddlers, baked chicken breasts are good to purée or chop and can be frozen.

SERVES 2

Sides (pages 320–43)
Any you fancy
Prep/cooking 14–16 mins, plus 5 mins resting
Active time 1 min

2 skinless, boneless chicken breasts, about 150g each
1 tsp vegetable oil
Salt
Freshly ground black pepper or other seasoning (see right)

1. Preheat your oven to 200°C/Gas 6, position upper middle shelf.

2. Get a baking tray. Put the chicken breasts on the tray. Sprinkle salt and pepper, or something instead of pepper, evenly over both sides. Brush the breasts with the oil to push the seasoning into the flesh and coat it evenly.

3. Turn each breast shiny side up with the fatter end facing away from you. Put the tray in the oven with the breast's fatter end towards the back.

4. Bake for 14–16 minutes. A just-cooked chicken breast feels firm to the touch. It should be 70–72°C inside, which will rise to 74–76°C as it rests.

5. Turn the oven off. Open the door and leave it slightly ajar while the chicken rests inside for at least 5 minutes. Depending on the recipe, this resting is either done on the baking tray, or in the sauce/dressing.

Instead of pepper

Try allspice, cayenne pepper, chilli powder, Chinese five-spice, cinnamon, cumin, cardamom, curry powder, crushed fennel seeds, nutmeg, ginger, jerk spice, ras-el-hanout, smoked paprika, turmeric, sumac, za'atar, mustard, tamarind, citrus juice or citrus zest.

Cooking and resting times for larger chicken breasts

150–175g: 14–16 mins, 5 mins rest
175–200g: 16–18 mins, 5 mins rest
200–250g: 18–22 mins, 5 mins rest
Interior temperature: Bake to 70–72°C; rest to 74–76°C (use your probe)

Magic adventures

Serve with pesto, tapenade, tomato compote, soft, sweet, sticky onions, green curry paste or garlic butter.

Cook extra

Use for a sandwich or a wrap the next day, and a salad the day after.

1/ Chicken with porcini, parsley sauce & spinach

Once you taste the voluptuous porcini cream that caresses the chicken's curves you'll see why the story of this dish has to start with the sauce. Dried porcini were my first wild mushrooms, and I have been making a version of this sauce for more than twenty years. After all that time, I am as hungry for it as ever, if anything I love it more because of its warm and familiar feel. The key to making the chicken and sauce marry blissfully is to roll, soak and then rest them together before serving.

For younger kids, the spinach is best wilted 30 seconds longer and chopped very finely, even puréed. In my experience younger kids like the taste of the sauce but not the texture of the porcini, so eat them all yourself. Good to purée or chop and freeze for babies and toddlers.

SERVES 2

Sides (pages 320–43)

A sauce soaker, such as rice or bread

Prep/cooking 30–35 mins

Active time 15–20 mins

2 skinless, boneless chicken breasts, about 150g each

1 tsp vegetable oil

12–15g dried porcini (½ small pack)

150ml plus 2 tbsp water

1 garlic clove, peeled and finely chopped

100ml chicken stock

100ml double cream

4 tbsp sliced flat-leaf parsley

120g spinach (1 small packet), washed if gritty

Salt and freshly ground black pepper

1. Preheat your oven to 200°C/Gas 6, position upper middle shelf. Boil your kettle.

2. Start with the chicken. Get a baking tray. Put the breasts on the tray. Season with salt and pepper. Brush with oil. Bake for 14–16 minutes.

3. Meanwhile, put the dried porcini into a measuring jug. Pour 150ml boiling water over them. Leave to soak for 10 minutes. Lift the porcini out. Chop them into small pieces. Get a medium-sized ovenproof frying pan. Add the porcini. Pour the clear soaking liquid gently over the top. Discard the last murky bit if there is any grit.

4. Put the pan on a high heat. Add the garlic and chicken stock. Bring to the boil and boil for 2 minutes or until the liquid has reduced by half. Stir in the cream. Bring back to the boil and boil for 20–30 seconds or until the sauce is thick enough to coat the back of the spoon. Season to taste. Take the pan off the heat.

5. Once the chicken breasts are baked, get them out of the oven and add them to the sauce. Add the parsley. Turn the chicken breasts in the sauce until they are well coated. Turn the oven off. Put the pan back in the oven and leave the door slightly ajar. Let the chicken rest for 5 minutes.

6. After 2 minutes, get a large shallow pan. Add 2 tbsp of water. Bring to the boil over a high heat. Add the spinach. Cover and cook for 30 seconds. Take the lid off. Stir for 10 seconds until the leaves all wilt. Season to taste.

7. Once the chicken has rested, warm it over a gentle heat for 1 minute until the sauce just starts to bubble. If it is too thick, stir in hot water, 1 tbsp at a time, until it is spoon coating consistency. Serve with the spinach.

Cook extra

Bake extra chicken breast(s) and leave them to cool on your baking tray to use for a sandwich, salad or wrap the next day.

2/ Curried chicken with tomato, lemon & almond dressing

My time in Provence taught me that citrus is the sunshine seasoning. Years of cooking and tasting showed me that it can sometimes have more impact when its sharp flavour is softened. I boil the lemon and orange juice in this recipe to make it more concentrated, just sour enough to refresh and just sweet enough to revitalise. The chicken is then more intensely flavoured but less overpowered by citrus than if the juice was raw. The curry and turmeric add a jolly little twang; feel free to add more if you like it hot.

For younger kids, leave out or put in less of the spice mixture and chop the mint very finely. Add the almonds to your dressing but not theirs, then give the kids a taste. Without the almonds this is good to purée or chop and freeze for babies and toddlers.

SERVES 2

Sides (pages 320–43) Tasty grains or chickpeas and/or leafy veg

Prep ahead Dressing, except mint. Spice mixture, 4 hours ahead

Prep/cooking 35–40 mins

Active time 20–25 mins

6 tbsp orange juice (fresh or from a carton)

Zested or grated zest and juice of 1 lemon (4 tbsp)

1 garlic clove, peeled and finely chopped

2 tsp grated ginger

1 tsp curry powder

½ tsp ground turmeric

2 skinless, boneless chicken breasts, about 150g each

3 heaped tbsp flaked almonds

4 tbsp extra virgin olive oil

8 dried apricots, chopped into 1cm pieces

2 large plum tomatoes, cut into 1cm dice

4 tbsp sliced mint

4 tbsp plain yoghurt

Salt and sugar

1. Preheat your oven to 200°C/Gas 6, position upper middle shelf.

2. Start with the spice mixture. Get a medium-sized ovenproof frying pan. Add the orange juice, lemon zest, lemon juice, garlic, ginger, curry powder and turmeric. Put the pan on a high heat. Bring to the boil and boil for 1 minute or until the mixture is just thick enough to lightly coat the back of a spoon. Take the pan off the heat.

3. Get a baking tray. Put the chicken breasts on the tray. Spoon 1 tbsp of the spice mixture over each chicken breast. Brush the mixture all over both sides of the breasts. Season with salt. Bake for 9 minutes.

4. Take the tray out of the oven. Sprinkle the almonds on the tray next to the pointy ends of the breasts. Put the tray back into the oven for 5–7 minutes (or as much extra time as the larger weights need, removing the almonds when they are toasted).

5. While the chicken bakes, make the dressing. Get a medium bowl. Add the extra virgin olive oil, dried apricots, tomatoes and mint.

6. Once the chicken breasts are baked, get them out of the oven. Add them and the almonds to the spice mixture in your pan. Turn the breasts in the mixture until they are well coated. Turn the oven off. Put the pan back in the oven and leave the door slightly ajar. Let the chicken rest for 5 minutes.

7. Roll the chicken breasts in the pan juices and almonds. Thickly slice the breasts (or leave them whole if you prefer). Put the chicken on your plates. Use a heatproof spatula to scrape the sticky pan juices and almonds into the dressing. Season to taste with salt and sugar. Spoon the dressing over the chicken breasts. Serve the yoghurt in a bowl on the side.

Cook extra

Bake extra chicken breast(s) and leave them to cool in the citrus mixture. Chop the breasts and mix with the equivalent extra dressing for a pita bread or salad with tasty grains and/or crisp lettuce, peppers or cucumber.

3/ Sesame chicken with soy, honey, orange & ginger

Soy, honey, orange and ginger is one of the first combinations I can remember using to flavour chicken. It must have been the start of my love affair with the irresistible contrast of sweet and sour that sets this chicken alight. It's a lively pick-me-up; the breasts absorb and are enrobed by the flavour while they bake and rest in the glaze.

For younger kids, leave out three-quarters of the ginger and all of the chilli. Boil the sliced spring onions for a minute or so to soften their flavour. Once you've dished theirs up, add the extra ginger and chilli to yours. Without the salad and sesame seeds, the chicken breast is good to purée or chop and freeze for babies and toddlers.

SERVES 2

Sides (pages 320–43)
Rice or egg noodles and/or glazed carrots

Prep ahead Soy, honey, orange and ginger mixture, up to 2 days ahead

Prep/cooking 30–35 mins

Active time 20–25 mins

4 tbsp dark soy sauce

2 tbsp honey

2 heaped tsp grated ginger

2 tsp sesame oil

2 medium oranges

2 skinless, boneless chicken breasts, about 150g each

4 spring onions, trimmed and thinly sliced diagonally

½ mild red chilli, deseeded and finely chopped

3 heaped tsp sesame seeds

1. Preheat your oven to 200°C/Gas 6, position upper middle shelf.

2. Start with the soy mixture. Get a medium-sized ovenproof frying pan. Add the soy sauce, honey, ginger and 1 tsp of the sesame oil. Grate the zest of 1 orange into the pan. Cut the orange in half. Squeeze its juice. Add the juice (4–5 tbsp) to the pan. Bring to the boil over a high heat. Boil for 1 minute or until the mixture is thick enough to lightly coat the back of a spoon. Take the pan off the heat.

3. Get a baking tray. Put the chicken breasts on the tray. Spoon 1 tbsp of the soy mixture over each breast. Brush the mixture over both sides. Bake for 14–16 minutes.

4. Next, make the spring onion mixture. Get a medium bowl. Zest or grate the zest of half the second orange into it. Peel the orange and separate into segments (as if you were going to eat it). Slice each segment widthways into 5mm slices. Add them to the bowl. Add the spring onions, chilli, 1 tsp of the sesame seeds and the remaining 1 tsp of sesame oil. Stir together. Scatter the mixture around the edge of your plates.

5. Once the chicken breasts are baked, get them out of the oven. Add them to the frying pan with the soy glaze. Sprinkle 1 tsp of sesame seeds over each chicken breast. Put the pan back in the oven and leave the door slightly ajar. Let the chicken rest for 5 minutes.

6. Brush the chicken with the soy glaze; don't worry if you move the seeds around a bit. Put the chicken breasts on your plates. Warm the glaze; if it's too thick, stir in hot water, 1 tbsp at a time, until it is spoon coating consistency. Spoon the glaze around the breasts.

Cook extra

Make extra soy glaze. Bake extra chicken breast(s) and leave them to cool in the glaze. Chop the breasts and combine with the equivalent extra spring onion mixture to use in a wrap, or rice or noodle salad with one or a mixture of bean sprouts, chopped peppers or cucumber.

4/ Chicken with mustard, chives, runner beans & peas

This combination of feisty mustard, perky chives, peppery watercress, sweet peas and runner beans is a great way to serve chicken in summer. I like using watercress, both as an aromatic herb and as a vegetable, and I prefer to slice it before adding it to a sauce so the flavour wraps its goodness around all of the other ingredients. Oh, and every bit of this recipe loves butter, so feel free to lash in a little or a lot more.

    For younger kids, put a tiny amount of the mustard and lemon mixture on the chicken breast but either leave off the topping or grate the zest finely, rather than using a zester. Chop rather than slice the onions for the vegetables and chop the watercress extremely finely or leave it out of theirs. Good to purée or chop and freeze for babies and toddlers.

SERVES 2

Sides (pages 320–43)
None needed. For bulk, simmered or glazed potatoes
Prep ahead Onion and stock mixture, a day ahead
Prep/cooking 30–35 mins
Active time 20–25 mins

5 tbsp sliced chives
Zested or grated zest and
   juice of ½ lemon (2 tbsp)
2 skinless, boneless
   chicken breasts, about
   150g each
2 heaped tsp English or
   Dijon mustard
1 medium onion, peeled
   and cut into 5mm slices
40g butter
2 tbsp water
200ml chicken stock
100g frozen peas
125g young runner beans,
   topped and cut into 1cm
   slices diagonally
80–90g watercress
   (1 small packet/bunch),
   cut into 5mm slices
Salt and freshly ground
   black pepper

1. Preheat your oven to 200°C/Gas 6, position upper middle shelf. Boil your kettle. Put a colander in your sink.

2. Start with the chives and lemon zest. On a small plate, mix them together. Put them next to your cooker.

3. Get a baking tray. Put the chicken breasts on the tray. In a small bowl, mix the mustard and lemon juice together. Season with salt and pepper. Brush the mixture over both sides of the chicken breasts. Bake for 14–16 minutes.

4. While the chicken bakes, get a medium saucepan. Add the onion, 20g of the butter and the 2 tbsp of water. Cover and sweat over a medium heat for 7–10 minutes, stirring occasionally, until the onion is soft but not brown. Add the chicken stock. Bring to the boil and simmer for 4 minutes or until the liquid has reduced by a third. Take the pan off the heat.

5. While the onions sweat, get a large pot. Add boiling water and bring back to the boil. Add the peas and runner beans. Cover, bring back to the boil and boil for 3 minutes or until tender. Drain into your colander. Shake dry.

6. Once the chicken breasts are baked, turn the oven off. Open the door and leave it slightly ajar while the chicken rests inside for 5 minutes.

7. Add the peas and beans to the onion and chicken stock. Bring to the boil. Stir in the watercress and remaining 20g butter. Season to taste.

8. Put the chicken breasts and their resting juices into the pan. Spoon a little sauce over them. Cover the breasts with the lemon zest and chive mixture. Transfer them to your plates with the vegetables and sauce.

Cook extra

Make extra chive and lemon mixture. Brush extra chicken breast(s) with the mustard and lemon and leave them to cool to use for a sandwich, wrap, pita bread or salad the next day. Chop the breasts and mix with the chives and lemon. This is good mixed with potatoes, mayonnaise and mustard.

5/ Casey's glazed chicken with corn & chilli relish

This dish is a punchy, boldly flavoured beauty: sweet and sour, fresh, exciting and bursting with colour. My goddaughter Casey asked me if it was barbecue sauce on the chicken and I realised that was exactly how it tasted. The fresh crunch of the relish livens up the chicken and sauce. It tastes like barbecue and feels like sunshine.

For younger kids, chop the chicken into chunks and separate a little of the relish for them before you add the chilli. Baby gem ribs are juicy, which makes them good to squash, suck and chew for little ones who are just starting to hold and eat things themselves. Except the lettuce, this is good to purée or chop and freeze for babies and toddlers.

SERVES 2

Sides (pages 320–43)
None needed. For bulk, plain or tasty grains
Prep ahead Glaze and relish, except coriander, up to 4 hours ahead
Prep/cooking 30–35 mins
Active time 20–25 mins

100ml tomato juice
2 tbsp Worcestershire sauce
2 tbsp marmalade
1 garlic clove, peeled and finely chopped
2 skinless, boneless chicken breasts, about 150g each
200g tin sweetcorn, drained
3 tbsp extra virgin olive oil
Grated zest and juice of ½ lime (1½ tbsp)
½ mild red chilli, deseeded and finely chopped
4 tbsp sliced coriander
1 baby gem lettuce, leaves separated
Salt, cayenne pepper and caster sugar

1. Preheat your oven to 200°C/Gas 6, position upper middle shelf.

2. Start with the glaze. Get a medium-sized ovenproof frying pan. Add the tomato juice, Worcestershire sauce, 1 tbsp of the marmalade and the garlic. Put the pan on a high heat. Bring to the boil and boil for 1 minute or until the mixture is just thick enough to lightly coat the back of a spoon. Take the pan off the heat.

3. Get a baking tray. Put the chicken breasts on the tray. Spoon 1 tbsp of the glaze over each breast. Brush the mixture all over both sides of the breasts. Season with salt. Bake for 14–16 minutes.

4. Once the chicken breasts are baked, get them out of the oven. Put them in the pan with the rest of the glaze. Turn the breasts in the glaze until they are well coated. Turn the oven off. Put the pan in the oven and leave the door slightly ajar. Let the chicken rest for 5 minutes.

5. While the chicken rests, make the corn and chilli relish. Get a small pan. Add the sweetcorn, remaining 1 tbsp of marmalade, the extra virgin olive oil, lime zest, lime juice and chilli. Put the pan on a medium heat. Warm for 1 minute until the sweetcorn is hot. Take the pan off the heat. Add the coriander. Season to taste with salt, cayenne and sugar.

6. Once the chicken has rested, put the pan on a medium heat. Warm for a minute or so until you see a few bubbles in the glaze. If the glaze is too thick, stir in hot water 1 tbsp at a time until it is spoon coating consistency. Brush the chicken breasts with the glaze. Put the chicken breasts on your plates with the lettuce leaves and the corn and chilli relish. Spoon any remaining glaze over the top.

Cook extra

Make extra glaze. Bake extra chicken breast(s) and leave them to cool in the glaze. Chop the chicken breasts and combine with the equivalent extra relish to mix with grains, potatoes or baby gem lettuce for a salad, wrap or pita bread.

6/ Chilli chicken, sweet & sour kidney beans & avocado salsa

The chilli and lime make this chicken very perky. It's a combination of ingredients I love, and the secret is in the seasoning. The salsa needs sugar to balance and accentuate the lime juice. The beans turn from stodge to superstar when they are lightly fried and then highly seasoned with the same flavours as the salsa and chicken. Little things, lovely tastes.

For younger kids, leave the chilli off the chicken. With most spices I'll say use a tiny amount, but chilli is a bit too scary. My kids aren't keen on the beans – it's the texture and thickness of the skin rather than the taste. If yours are the same, just warm a few low-salt, low-sugar baked beans to serve with the chicken. This recipe is no good to purée or freeze.

SERVES 2

Sides (pages 320–43)
None needed. For bulk, tortilla chips, popcorn or rice
Prep ahead Salsa, except mint, an hour ahead; cover directly with cling film
Prep/cooking 30–35 mins
Active time 20–25 mins

2 skinless, boneless
   chicken breasts, about
   150g each
½ tsp chilli powder
   (or more if you like)
3 tsp vegetable oil
Zested or grated zest and
   juice of 1 lime (3 tbsp)
3 tbsp extra virgin olive oil
125g baby plum tomatoes
   (½ punnet), cut into thin
   wedges
1 large ripe avocado
2 tbsp sliced mint
400g tin red kidney beans,
   drained and rinsed
4 tbsp soured cream or
   plain yoghurt
Salt, chilli powder and
   caster sugar

1. Preheat your oven to 200°C/Gas 6, position upper middle shelf.

2. Start with the chicken. Get a baking tray. Put the chicken breasts on the tray. Sprinkle salt and ¼ tsp of chilli powder evenly over both sides of each one. Brush each breast with ½ tsp of vegetable oil. Bake for 14–16 minutes.

3. While the chicken bakes, make the salsa. Get a medium bowl. Add the lime zest, half the lime juice, the extra virgin olive oil, ½ tsp of sugar and ¼ tsp of salt. Stir it all together. Add the tomato wedges.

4. Cut the avocado in half lengthways. Twist to separate the two halves and remove the stone. Peel each half and then cut the avocado into pieces, roughly the size of the tomato wedges. Add the avocado and mint to the salsa. Fold rather than stir the ingredients together, just enough to combine them without mashing the avocado.

5. Once the chicken breasts are baked, turn the oven off. Open the door and leave it slightly ajar while the chicken rests inside for 5 minutes.

6. Next, get a medium-sized frying pan. Put it on a high heat. Add 2 tsp of vegetable oil. When it is hot, add the kidney beans. Sauté for 2 minutes or until they are hot but not breaking up. Add the rest of the lime juice. Fry for 1 minute more. Season to a sweet, sour and spicy taste with salt, chilli and sugar.

7. Once rested, cut the chicken breasts in half (or leave them whole if you prefer). Put the chicken on your plates. Spoon on the kidney beans and salsa. Serve with soured cream or yoghurt.

Cook extra

Make extra portion(s) of the whole recipe. Chop the chicken. Drain the salsa and beans. Mix together and roll into wraps with grated cheese for tortillas to eat hot or cold the next day.

BAKED SALMON FILLETS

Farmed salmon needs more culinary help than wild, so I've come up with some highly seasoned recipes to energise its flesh and excite your tongue. Inspired by my friend Justin North of Becasse in Sydney, I'm using a method of cooking the salmon at a low temperature. The result is the succulent equal of pink meat. The flesh is cooked through, slowly and evenly to 55–60°C. There is no raw, no rare, nor is there any well done and the exterior seasoning has time to take hold of and flavour the flesh.

If you can buy only pre-cut salmon and the fillets are smaller than I suggest, don't worry. The cooking time is determined by the thickness of the fish rather than the weight. I rub the seasonings into the salmon with a pastry brush to gently push the flavour into the flesh. Use a non-stick tray and you don't need any oil.

Sometimes fish needs a crisp exterior to tempt kids, so if baking fails don't assume they dislike salmon, try frying it. Good to purée or chop and freeze for babies and toddlers.

SERVES 2

Sides (pages 320–43)
Any you fancy

Prep/cooking 23 mins

Active time 1 min

2 skinless farmed salmon
   fillets, 130–140g each and
   2–2.5cm thick
Salt
Freshly ground black
   pepper or other
   seasoning (see right)

1. Preheat your oven to 120°C/Gas ½, position middle shelf.

2. Get a non-stick baking tray, or if you don't have one, line a baking tray with non-stick paper. Put the salmon fillets on the tray. Pat them as dry as you can with kitchen paper.

3. Season all sides of the salmon with salt and pepper, or something instead of pepper. Bake for 22 minutes. If you are not quite ready to eat your salmon, turn off the oven, leave the door slightly ajar and the salmon will happily sit for at least 5 minutes. Because it is slowly baked, the salmon is warm rather than red hot.

4. If there is a little milky residue around the outside of the salmon, don't worry, it is just the salmon's blood that sets in the heat, in the same way an egg does. Just brush it off for appearance's sake. If you look carefully, you can see my brush marks on the tray.

Instead of pepper
Try cayenne pepper, chilli powder, curry powder, Chinese five-spice, cinnamon, crushed fennel or dill seeds, garam masala, jerk spice, ras-el-hanout, smoked paprika, turmeric, sumac berries, vanilla, citrus juice and zest, mustard, harissa, grated horseradish or horseradish cream.

Magic adventures
Serve with pesto, tapenade, tomato compote, soft, sweet, sticky onions, green curry paste or garlic butter.

Cook extra
Slowly baked salmon is ideal to serve cold, or use to make fish cakes, because it stays very moist. Put one or two extra fillets on the tray to use cold and flaked for salads, sandwiches, pita or wraps the next day.

1/ Paprika salmon with fennel & balsamic tomato dressing

My obsession with tomatoes means that I have made endless tomato dressings, but as I live in England, I often need to trick cold weather tomatoes into tasting like sun-drunk southern beauties. This dressing lifts and softens the tomatoes, and by mixing the warm appeal of the cooked with the fresh vigour of the raw, it flatters the salmon into pink-fleshed flakiness. As much as I love tinned tomatoes, they are no good for this recipe.

For younger kids, take half of the vinegar out of the recipe. Use a tiny amount of the paprika on their salmon. Give them the tender centre of the fennel in sticks to pick up and dip in the dressing. Without the fennel salad this is good to purée or chop and freeze for babies and toddlers.

SERVES 2

Sides (pages 320–43)
Soft polenta or chickpea purée, olive oil mashed potato, plain or tasty grains or bread

Prep ahead Dressing, up to 2 hours ahead

Prep/cooking 30–35 mins

Active time 20–25 mins

2 skinless salmon fillets, 130–140g each and 2–2.5cm thick
1 fennel bulb, trimmed
Zested or grated zest of ½ lemon and 2 tsp juice
3 tbsp extra virgin olive oil
14 black olives, pitted and halved
1 tbsp balsamic vinegar
4 tbsp tomato juice
1 garlic clove, peeled and finely chopped
2 very ripe, large tomatoes (preferably plum), cut into 1cm dice
Salt, sugar and paprika

1. Preheat your oven to 120°C/Gas ½, position middle shelf. Boil your kettle.

2. Start with the salmon. Get a non-stick baking tray. Put the salmon on the tray. Season each fillet with salt and ¼ tsp of paprika. Brush the seasoning into the flesh. Bake for 22 minutes.

3. While the salmon bakes, prepare the fennel. Get a small pan. Fill it with boiling water. Add salt and bring back to the boil. Put a colander in your sink. Cut the fennel bulb in half lengthways. Cut one half in two. Add the two fennel quarters to the boiling water and simmer for 8–10 minutes until tender. Drain in your colander. Put the fennel quarters back in the pan. Keep warm.

4. Next, make the dressing. Get a medium-sized shallow bowl. Add the lemon zest, lemon juice and a pinch of sugar. Whisk in 1 tbsp of the extra virgin olive oil.

5. For the fennel salad, lay the second fennel half, cut side down, on your board. Slice it very thinly lengthways. Toss the fennel slices with the dressing and olives. Season to taste.

6. To make the tomato dressing, get a small saucepan. Add the balsamic vinegar. Bring to the boil over a high heat. Boil for 10 seconds or until it is sticky and nearly dry. Add the tomato juice and garlic. Bring to the boil and boil for 30 seconds. Add the diced tomatoes. Bring back to the boil. Turn the heat to medium. Simmer rapidly for 2 minutes. Take the pan off the heat. Stir in the remaining 2 tbsp of extra virgin olive oil. Season to taste with salt, sugar and a tiny pinch of paprika.

7. Put the salmon fillets on your plates. Spoon the tomato dressing alongside. Put the cooked fennel and fennel salad on the other side of the salmon.

Cook extra

Bake extra salmon fillet(s) and make extra dressing to use cold and flaked in a salad with grains, pasta or leaves, or in a baguette or wrap.

2/ Salmon with apple, grapefruit, crème fraîche & watercress

This recipe was inspired by a Raymond Blanc dish. I cooked my version for him one evening in spring and he loved it. Salmon and apples are often paired and this dressing takes their relationship to new heights. I boil the apple juice to concentrate its flavour and acidity, then whisk in extra virgin olive oil. The reward is a taste like apple honey – both a luscious coating and tangy dressing for the salmon. The watercress gives the apple some bite and the crème fraîche smooths and soothes.

For younger kids, chop rather than slice the apples and purée or very finely chop the basil and watercress. For babies and toddlers, you can purée or chop and freeze the salmon.

SERVES 2

Sides (pages 320–43)
None needed. For bulk, olive oil glazed potatoes or plain or tasty grains
Prep ahead Glaze, up to 2 days ahead. Apples can sit in the dressing for up to an hour
Prep/cooking 40–45 mins
Active time 25 mins

400ml apple juice
2 tbsp extra virgin olive oil
1 large ruby grapefruit
4 heaped tbsp crème fraîche
4 tbsp sliced basil
2 skinless salmon fillets, 130–140g each and 2–2.5cm thick
1 small crisp apple (Gala, Cox or Braeburn)
80g mangetout
40g watercress (½ small packet/bunch)
Salt and freshly ground black pepper

1. Preheat your oven to 120°C/Gas ½, position middle shelf. Boil your kettle.

2. Start with the apple glaze. Get a medium-sized saucepan. Add the apple juice. Put the pan on a high heat. Bring to the boil and boil until the juice is reduced to 4–5 tbsp; this takes about 10 minutes and the juice should be thick enough to coat the back of a spoon. Watch carefully; if you reduce it too far it will caramelise. Pour the glaze into a bowl. Whisk in the extra virgin olive oil. Season to taste with salt and pepper.

3. While the glaze reduces, prepare the grapefruit. Cut the top and bottom off the fruit. Cut away the peel and pith in strips. Cut the segments free from their white membranes.

4. Get a small bowl. Add the crème fraîche and 2 tbsp of the basil. Mix well. Season to taste.

5. Get a non-stick baking tray. Put the salmon on the tray. Season. Spoon 1 tsp of apple glaze onto each fillet. Brush into the flesh. Bake for 22 minutes.

6. While the salmon bakes, halve the apple and cut out the core. Slice the apple thinly. Add the slices to the rest of the apple glaze with the remaining 2 tbsp of basil. Gently turn and coat the apples in the dressing.

7. Get a large pot. Fill it with boiling water. Add salt and bring back to the boil. Put a colander in your sink. Boil the mangetout for 3 minutes or until they are tender. Drain. Return the mangetout to the pan. Sauté over a medium heat for 10–30 seconds to remove excess water.

8. Put the salmon fillets on plates. Spoon the crème fraîche alongside. Surround with the grapefruit, apple, mangetout and a little watercress. Spoon the apple dressing over everything. Serve the remaining watercress in a bowl on the side to soak up any dressing left on the plates.

Cook extra
Make extra portion(s) of the whole recipe. Use for a cold salad with quinoa or couscous, or wrap in a tortilla, rice paper or large lettuce leaf.

3/ Salmon, mushy peas & chunky sunblush tomato ketchup

This recipe is like a kitchen full of happy people. Salmon and peas, tomatoes and basil, honey and pine nuts are all lifelong friends that bring out the best in each other. Together on a plate they create a carnival of colour and taste. The sunblush tomatoes pick up on the sweetness of the peas and I've added wine vinegar for a sour tingle to balance it all. The cayenne pepper is just a seasoning; the salmon is not meant to be spicy hot.

This is an excellent meal for kids. Just make the dressing without the vinegar, split it in two and add less vinegar to theirs. Cut the sunblush tomatoes into smaller pieces and introduce them as 'a bit like tomato raisins'. Use the mushy peas as a base for presenting new flavours to kids in small quantities; I've added fish, herbs and root vegetables to them with great success. Good to purée or chop and freeze for babies and toddlers.

SERVES 2

Sides (pages 320–43)
Olive oil glazed potatoes or polenta chips or bread
Prep ahead Mushy peas and tomato relish without the basil, a day ahead
Prep/cooking 30–35 mins
Active time 20–25 mins

2 skinless salmon fillets, 130–140g each and 2–2.5cm thick
150ml plus 2 tbsp water
3 tbsp extra virgin olive oil
200g frozen peas (straight from the freezer)
6 tbsp sliced basil
1 tbsp honey
1 tbsp white or red wine vinegar
1 tsp tomato purée
8 sunblush tomatoes, each cut into 3
2 tbsp pine nuts (optional)
Salt and cayenne pepper

1. Preheat your oven to 120°C/Gas ½, position middle shelf. Boil your kettle.

2. Start with the salmon. Get a non-stick baking tray. Put the salmon on the tray. Season each fillet with salt and cayenne. Brush the seasoning into the flesh. Bake for 22 minutes.

3. While the salmon bakes, prepare the mushy peas. Get a medium-sized pan. Add 150ml water and 1 tbsp of the extra virgin olive oil. Bring to the boil. Add the peas. Cover and bring back to the boil. Take the lid off. Boil rapidly for 4 minutes until all but 3 tbsp of the liquid has evaporated. Add 3 tbsp of the basil. Mash or blend the pea mixture to a chunky texture. Season to taste.

4. Next, make the sunblush tomato ketchup. Get a small pan. Add the honey, wine vinegar, tomato purée, 2 tbsp of water and the remaining 2 tbsp of extra virgin olive oil. Whisk together. Add the sunblush tomatoes and pine nuts if you are using them. Put the pan on a medium heat for 30 seconds or so until the relish is warm but not boiling. Add the remaining 3 tbsp of basil. Take the pan off the heat. Season to taste.

5. Put the mushy peas on one side of your plates. Put the salmon next to them. Spoon the sunblush tomato ketchup over and around the salmon.

Cook extra

Make extra portion(s) of the whole recipe. Flake the salmon and combine with the mushy peas and sunblush tomato ketchup (without the oil) for a wrap or sandwich. For a creamy touch, add a little mayonnaise, yoghurt, soured cream or crème fraîche. Or, to make a salad, flake the salmon and mix it with the peas, some warm simmered potatoes, the sunblush tomato ketchup and mayonnaise.

4/ Salmon with the great white butter sauce, leek & asparagus

The sauce known as *beurre blanc* comes from a place in France where the river Loire meets the Atlantic sea. It is perhaps this provenance that makes *beurre blanc* the perfect sauce for salmon. It is a legendary sauce, a great French lady; the white wine and vinegar give her bite and the butter gives her beauty. I give her a veil of practicality with a splash of cream to make her less delicate or prone to separation as she would be with butter alone. It also means she can be kept warm for a while. Asparagus and leek party together on the side; both love the sauce as much as the salmon.

    The sauce is fine for kids as the wine has its alcohol boiled out. Leeks can be a tricky texture, so chop them finely and boil them until they are completely soft. Start kids on the more tender asparagus tips. Good to purée or chop and freeze for babies and toddlers.

SERVES 2

Sides (pages 320–43)
Simmered potatoes, rice or bread and/or crisp asparagus salad, if you've any left over

Prep ahead Sauce, an hour ahead; keep warm

Prep/cooking 30–35 mins

Active time 20–25 mins

2 skinless salmon fillets, 130–140g each and 2–2.5cm thick
100ml dry white wine
2 tsp white wine vinegar
2 shallots, peeled and very finely chopped
2 tbsp whipping cream
1 tbsp water
60g butter
1 large leek (about 200g), trimmed and cut into 2cm slices diagonally
1 bunch of asparagus (about 10 spears), woody ends removed, each cut into 3 diagonally
Salt, freshly ground black pepper and sugar

1. Preheat your oven to 120°C/Gas ½, position middle shelf. Boil your kettle.

2. Start with the salmon. Get a non-stick baking tray. Put the salmon on the tray. Season each fillet with salt and pepper. Brush the seasoning into the flesh. Bake for 22 minutes.

3. While the salmon bakes, prepare the sauce. Get a small saucepan. Add the wine, wine vinegar and shallots. Put the pan on a high heat. Bring to the boil and boil until the liquid is reduced by three-quarters. When it is ready, there will be about 2 tbsp of liquid left in the pan and it will be quite dark. Turn down the heat, whisk in the cream and the 1 tbsp of water. Don't worry if it looks a bit curdled, it will be fine. Add the butter, 20g at a time, whisking as you go. Don't let the sauce boil or it will separate. Season to taste with salt, pepper and sugar. Keep the sauce warm over a very low heat for a few minutes or sit the pan in another pan of hot water for up to an hour, whisking occasionally.

4. Next, get a large saucepan. Fill it with boiling water. Add salt and bring back to the boil. Put a colander in your sink. Add the leek slices to the boiling water. Cover and bring back to the boil. Take off the lid. Boil for 2 minutes. Add the asparagus stalks and boil for 3 minutes. Add the tips and boil for another 2 minutes or until everything is tender. Drain in your colander. Shake it to remove as much water as possible. Add the vegetables to the sauce. Season to taste.

5. Put the salmon on one side of your plates. Put the leek and asparagus next to it. Spoon the sauce over everything.

Cook extra
Bake extra salmon fillet(s) to eat cold the next day with a potato or green salad and herb mayonnaise. Or flake the salmon and mix it with cress for a sandwich or wrap; try adding grated pear.

5/ Salmon with sprouts, bacon & mustard cream sauce

The slightly salty, meaty combination of bacon and salmon came from a brunch of bacon, eggs and a salmon steak we served at Brasserie Flipp in Wellington. It is a real comfort dish, one that leaves you feeling satisfied and sleepy. The key to the sauce is to catch the flavours of the bacon and mushrooms in the bottom of the pan, then boil the stock before adding the cream. I use chicken stock because I like it with the bacon; fish or vegetable stock would be fine too. The sauce also works with beef, chicken and pork.

For younger kids, don't put the mustard onto the salmon, but leave it in the sauce. The bacon may be too chewy so fry it for a minute less and then give it a go. Without the bacon the recipe is good to purée or chop and freeze for babies and toddlers.

SERVES 2

Sides (pages 320–43)
Mashed or simmered potatoes, or bread
Prep ahead Sauce, except mustard and rosemary, up to 2 hours ahead
Prep/cooking 30–35 mins
Active time 20–25 mins

2 skinless salmon fillets, 130–140g each and 2–2.5cm thick
4 tsp grain mustard
2 tsp vegetable oil
100g bacon lardons or streaky bacon, cut into 2cm chunks
150g small button mushrooms, halved
½ medium red onion, peeled and cut into 1cm dice
15g butter
100ml chicken stock or water
6 tbsp double cream
1 tbsp chopped rosemary
12 Brussels sprouts (120g), trimmed and halved
Salt and freshly ground black pepper

1. Preheat your oven to 120°C/Gas ½, position middle shelf. Boil your kettle.

2. Start with the salmon. Get a non-stick baking tray. Put the salmon on the tray. Season each fillet with salt. Spoon 1 tsp of the mustard onto each fillet. Brush the mustard evenly all over the flesh. Bake for 22 minutes.

3. While the salmon bakes, make the sauce. Get a medium-large frying pan. Put the pan on a high heat. Add the oil and get it really hot. Add the bacon and fry for 2 minutes until lightly browned. Add the mushrooms, red onion and butter. Fry for 3–4 minutes until the mushrooms are golden, but be careful not to burn the onion. Add the chicken stock and bring to the boil. Stir in the cream. Bring back to the boil. Stir in the remaining 2 tsp of mustard and the rosemary. The sauce should be thick enough to coat the back of a spoon; if it's not, boil for a little longer. If the salmon is not ready, take the pan off the heat.

4. Get a large pot. Fill it with boiling water. Add salt and bring back to the boil. Put a colander in your sink. Boil the Brussels sprouts for 3–5 minutes or until tender. Drain and return them to the pan. Sauté over a medium heat for 10–30 seconds to remove excess water.

5. Once the salmon is cooked, bring the sauce to the boil. If the sauce is too thick when you reheat it, stir in hot water, 1 tbsp at a time, until it is a spoon coating consistency. Turn off the heat. Put the salmon into the sauce. Brush the sauce all over the salmon. Scatter the Brussels sprouts around the salmon. Take it to your table in the pan.

Cook extra

Bake extra salmon fillet(s) brushed with mustard. The mustard coated salmon makes a great sandwich or wrap with cress or rocket and mayonnaise, or a salad with grains, potatoes or pasta.

6/ Salmon curry with chickpeas, mango salsa & mint yoghurt

This salmon has all the comfort and fun of an evening in with a curry and at the same time it is light, fresh, feisty and fast. The toasted chickpeas are spiced up by the curry powder and the yoghurt's creamy comfort softens everything into glorious harmony. In place of the traditional mango chutney I've made a vibrant salsa; if you can't find a ripe mango, replace it with an apple or a small red pepper.

For younger kids, use a quarter of the quantity of curry powder on the salmon the first time you make this. They may also find the lemon too acidic in the salsa, so make it with the orange juice only, separate theirs, then add the chilli and lemon juice to yours. Good to purée or chop and freeze for babies and toddlers.

SERVES 2

Sides (pages 320–43) None needed. For bulk, naan bread. Spinach salad, if you've any left over from the main meal

Prep ahead Yoghurt and mango salsa, except mint, up to 2 hours ahead

Prep/cooking 30–35 mins

Active time 25–30 mins

2 skinless salmon fillets, 130–140g each and 2–2.5cm thick

2 tsp curry powder

Zested or grated zest and juice of ½ orange (3 tbsp)

Zested or grated zest and juice of ½ lemon (2 tbsp)

4 tbsp plain yoghurt

4 tbsp sliced mint

½ mild red chilli, deseeded and finely chopped

2 tbsp extra virgin olive oil

1 small or ½ large ripe mango

1 tbsp vegetable oil

400g tin chickpeas, well drained and patted dry

100–120g baby spinach

Salt and sugar

1. Preheat your oven to 120°C/Gas ½, position middle shelf. Boil your kettle.

2. Start with the salmon. Get a baking tray. Put the salmon on the tray. Season each fillet with salt and ½ tsp of curry powder. Brush the seasonings into the flesh. Bake for 22 minutes.

3. Next, make the salsa and yoghurt dressing. Get two medium bowls. Divide the citrus zest and juices between them. Add the yoghurt and half of the mint to one bowl. Season to taste with salt.

4. Add the remaining mint to the second bowl. Stir in ½ tsp of sugar, the chilli and extra virgin olive oil. Next, cut the top and tail from the mango, then peel it with a speed peeler. Slice the flesh from the wide sides of the mango, cutting as close to the flat side of the stone as you can. Cut thinner wedges away from the tapered sides of the stone. Then just scrape the remaining flesh from the stone as best you can. Cut the mango into 1.5cm dice. Stir the mango into the dressing. Season to taste with salt and sugar. Put this salsa and the yoghurt dressing on your table.

5. Heat a large sauté pan. Add the vegetable oil and get it really hot. Add the chickpeas. Sauté for 2 minutes. Sprinkle the remaining 1 tsp of curry powder over the chickpeas. Sauté for another 1–2 minutes until the chickpeas are toasted and golden. Add the spinach. Stir for 30 seconds until it wilts.

6. Spoon the chickpeas and spinach onto your plates. Put the salmon on top. Add your salsa and yoghurt dressing when you sit down.

Cook extra

Make extra portion(s) of the recipe. Flake the salmon. Drain the salsa. Fold the salmon, chickpeas, yoghurt and drained salsa together and use this mixture to fill a wrap. Or, to make a salad, keep the spinach on one side and the salsa juice in a little pot. Toss and dress the salad when you're ready to eat it.

ROAST AUBERGINE

There is something very sexy about eating these aubergines – something about the way their chewy, dark skin gives way to juicy, soft and highly seasoned flesh. I think of them as juicy vegetarian steaks, and they are for everyone, not just for vegetarians.

An aubergine with smooth and blemish-free skin that feels firm indicates creamy flesh with few seeds. Roasting is an outstanding and simple way to cook aubergines. Criss-crossing the flesh helps the aubergine soak up the seasonings, which I add both before and after cooking to get flavours that are richly cooked into the flesh and freshly brushed over. Aubergines must be cooked through, soft and creamy – the cooking time will vary slightly according to the thickness, seediness and ripeness of the aubergine. I cut the skin off the bottom of each half aubergine for a better balance of skin and flesh, to season it in places I couldn't otherwise reach and so that it sits flat.

For young kids, I'd suggest scooping the aubergine flesh out of the skin and chopping it up. This applies to the following recipes too. Or start them off with the aubergine pizza. The scooped out aubergine flesh is excellent to purée, and the purée can be frozen.

SERVES 2

Sides (pages 320–43)
Mozzarella or goat's cheese with roast peppers, tomatoes and/or sautéed courgettes. Pasta, or plain or tasty grains with tomato compote or garlic butter

Prep ahead Aubergines can be roasted up to 2 days ahead

Prep/cooking 25–30 mins

Active time 5 mins

2 tbsp extra virgin olive oil
2 tbsp lemon juice
1 large, firm aubergine
Salt
Sugar
Freshly ground black
   pepper or cayenne
   pepper or other
   seasoning (see right)

1. Preheat your oven to 220°C/Gas 7, position upper middle shelf.

2. Start with the dressing. Get a small bowl. Add the extra virgin olive oil and lemon juice. Mix with a fork. Season to taste with salt and sugar.

3. Next, prepare the aubergine. Cut it in half lengthways. Score the flesh side in a criss-cross pattern. Peel or slice a 10cm long, 3cm wide strip of skin off the bottom of each half. Get a small baking tray. Line it with greaseproof or non-stick baking paper. Put the aubergine halves on the baking tray. Brush the top and bottom of the aubergine vigorously with half the dressing. Make sure the aubergine is criss-cross side up. Roast for 20–25 minutes until the flesh is soft. While the aubergine is still hot, brush the remaining dressing over the top.

Instead of pepper
Try cardamom, cumin, chilli powder, Chinese five-spice, cinnamon, caraway, crushed fennel seeds, allspice, jerk spice, sumac, tamarind, za'atar, ginger, garlic, harissa, smoked paprika, soy and honey, barbecue sauce, citrus juice or citrus zest.

Magic adventures
Serve with pesto, tapenade, tomato compote, soft, sweet, sticky onions, green curry paste or garlic butter.

Cook extra
The aubergines are good hot or cool in salads. If you serve them cool, then add more lemon juice, or replace it with balsamic vinegar. Scoop out the aubergine flesh and purée it with olive oil and lemon juice to make a good accompaniment, dip or spread for grilled bread, sandwiches or wraps.

1/ Aubergine with ricotta, Parmesan & orange pepper

I first ate this with the plate perched on my laptop keyboard during a cold afternoon in January. It felt like a firework display in my mouth, glamorous comfort food with the contrasting delights of currants and capers. The ricotta mixture is nostalgic for me: it was the cement in great layered towers of vegetables that I served in my cheffy 90s – the higher the better. I still can't look at an aubergine without wanting to stack it somehow.

For younger kids, chop rather than slice the onions and peppers. Use less vinegar and leave out the capers if you need to, though I've found most kids like them in a tomato sauce. Can be puréed or chopped and frozen for babies and toddlers.

SERVES 2

Sides (pages 320–43)
Plain grains or chickpeas
or polenta with olive oil
Prep ahead Peppers, a day
ahead
Prep/cooking 30–35 mins
Active time 25–30 mins

4 tbsp plus 2 tsp extra
   virgin olive oil
2 tbsp red wine vinegar
1 large aubergine
½ medium red onion, peeled
   and cut into 5mm slices
2 garlic cloves, peeled and
   finely sliced
1 orange pepper, quartered,
   deseeded and cut across
   into 1cm slices
3 tbsp currants
2 tbsp water
1 heaped tsp tiny salted
   or brined capers, rinsed
½ x 400g tin chopped
   tomatoes
8 tbsp grated Parmesan
125g ricotta
4 tbsp sliced basil
Salt, freshly ground black
   pepper and sugar

1. Preheat your oven to 220°C/Gas 7, position upper middle shelf.

2. Start with the dressing. Get a small bowl. Add 2 tbsp of the extra virgin olive oil and 1 tbsp of the wine vinegar. Mix them together with a fork. Season to taste with salt and sugar.

3. Next, prepare the aubergine. Cut it in half lengthways. Score the flesh side in a criss-cross pattern. Peel or slice a 10cm long, 3cm wide strip of skin off the bottom of each half. Get a small baking tray. Line it with greaseproof or non-stick baking paper. Put the aubergine halves on the baking tray. Brush the top and bottom of the aubergine vigorously with half the dressing. Make sure the aubergine is criss-cross side up. Roast for 20–25 minutes until the flesh is soft. While the aubergine is still hot, brush the remaining dressing over the top.

4. While the aubergine roasts, prepare the pepper mixture. Get a medium-sized frying pan. Add the red onion, garlic, orange pepper, currants, 2 tbsp of the extra virgin olive oil, the remaining 1 tbsp of wine vinegar, the 2 tbsp of water, a pinch of salt and a pinch of sugar. Cover the pan and put it on a medium heat. Sweat for 10 minutes or until soft, checking a few times; if the mixture looks a bit dry, add 1–2 tsp of water. Add the capers and tomatoes. Turn up the heat. Bring to the boil. Simmer for 2 minutes. Season to taste.

5. Get a medium bowl. Add the Parmesan, ricotta and 2 tbsp of the basil. Mix together. Season to taste. When you are ready to serve, spread this mixture over the cooked aubergine halves. Trickle 1 tsp of extra virgin olive oil over each aubergine half. Roast for 3 minutes.

6. Use a fish slice to lift the aubergines onto your plates. Add the remaining basil to the orange pepper mixture. Spoon it over the aubergines.

Cook extra
Make extra portion(s) of the recipe. Cut the aubergine into chunks. Toss with the pepper mixture. Use the ricotta mixture to butter a baguette and fill it with the aubergine and pepper.

2/ Aubergine with glazed tofu, fried broccoli & chilli

Once a year, I have an eating holiday with my dear friend Justin North. This time it was Tokyo. We ate sweet and sour, glazed and glorious teriyaki aubergines at Hideki Ishikawa's 3 star Michelin restaurant. I just had to adapt it for this chapter.

We often go to great lengths to describe things that are not meat as being meaty – a very meaty fish or fat, meaty mushrooms, for example. I'm desperate to find another way, a vegetarianism. This isn't like meat at all but it's big, bold, gutsy, juicy and masculine – an oddly elegant combination that doesn't taste elegant at all. It just tastes good.

For younger kids, make sure the ginger and garlic are very finely chopped or grated. Start with a little less hoisin sauce for theirs. Letting them paint the aubergine is a good idea too. Can be puréed or chopped and frozen for babies and toddlers.

SERVES 2

Sides (pages 320–43)
None needed. For bulk, rice or egg noodles

Prep ahead Dressing, up to 2 days ahead

Prep/cooking 30–35 mins

Active time 25–30 mins

4 tbsp hoisin sauce
4 tsp grated ginger
1 garlic clove, peeled and
   finely chopped
5 tsp sesame oil
1 large aubergine
120g medium chestnut
   or button mushrooms,
   halved
150g tofu, drained and
   cut into 4 pieces
1 tbsp lime juice
1 tbsp soy sauce
4 tbsp sliced coriander
5 tbsp water
150g broccoli (¼–½ head),
   cut into small florets,
   stalk into 5mm strips
½ mild red chilli, deseeded
   and finely diced

1. Preheat your oven to 220°C/Gas 7, position upper middle shelf.

2. Start with the dressing. Get a medium bowl. Add the hoisin sauce, 2 tsp of the grated ginger, half the garlic and 2 tsp of the sesame oil. Mix with a fork.

3. Next, prepare the aubergine. Cut it in half lengthways. Score the flesh side in a criss-cross pattern. Peel or slice a 10cm long, 3cm wide strip of skin off the bottom of each half. Get a small baking tray. Line it with greaseproof or non-stick baking paper. Put the aubergine halves on the baking tray. Brush the top and bottom of the aubergine vigorously with a third of the dressing. Make sure the aubergine is criss-cross side up. Roast for 15 minutes.

4. While the aubergine roasts, prepare the mushrooms and tofu. Brush them with half of the remaining dressing. When the aubergine has been in the oven for 15 minutes, add the mushrooms and tofu to the baking tray. Roast for another 10 minutes.

5. Add the lime juice, soy sauce, coriander and 2 tsp of the remaining sesame oil to the rest of the dressing.

6. Get a large pan. Add the remaining 1 tsp of sesame oil and 5 tbsp of water. Bring to the boil. Add the broccoli. Cover and boil over a high heat for 3 minutes. Add water, 1 tbsp at a time, if the pan dries out. Take off the lid. Add the remaining 2 tsp of grated ginger, the rest of the garlic and the chilli. Stir-fry for 1–2 minutes until the water has evaporated and the broccoli is tender, being careful not to burn the ginger and garlic.

7. Cut each aubergine half into 3 pieces (or leave them whole if you prefer). Divide the aubergine, mushrooms, tofu and broccoli between your plates. Spoon and then brush the dressing over everything.

Cook extra

Make extra portion(s) of the recipe. Chop the aubergine. Mix it with the other ingredients, cooked egg noodles and extra lime juice. Eat hot or cold.

3/ Aubergine with chickpeas & cranberry & orange relish

This dish is all luxury, flirtatious flavours and creamy textures, but there is no cream. I've loved tinned chickpeas for a long time and boiling them with their liquid is enough to make a creamy textured sauce. Feel free to replace the dried cranberries with dried apricots or raisins – they are there for a sweet bit of chew and a flash of red. And you can replace the ras-el-hanout with curry powder.

This is a good meal for younger kids. The chickpeas are tasty without being fiery, but halve the kids' spices to start. Let kids put their own yoghurt on at your table. An excellent dish to purée or chop and freeze for babies and toddlers.

SERVES 2

Sides (pages 320–43)
None needed. For bulk, pita.
Crisp leaf or raw mangetout
salad is also good

Prep ahead Chickpeas, a day
ahead. Relish, an hour ahead

Prep/cooking 30–35 mins

Active time 20–25 mins

4 tbsp extra virgin olive oil
3 tbsp lemon juice
1 large aubergine
1 medium onion, peeled
    and cut into 5mm dice
1 garlic clove, peeled and
    finely chopped
3 tsp grated ginger
½ tsp ground turmeric
400g tin chickpeas
1 small orange
2 heaped tbsp dried
    cranberries (or raisins)
2 tbsp sliced mint
4 tbsp plain yoghurt
Salt, sugar and
    ras-el-hanout

1. Preheat your oven to 220°C/Gas 7, position upper middle shelf.

2. Start with the dressing. Get a small bowl. Add 2 tbsp of the extra virgin olive oil, 2 tbsp of the lemon juice and 1 tsp of ras-el-hanout. Mix together well. Season to taste with salt and sugar.

3. Next, prepare the aubergine. Cut it in half lengthways. Score the flesh side in a criss-cross pattern. Peel or slice a 10cm long, 3cm wide strip of skin off the bottom of each half. Get a small baking tray. Line it with greaseproof or non-stick baking paper. Put the aubergine halves on the baking tray. Brush the top and bottom of the aubergine vigorously with half the dressing. Make sure the aubergine is criss-cross side up. Roast for 20–25 minutes until the flesh is soft. While the aubergine is still hot, brush the remaining dressing over the top.

4. While the aubergine roasts, prepare the chickpeas. Get a medium-sized pan. Add 1 tbsp of the remaining extra virgin olive oil, the onion, garlic, 1 tsp of the grated ginger and the turmeric. Cover and sweat over a medium heat for 7–10 minutes until the onion is soft. Add the chickpeas and their liquid. Cover and bring to the boil. Remove the lid. Turn the heat down to low. Simmer for 4–5 minutes until the liquid thickens (to look slightly thicker than orange juice you buy with bits in.) Take the pan off the heat. Cover.

5. Next, make the relish. Get a medium bowl. Grate the zest of the orange into it. Peel the orange and separate into segments. Slice each segment widthways into 5mm slices and add to the bowl. Stir in the cranberries, the remaining 1 tbsp of lemon juice, 1 tbsp of extra virgin olive oil and 1 tsp of grated ginger, and half the mint. Mix the remaining mint and 1 tsp of ginger with the yoghurt. Season to taste. Put the yoghurt on your table.

6. Put an aubergine half on each plate. Spoon the chickpeas and relish over and around the aubergine. Serve with the yoghurt.

Cook extra
Make extra portion(s) of the recipe. Drain the chickpeas. Cut the aubergine into chunks. Mix with the relish. Stuff into pita, wraps or big lettuce leaves.

4/ My Mum's spiced eggplant with creamy lentils & grapes

This is a very special meal for me as it is the only one in the book that mum and I ate together when she was here in England on holiday. Mum loves aubergines, or eggplants as they're called in New Zealand. This one's for you mum. If you can't find ground cardamom, add 2 tsp of crushed seeds to the sauce instead.

The texture and taste of the lentils make this an excellent dish for kids. Try starting them with curry powder if it is more familiar than the spices I've used. I asked Jake to smell the dry spices and he didn't like the scent, but he really liked their flavour in the lentils. By all means chop the aubergine and mix it through the lentils. Purée or chop for babies and toddlers, but don't freeze, as the cream will separate.

SERVES 2

Sides (pages 320–43)
None needed. For bulk, rice or naan bread
Prep ahead Lentils, a day ahead
Prep/cooking 35–40 mins
Active time 35–40 mins

1 tsp ground cumin
1 tsp ground cardamom
2 tbsp extra virgin olive oil
250ml plus 2 tbsp white or black grape juice
1 large aubergine
1 medium onion, peeled and cut into 1cm dice
2 garlic cloves, peeled and thinly sliced
1½ tbsp grated ginger
1 heaped tbsp tomato purée
4 tbsp ground almonds
1 tsp vegetable bouillon powder
100ml whipping cream
400g tin Puy lentils, drained (250g drained weight)
12 grapes, quartered
4 tbsp sliced basil
4 tbsp plain yoghurt
Salt

1. Preheat your oven to 220°C/Gas 7, position upper middle shelf.

2. Start with the dressing. Get a small bowl. Add ½ tsp of the cumin, ½ tsp of the cardamom, 1 tbsp of the extra virgin olive oil and the 2 tbsp of grape juice. Mix together well. Season to taste with salt.

3. Next, prepare the aubergine. Cut it in half lengthways. Score the flesh side in a criss-cross pattern. Peel or slice a 10cm long, 3cm wide strip of skin off the bottom of each half. Get a small baking tray. Line it with greaseproof or non-stick baking paper. Put the aubergine halves on the baking tray. Brush the top and bottom of the aubergine vigorously with a third of the dressing. Make sure the aubergine is criss-cross side up. Roast for 20–25 minutes until the flesh is soft. While the aubergine is still hot, brush half the remaining dressing over the top.

4. While the aubergine roasts, make the creamy lentils. Get a medium-sized shallow pan. Add the remaining 1 tbsp of extra virgin olive oil, the onion, garlic and ginger. Cover the pan and put it on a medium heat. Sweat for 7–10 minutes until soft. Add the tomato purée, remaining ½ tsp of cumin and ½ tsp of cardamom, and the ground almonds. Turn the heat to high and fry for 2 minutes, stirring constantly so it doesn't burn. Whisk in 250ml grape juice, the bouillon powder and whipping cream. Bring to the boil. Turn the heat to low and simmer for 5 minutes.

5. Add the lentils to the pan. Bring back to the boil. Simmer for 2 minutes. Season to taste with salt. Now add the roasted aubergine halves.

6. Mix the grapes and basil with the remaining dressing. Scatter them over the lentils and aubergine. Spoon on the yoghurt. Take the pan to your table.

5/ Aubergine 'burger' with smoked paprika & Greek salad

This is a plateful of playtime. The chutney perks up the aubergine and helps stick the 'burger' together, and I love the way the feta's salty crumbles get cosy with the chutney. There's no need to make your own, there are some very nice tomato chutneys available in delis and supermarkets. Once you've got the hang of it you can try all sorts of variations: mozzarella and rich tomato sauce; goat's cheese and beetroot; or any combination of cheese, sunblush, sun-dried, confit or compote tomato.

For younger kids, leave the red onion out completely. The feta will also be a hard sell, more because of the texture than taste, but let them try it and have some grated Cheddar or cream cheese to hand. I've been surprised that most of the kids I've cooked for like olives. This meal is no good to purée or freeze.

SERVES 2

Sides Polenta chips (page 340)

Prep ahead Salad, except basil, 2 hours ahead

Prep/cooking 40 mins

Active time 30 mins

3 tbsp plus 1 tsp extra virgin olive oil

Zested or grated zest of ½ small lemon and 2 tbsp plus 1 tsp juice

1 large aubergine, green tip cut off

¼ medium red onion, peeled and finely sliced

¼ cucumber, halved, deseeded and cut into 5mm slices

100g feta, cut into 2cm cubes

12 black olives, pitted

4 heaped tbsp sliced basil

1 beefsteak tomato

4 heaped tsp tomato chutney

Salt, sugar and smoked paprika

1. Preheat your oven to 220°C/Gas 7, position upper middle shelf.

2. Start with the dressing. Get a small bowl. Add the 3 tbsp of extra virgin olive oil, lemon zest, 2 tbsp of lemon juice and ½ tsp of smoked paprika. Mix together well. Season to taste with salt and sugar.

3. Next, prepare the aubergine. Cut it in half lengthways. Score the flesh side in a criss-cross pattern. Peel or slice a 10cm long, 3cm wide strip of skin off the bottom of each half. Cut each half across into two. Get a small baking tray. Line it with greaseproof or non-stick baking paper. Put the aubergine quarters on the baking tray. Brush the top and bottom of the aubergine vigorously with half the dressing. Make sure the aubergine is criss-cross side up. Roast for 20–25 minutes until the flesh is soft.

4. While the aubergine roasts, prepare the Greek salad. Get a medium-sized shallow bowl. Add the onion, a pinch of salt, a pinch of sugar and the 1 tsp of lemon juice. Toss to mix. Let sit for 5 minutes. Next, add the cucumber, half the feta, the olives, basil and remaining dressing. Mix together very gently so you don't break up the feta too much. Season to taste.

5. Cut the beefsteak tomato in half. Slice it very thinly. Spread the tomato slices over your plates. Season the slices with salt and smoked paprika.

6. Once the aubergine quarters are ready, spread 2 heaped tsp of chutney on two of them. Top with the remaining feta. Put a second quarter aubergine on top of each. Press down gently. Roast for 2 minutes.

7. Put the aubergine 'burgers' on top of the tomatoes. Brush each 'burger' with ½ tsp of olive oil. Spoon the Greek salad to one side. Serve with the polenta chips.

Cook extra

Make extra portion(s) of the recipe. Cut the roast aubergine into cubes. Mix with the other ingredients to make a salad or stuffing for a wrap.

6/ Aubergine, tomato & mozzarella 'pizza'

I'm cheating slightly here, but doing so in your service. The aubergine has to be dryer and wider than it does for the other recipes, so it needs to be cut more thinly before being cooked. This recipe gives you a tart or pizza base for anyone who doesn't eat wheat, and you can use these aubergines as a base for any of the onion tarts on page 168.

The key to this recipe is to get the tomatoes and mozzarella very dry. The method of salting the tomatoes to get their moisture out and intensify their taste is the same for a home-baked pizza and works with a pizza dough, puff pastry, wrap or pita base.

This is an excellent way to introduce kids of all ages to aubergines. You can have a pizza party and get them to put their own toppings on; sweetcorn and olives are popular in our house. No good to purée or freeze.

SERVES 2

Sides (pages 320–43)
Potato salad or garlic bread and/or leaf or tomato salad
Prep ahead Aubergines can be roasted a day ahead; finish with topping to serve
Prep/cooking 45 mins
Active time 10–15 mins

1 aubergine, green tip cut off
2 tbsp plus 2 tsp extra virgin olive oil
2 large, ripe plum tomatoes (110–120g each)
2 tsp tomato purée
6 sunblush tomatoes, cut into 2cm dice
1 garlic clove, peeled and finely chopped
1 mozzarella ball (about 125g)
2 tbsp grated Parmesan
2 tbsp sliced basil
1 tsp balsamic vinegar
Salt, cayenne pepper and sugar

1. Preheat your oven to 230°C/Gas 8, position upper middle shelf.

2. Start with the aubergine. Cut it in half lengthways. Lay the halves cut side down on your chopping board. Cut each half lengthways in two, to give 4 thinner slices. Get a baking tray. Line it with a non-stick mat. Lay the aubergine slices on the tray close together in pairs to make 2 'pizza' bases. Brush both sides of the aubergine slices with the 2 tbsp of olive oil. Season with salt. Roast for 8 minutes. Turn the aubergine slices over. Roast for 8 minutes or until golden.

3. To prepare the plum tomatoes, cut out the dark tops and then cut the tomatoes in half. Cut 2 halves into 5 slices each. Sprinkle these slices lightly with salt. Chop the remaining 2 tomato halves into 2cm dice.

4. Get a medium bowl. Add the diced tomato, tomato purée, sunblush tomatoes, garlic, ⅛ tsp of salt, a pinch of cayenne and ¼ tsp of sugar. Stir well. Leave to sit until the aubergine is roasted.

5. Drain and halve the mozzarella. Cut each half into 5 even slices. Pat very dry with kitchen paper. Once the aubergine is ready, take it out of the oven. Turn your oven up to 240°C/Gas 9.

6. Pat the tomato slices dry. Drain the diced tomato mixture in a sieve over a bowl, pushing gently on the tomatoes with the back of a spoon to make sure they are as dry as possible. Put the juice to one side.

7. Spread the diced tomato over the cooked aubergine. Lay the mozzarella and sliced tomato on top. Sprinkle over the Parmesan. Roast for 15–18 minutes until the cheese is melted and golden. Don't worry if it burns a bit around the edge. Scatter the basil on top.

8. Add the 2 tsp of olive oil and 1 tsp of balsamic vinegar to the strained tomato juice. Spoon the dressing onto your plates. Use a fish slice to transfer the pizza to the plates.

PAN-FRIED PORK CHOPS

Pork chops vary greatly in size and you will need to adjust the cooking time accordingly (see below). I prefer shoulder chops or steaks because they have more flavour and a better marbling of fat; they are also cheaper. You will get a better, more golden crust if the surface of the pork is very dry, so keep chops uncovered in the fridge before cooking.

For younger kids, slice the pork. Purée or chop and freeze for babies and toddlers.

SERVES 2

Sides (pages 320–43)
Any you fancy

Prep/cooking 15–20 mins
Active time 15–20 mins

2 pork chops, about 200g each, skin cut off leaving a 5mm–1cm layer of fat
2 tsp vegetable oil
20g butter, cut into 8 pieces
4 tbsp water
Salt
Freshly ground black pepper or other seasoning (see right)

1. Preheat your oven to 50°C/lowest Gas. Put a plate with a rack on it in the oven to rest the pork on. Put a bowl next to the cooker to drain the fat into.

2. Cut through the fat around the pork chops at 1cm intervals. Season the chops with salt and pepper, or something instead of pepper.

3. Get a medium-sized frying pan. Add the oil and get it really hot. Use tongs to hold the chops fat side down in the pan. You should hear a big sizzle; if not take out the chops and get the pan hotter. Fry for 30 seconds until the fat is pale golden. Lay the chops on one side. If they curl a bit as they hit the heat, press them flat with your tongs. Fry for 2–3 minutes over a medium-high heat. Turn. Fry for another 2–3 minutes. Lower the heat to medium. Put the chops on the rack. Drain the fat. Return the chops to the pan. Add 6 pieces of butter. Fry for 1 minute on each side; don't let the butter burn.

4. Turn the oven off. Put the chops on the rack in the oven to rest for 3–5 minutes, leaving the door slightly ajar.

5. Add the 4 tbsp of water to the pan. Bring to the boil, stirring and scraping up the juices off the bottom of the pan. Take the pan off the heat. Stir in the rest of the butter. Once the chops have rested, add their juices to the pan. Turn the chops in the juices and brush until glossy. Serve with the juices.

Instead of pepper
Try chilli or curry powder, Chinese five-spice, cinnamon, caraway, cumin, cardamom, ground fennel seeds, allspice, ginger, jerk spice or paprika.

Cooking and resting times for different pork chop weights
180–220g: 2 mins each side in oil, 1 min each side in butter, 3 mins rest
220–260g: 2½ mins each side in oil, 1 min each side in butter, 4 mins rest
260–300g: 3 mins each side in oil, 1 min each side in butter, 5 mins rest
Interior temperature: Fry to 61–63°C; rest to 63–65°C (use your probe)

Magic adventures
Serve with pesto, tapenade, tomato compote or soft, sweet, sticky onions.

Cook extra
A cold pork chop can be sliced and brushed with hoisin sauce for chow mein or fried rice. They are also good plain, glazed or spiced in a sandwich or wrap.

1/ Paprika pork with toasted chickpeas, red pepper & beans

I first ate this enchanting summer stew served with tripe in San Sebastian. It's a tasty, colourful, highly versatile combination. You can exchange the pork for baked chicken, salmon fillets, roast aubergine, lamb chops, mackerel or grilled haloumi. The toasted chickpea mixture makes a great little snack with drinks.

The toasted mixture is a good way to get younger kids into chickpeas, almonds and garlic. You can also add little cubes of bread, or my croûtons (see page 343). Leave out the almonds to purée or chop and freeze for babies and toddlers.

SERVES 2

Sides Bread

Prep ahead Pepper sauce, up to a day ahead

Prep/cooking 35–45 mins

Active time 20–25 mins

4 garlic cloves, peeled and thinly sliced

1 red pepper, quartered, deseeded and cut across into 1cm slices

2 tbsp extra virgin olive oil

2 tsp red wine vinegar

1 ripe tomato, cut into 1cm dice

4 tbsp tomato juice

2 tsp vegetable oil

2 pork chops, about 200g each, skin cut off, leaving a 5mm–1cm layer of fat

20g butter, cut into 8 pieces

½ x 400g tin chickpeas, well drained

4 tbsp flaked almonds (optional)

4 tbsp water

100g runner beans, cut into 4cm chunks

Salt and smoked paprika

1. Preheat your oven to 50°C/ lowest Gas. Put a plate with a rack on it in the oven to rest the pork on. Put a bowl next to the cooker to drain the fat into. Boil your kettle. Put a colander in your sink.

2. Start with the pepper sauce. Get a medium-sized saucepan. Add half the garlic, the red pepper, ¼ tsp of smoked paprika and the extra virgin olive oil. Cover and sweat over a medium heat for 12 minutes until the pepper softens. Add the wine vinegar. Boil for 30 seconds. Add the tomato and tomato juice. Simmer for 1 minute until the tomato softens and the juice thickens a little. Take the pan off the heat.

3. Get a medium-large frying pan. Add the vegetable oil and get it really hot. Season the chops with salt and smoked paprika. Use tongs to hold the chops fat side down in the pan and fry for 30 seconds. Lay the chops on one side. Fry for 2–3 minutes over a medium-high heat. Turn. Fry for 2–3 minutes. Lower the heat to medium. Drain the fat. Add 6 pieces of butter. Fry for 1 minute on each side. Rest the chops on the rack in the oven for 3–5 minutes, turning the oven off and leaving the door slightly ajar.

4. Add the chickpeas, almonds if you're using them, and the rest of the garlic to the frying pan. Season with salt and smoked paprika. Sauté over a low heat for 1–2 minutes until golden. Put them on the plate under the pork in the oven.

5. Add the pepper sauce and the 4 tbsp of water to the pan. Bring to the boil, scraping the bottom of the pan to get all the caramelised juices. Stir in the remaining 2 pieces of butter. Season to taste.

6. Rinse out your medium saucepan and fill it two-thirds full with water from your kettle. Add salt and bring to the boil. Add the runner beans and boil for 3–4 minutes or until tender. Drain well. Add the beans to the pepper sauce. Spoon onto your plates. Put the pork chops and their resting juices on the plates. Scatter the chickpeas, almonds and garlic over the top.

Cook extra
Make extra portion(s) of the recipe. Slice the pork and mix it with everything else for a delicious salad, sandwich or wrap.

2/ Pork chop with beetroot & sweet & sour rhubarb relish

Rhubarb is a good fruit to serve with pork because it gives the meat a sour sidekick that bites through the richness. The pork, sweet beetroot, sour rhubarb, spicy watercress and smooth yoghurt manage to be contrasting and happily harmonious at the same time. This is a meal where you're best to eat a bit of everything on each forkful. I've served it with duck in place of pork and it worked very well. The flavours would go nicely with game, goat's cheese, prawns and fried squid too.

For younger kids, slice the pork very thinly and slice or leave out the watercress. I've found that the rhubarb and beetroot are generally acceptable if the yoghurt is there to mellow the rhubarb. Good to purée or chop and freeze for babies and toddlers.

SERVES 2

Sides (pages 320–43)
None needed. For bulk, plain grains
Prep ahead Relish, up to 2 days ahead
Prep/cooking 35–40 mins
Active time 30–35 mins

200g rhubarb, trimmed
200ml orange juice
1 garlic clove, peeled and finely chopped
2 tsp grated ginger
3 tbsp caster sugar
3 tbsp extra virgin olive oil
1 tsp white wine vinegar
Zested or grated zest of ½ orange
2 tsp vegetable oil
2 pork chops, about 200g each, skin cut off, leaving a 5mm–1cm layer of fat
25g butter, cut into 6 pieces
200g cooked beetroot (see page 327), cut into 5mm slices
3 tbsp plain yoghurt
40g watercress (½ small packet/bunch)
Salt, cinnamon and sugar

1. Preheat your oven to 50°C/lowest Gas. Put a bowl next to the cooker to drain the fat into.

2. Start with the relish. Cut the rhubarb into 3mm sticks. Get a medium-sized shallow saucepan. Add the orange juice, garlic and ginger. Bring to the boil and boil rapidly for 4–5 minutes or until the liquid has reduced by half. Add the sugar. Stir until it dissolves. Add the rhubarb and 1 tbsp of the extra virgin olive oil. Cover and bring back to the boil. Lower the heat to medium. Gently poach the rhubarb for 3 minutes until it starts to soften.

3. Take the lid off the pan and turn the heat to high. Simmer rapidly for 1–2 minutes until the rhubarb is soft but still holding its shape and the liquid is the consistency of thin syrup. Turn off the heat. Add 1 tsp of the wine vinegar, the remaining 2 tbsp of extra virgin olive oil and the orange zest. Season to taste with salt, cinnamon and sugar. Put the pan in the oven. Lay a resting rack on top of the pan.

4. Get a medium-sized frying pan. Add the vegetable oil and get it really hot. Season the chops with salt and cinnamon. Use tongs to hold the chops fat side down in the pan and fry for 30 seconds. Lay the chops on one side. Fry for 2–3 minutes over a medium-high heat. Turn. Fry for 2–3 minutes. Lower the heat to medium. Drain the fat. Add the butter. Fry for 1 minute on each side; don't let the butter burn. Rest the chops on the rack on top of the pan in the oven for 3–5 minutes, turning the oven off and leaving the door slightly ajar.

5. Lay the beetroot slices on your plates. Put the rested pork chops on top. Brush the beetroot and pork with the relish juices. Spoon the rest of the relish around the chops. Spoon on the yoghurt and add some of the watercress. Serve the remaining watercress as a salad on the side.

Cook extra

Make extra portion(s) of the recipe. Slice the cold pork and mix it with the other ingredients for an excellent and unusual salad, sandwich or wrap.

3/ Pork chop with braised fennel & red onions

Pork and anise of any sort make fine companions. The braised fennel is intensely scented, and the red onions are flavoured with the sweet caramelised juices in the pan. If you have the good fortune to be able to pick a few fennel fronds from your garden, use these in place of the parsley. The nutty butter, onions and herbs, combined with the juices of the pork, are almost as good as the meat itself.

For younger kids, slice the pork thinly. Give them the more tender hearts of the fennel. Omit the fennel seeds and chop onions and parsley extra finely, or if they're finding leafy things difficult, leave the parsley out for now. Good to purée or chop and freeze for babies and toddlers.

SERVES 2

Sides (pages 320–43)
Olive oil mashed potato
or soft polenta, a pulse or
vegetable purée
Prep ahead Fennel, cook up
to a day ahead
Prep/cooking 30–35 mins
Active time 25–30 mins

1 large fennel bulb,
   trimmed
150ml chicken stock
2 garlic cloves, peeled and
   finely sliced
2 tsp fennel seeds
45g butter
2 tsp vegetable oil
2 pork chops, about 200g
   each, skin cut off, leaving
   a 5mm–1cm layer of fat
2 medium red onions,
   peeled and cut into
   1.5cm dice
100ml water
6 heaped tbsp sliced
   flat-leaf parsley
Salt and freshly ground
   black pepper

1. Preheat your oven to 50°C/lowest Gas. Put a plate with a rack on it in the oven to rest the pork on. Put a bowl next to the cooker to drain the fat into.

2. Start with the fennel. Cut the bulb in half lengthways. Cut each half into three slices. Lay the fennel slices flat in a medium-sized shallow pan. Cover the fennel with the chicken stock. Add the garlic, 1 tsp of the fennel seeds and 20g of the butter. Season lightly with salt and pepper. Cover and bring to the boil. Turn the heat to low. Simmer for 10–12 minutes or until the fennel is just tender. Take the lid off and boil rapidly for 3–5 minutes until all of the liquid has evaporated and the fennel is glazed. Turn off the heat.

3. While the fennel simmers, get a medium-sized frying pan. Add the oil and get it really hot. Season the chops with salt and pepper. Use tongs to hold the chops fat side down in the pan and fry for 30 seconds. Lay the chops on one side. Fry for 2–3 minutes over a medium-high heat. Turn. Fry for 2–3 minutes on the other side. Lower the heat to medium. Drain the fat. Add the remaining 25g butter, cut into 6 pieces. Fry for 1 minute on each side; don't let the butter burn. Rest the chops on the rack in the oven for 3–5 minutes, turning the oven off and leaving the door slightly ajar.

4. Add the diced red onions and remaining 1 tsp of fennel seeds to the frying pan along with the 100ml water. Boil for 3–4 minutes or until the liquid has evaporated and the onions are soft and starting to caramelise. Add the parsley. Season to taste. Finally, add any resting juices from the chops.

5. Put the pork chops and braised fennel on plates. Spread the onion mixture over the chops.

4/ Pork chop with Cox's apple, sage & cream sauce

I first made this sauce with apple juice given to me by Chris Lanczak, who has looked after the orchards at the glorious Waterperry gardens, a few miles from my house in Oxfordshire, for his whole working life. The sauce is a suave delight, good and rich, creamy and flavoursome, and the pork loves being smothered in its depths. It's the kind of sauce that is often based on Calvados or cider, but I've made it alcohol free without any compromise to the flavour. Cox's Orange Pippin is a perfect apple for this one, with just the right combination of sweet and sharp; it will also fry without falling apart.

For younger kids, slice the pork thinly. For the sauce, chop the cooked apple finely and the sage extremely finely or leave it out; apart from that you won't need to change anything. Good to purée or chop and freeze for babies and toddlers.

SERVES 2

Sides (pages 320–43)
Parsnip purée or mashed potato, quinoa or basmati rice

Prep/cooking 25–30 mins
Active time 20–25 mins

200ml apple juice
2 tsp vegetable oil
2 pork chops, about 200g each, skin cut off, leaving a 5mm–1cm layer of fat
15g butter, cut into 6 pieces
1 medium Cox's Orange Pippin, peeled, halved and cored, each half cut into 5 wedges
2 tbsp finely sliced sage
125g crème fraîche
Salt, freshly ground black pepper and sugar

1. Preheat your oven to 50°C/lowest Gas. Put a plate with a rack on it in the oven to rest the pork on. Put a bowl next to the cooker to drain the fat into.

2. Start with the sauce. Get a medium-sized saucepan. Pour the apple juice into it. Put the pan on a high heat. Bring to the boil and boil until the juice has reduced by half. Take the pan off the heat.

3. While the juice reduces, get a medium-sized frying pan. Add the oil and get it really hot. Season the chops with salt and pepper. Use tongs to hold the chops fat side down in the pan and fry for 30 seconds. Lay the chops on one side. Fry for 2–3 minutes over a medium-high heat. Turn. Fry for 2–3 minutes on the other side. Lower the heat to medium. Drain the fat. Add the butter. Fry for 1 minute on each side; don't let the butter burn. Rest the chops on the rack in the oven for 3–5 minutes, turning the oven off and leaving the door slightly ajar.

4. Add the apple wedges to the frying pan. Fry over a low heat for 2 minutes. Turn and fry for 2 minutes until golden brown on both sides. Add the sage. Pour over the reduced apple juice. Bring to the boil and boil for 1 minute until the juice is thick and almost syrupy. Stir in the crème fraîche and bring back to the boil. Turn off the heat. Season with salt, pepper and a touch of sugar. The sauce needs to be thick enough to richly coat the pork; if it becomes too thick, add hot water, 1 tbsp at a time, to thin it to a spoon coating consistency.

5. Add the pork and its resting juices to the pan. Turn the pork in the sauce and brush it all over the chops so they are well coated. Serve from the pan at your table.

5/ Pork chop with crunchy crumbs & cauliflower

I looked at my cauliflower and said, 'Show me what you can do, petal.' She showed me salad and purée so delicious that they enjoy equal billing with the pork. Parsley crumbs add another layer, their taste made rich by the brown butter. This nutty butter links the pork to the cauliflower purée, which I learnt to make with Jean Bardet in Tours. He served it as an *amuse gueule* with raspberry purée, a pretty shocking combination in the early 90s.

The soft, sweet cauliflower purée is ideal for kids. For younger kids, slice the pork thinly. Leave the shallot out of the salad, serve the kids, then add the shallot to yours. Chop the parsley very finely. Good to purée or chop and freeze for babies and toddlers.

SERVES 2

Sides (pages 320–43)
None needed. For bulk, plain grains or bread
Prep ahead Purée and salad, up to an hour ahead
Prep/cooking 35–40 mins
Active time 25–30 mins

400g cauliflower, with
    its small leaves
45g butter
120ml milk
2 tsp red wine vinegar
4 tsp extra virgin olive oil
1 shallot, peeled and
    thinly sliced
6 tbsp sliced flat-leaf
    parsley
2 tsp vegetable oil
2 pork chops, about 200g
    each, skin cut off, leaving
    a 5mm–1cm layer of fat
6 tbsp coarse, crisp
    breadcrumbs (either
    homemade, see page 21,
    or shop-bought)
2 tsp Dijon mustard
Salt, curry powder and
    freshly ground black
    pepper

1. Preheat your oven to 50°C/lowest Gas. Put a plate with a rack on it in the oven to rest the pork on. Put a bowl next to the cooker to drain the fat into. Boil your kettle. Put a colander in your sink.

2. Start with the purée. Fill a medium-sized saucepan with water from your kettle. Add salt. Bring to the boil. Chop 300g of the cauliflower, including all the stalk, into 3cm pieces. Add to the boiling water. Cover and bring back to the boil. Take the lid off. Boil for 8 minutes or until very soft. Drain in your colander. Add 20g of the butter to the pan and cook over a medium heat until pale brown; don't let it burn. Return the cauliflower to the pan. Add the milk and bring to the boil. Turn off the heat. Using a blender, purée the mixture for 3–4 minutes until very smooth. Scoop into a bowl. Season.

3. While the cauliflower boils, make the dressing and salad. Get a medium bowl. Cut the remaining 100g cauliflower florets into 5mm slices. Put them into the bowl with the small leaves. Add the wine vinegar, extra virgin olive oil, shallot and 2 tbsp of the parsley. Toss together. Season to taste.

4. Get a medium-sized frying pan. Add the vegetable oil and get it really hot. Season the chops with salt and curry powder. Use tongs to hold the chops fat side down in the pan and fry for 30 seconds. Lay the chops on one side. Fry for 2–3 minutes over a medium-high heat. Turn. Fry for 2–3 minutes on the other side. Lower the heat to medium. Drain the fat. Add the remaining 25g butter, cut into 6 pieces. Fry for 1 minute on each side; don't let the butter burn. Rest the chops on the rack in the oven for 3–5 minutes, turning the oven off and leaving the door slightly ajar.

5. Add the breadcrumbs to the frying pan. Stir and scrape until they absorb all of the pan juices. Put the pan back on a medium heat and toast the crumbs for 30 seconds until golden. Stir in the remaining 4 tbsp of parsley. Season with salt and pepper. Take the pan off the heat.

6. Heat the cauliflower purée in your microwave or in a pan for 1–2 minutes. Brush the chops with their resting juices, then the mustard. Coat them with the breadcrumbs. Serve with the cauliflower purée and salad.

6/ Glazed pork chop with crisp lettuce & carrot salad

I first used a Worcestershire sauce, honey and ginger glaze on chicken for a competition when I was struggling for work one year. I was shortlisted, but didn't win because they controversially (in my mind) chose something with duck and raspberries. Once I'd got over my grump I was delighted to have another easy condiment to use as a seasoning.

The glaze is sweet and savoury, and there's not too much of it, so it's a good one for younger kids. My son Jake likes to make boats with baby gem lettuce, and it's not a bad way to serve this meal to kids. Slice the pork and then let them fill the baby gem leaf with pork, carrot and sunblush tomato. Only the pork is any good to purée or freeze.

SERVES 2

Sides (pages 320–43)
None needed. For bulk, garlic bread or plain or tasty grains
Prep ahead Dressing and glaze, at least a day ahead
Prep/cooking 30–35 mins
Active time 25–30 mins

3 tbsp Worcestershire sauce
2 tbsp liquid honey
2 tsp grated ginger
1 large carrot, peeled
1 tbsp plus 2 tsp vegetable oil
2 pork chops, about 200g each, skin cut off, leaving a 5mm–1cm layer of fat
1 tsp Dijon mustard
Zested or grated zest of 1 small lime and 2 tsp juice
10 sunblush or semi-dried tomatoes in oil
6 tbsp thickly sliced basil
1 head baby gem lettuce, leaves separated
Salt and freshly ground black pepper

1. Preheat your oven to 50°C/lowest Gas. Put a plate with a rack on it in the oven to rest the pork on. Put a bowl next to the cooker to drain the fat into.

2. Start with the glaze. Get a shallow bowl. Add the Worcestershire sauce, honey and grated ginger. Whisk together. Put the glaze next to your cooker.

3. Slice the carrot lengthways into ribbons with a speed peeler. Set aside.

4. Get a medium-sized frying pan. Add the 2 tsp of oil and get it really hot. Season the chops with salt and pepper. Use tongs to hold the chops fat side down in the pan and fry for 30 seconds. Lay the chops on one side. Fry for 3 minutes over a high heat. Turn. Fry for 3 minutes. Take the pan off the heat. Put the chops on the rack. Drain the fat from the pan.

5. Add 4 tbsp of the glaze to the pan. Boil for 30 seconds until it thickens to the consistency of syrup. Put the pork chops in. Turn the heat to low. Fry/glaze the pork chops for 45 seconds to 1 minute. Turn and fry/glaze on the other side for 45 seconds to 1 minute until the chops are deeply coated. Don't let the glaze reduce too much and burn; take the pan off the heat if you're worried. Put the pork chops on the rack. Scrape the glaze in the pan over the top of the chops.

6. Put the chops on the rack in the oven to rest for 3–5 minutes, turning the oven off and leaving the door slightly ajar. (This glaze is a real pig so fill the empty frying pan with water to make it easier to wash up later!)

7. While the pork rests, make the dressing and salad. Add the 1 tbsp of oil, the mustard and lime zest and juice to the remaining glaze in the bowl. Add the carrot ribbons, sunblush tomatoes, basil and baby gem leaves. Toss together well. Put the salad onto large plates. Brush the pork chops with their resting juices. Put them next to the salad.

Cook extra
Make extra portion(s) of the recipe. Slice the cold pork, mix with the other ingredients and use to make a great sandwich, wrap or salad.

PASTA PILAF/RISOTTO

This is my pasta, cooked like a rice pilaf, to get a risotto consistency. The smaller the pasta, the quicker it cooks and the more naturally creamy the 'pilaf' will be. In the following recipes I've only used types of pastas and giant couscous that I've found to work for this method. The pastas are interchangeable; you just need to adjust the simmering times accordingly (see below). Always taste your pasta to check if it is cooked, as different brands vary and this cooking technique takes longer than boiling.

For younger kids, this pasta is good to use as a starting point to introduce them to new flavours. Try to cut and cook the ingredients you add to a similar size as the pasta you use.

SERVES 2

Good things to stir in Peas, beans, broccoli, peppers, mushrooms, dried porcini, sun-dried tomatoes, ham, bacon, smoked salmon, cooked chicken, any cheese

Prep/cooking 30 mins

Active time 15–20 mins

500ml vegetable or chicken stock

200g macaroni or other pasta (see right)

1 medium onion, peeled and cut into 5mm dice

2 garlic cloves, peeled and finely chopped

20g butter

4 tbsp mascarpone or other cream cheese (or quark for a lower fat version)

60g Cheddar, grated

Salt

Freshly ground black pepper or other seasoning (see right)

1. Start with the pasta. Get a small saucepan. Add the stock. Put the pan on a high heat. Bring to the boil. Add the pasta and bring back to the boil. Stir. Boil furiously for 1 minute. Turn the heat to low. Cover and simmer gently for 12 minutes, stirring occasionally so the pasta doesn't stick together.

2. Take the lid off. Simmer and stir for 3 minutes. By now the pasta should have absorbed most of the liquid, be slightly creamy and just cooked through. Take the pan off the heat and taste the pasta to check; if it is not quite cooked, simmer for another minute or two. If it looks too dry, add hot water, 1 tbsp at a time, but remember you'll add cream cheese later. Cover and leave to sit for 2 minutes, to finish cooking the pasta.

3. While the pasta simmers, get another small pan. Add the onion, garlic and butter. Cover the pan and put it on a medium heat. Sweat for 7–10 minutes, stirring occasionally, until the onion is soft but not brown. As soon as the onion and garlic are ready, add them to the pasta as it cooks.

4. Once the pasta's rested, stir in the mascarpone and Cheddar. If you like the consistency to be saucier, add hot water, 1 tbsp at a time. Season to taste.

Instead of pepper
Try curry powder, nutmeg, cayenne pepper or English or Dijon mustard.

Simmering times for different pastas
The approximate time the pasta or couscous takes *after* boiling for 1 min and *before* stirring for 3 mins and resting for 2 mins: penne 16 mins; macaroni/thin penne 12 mins; orzo 5 mins; giant couscous 5 mins.

Midnight macaroni cheese
Add an extra 2 tbsp of cream cheese. Season to taste. Scoop the pasta into an ovenproof dish. Scatter 40g grated Cheddar on top. Grill until golden.

Magic adventures
Stir in pesto, tapenade, tomato compote, sticky onions or garlic butter.

Cook extra
Double the recipe and freeze half.

1/ 'Creamy' tomato & basil macaroni, tomato & rocket salad

The idea of creamy pasta with no cream began with this recipe. I was writing about tomato sauce and looking for ways to make pasta with tomato sing a different song. After a while I remembered how annoyed I get when I blend tomato sauce and it goes creamy and orange when I want deep red. And there it was, to the tune of a tomato cream that coats and caresses pasta beautifully. I still add cheese because I love cheese, but you don't have to. The salad jumps on top and sings along in raw contrast and harmonious flavour.

For younger kids, serve the cherry tomatoes without the rocket on the side. That apart, this is an excellent recipe to introduce new vegetables, fish or meat to kids; chop what you're adding roughly to the size of the macaroni. No good to purée. Can be frozen.

SERVES 2

Sides None needed.
Baguette or garlic bread
to mop up the sauce
Prep ahead Tomato sauce,
up to 2 days ahead
Prep/cooking 30–35 mins
Active time 20–25 mins

4 tbsp extra virgin olive oil
2 tbsp tomato purée
200g macaroni or other
    pasta
400ml vegetable stock
    or water
2 garlic cloves, peeled and
    thinly sliced
½ x 400g tin chopped
    tomatoes
250g baby plum tomatoes
    (1 punnet), cut in half
40g rocket (½ small packet),
    cut into 1cm slices
6 heaped tbsp sliced basil
4 tbsp grated Parmesan
    (optional)
Salt, sugar and cayenne
    pepper

1. Start with the pasta. Get a medium-sized saucepan. Add 1 tbsp of the extra virgin olive oil, the tomato purée and the pasta. Put the pan on a medium heat. Stir for 1–2 minutes until the tomato purée smells richly roasted and the pasta is well coated; be careful, it can burn quickly. Add the stock and half the garlic. Bring to the boil. Stir. Boil furiously for 1 minute. Turn the heat to low. Cover the pan and simmer gently for 12 minutes, stirring occasionally.

2. While the pasta simmers, make the tomato sauce. Put the tinned tomatoes, remaining garlic and 1 tbsp of the extra virgin olive oil into a small pan. Bring to the boil. Turn the heat to low. Simmer for 5 minutes. Season to taste with salt, sugar and cayenne. Get your blender. Blend the tomato sauce for 3–4 minutes until it is totally smooth, creamy and pale orange.

3. Take the lid off the pasta pan. Add the tomato sauce. Simmer for 3 minutes. Take the pan off the heat. By now the pasta should have absorbed most of the liquid and be slightly creamy and just cooked through. Take the pan off the heat and taste the pasta to check. Cover and leave to sit for 2 minutes, to finish cooking the pasta.

4. Get a medium bowl. Add the baby plum tomatoes, rocket and remaining 2 tbsp of extra virgin olive oil. Tenderly mix with the basil. Season to taste.

5. Warm the pasta through for 1 minute. If you would like the consistency to be a bit saucier, add hot water, 1 tbsp at a time. Take the pan off the heat. Stir in the grated Parmesan if you're using it, and half the tomato, rocket and basil mixture. Spoon the pasta onto your plates. Top with the rest of the tomatoes, rocket and basil.

Cook extra
Double the pasta recipe and freeze half. The salad will not freeze.

2/ Creamy pasta with smoked salmon & horseradish

I had a hot introduction to horseradish the first time I encountered the fresh root. I was asked to purée it for a horseradish cream to serve with salmon at Pierre's restaurant in Wellington, then told to look carefully inside the bowl to see if it was fully puréed. As I did, my eyes felt like they'd been set on fire and I had an initiation of sorts. No such drama for you: I'm using bottled horseradish in this recipe.

Smoked salmon shows its cheaper side here. I use a packet of trimmings because it's just their flavour I'm after. Hot smoked mackerel or herring would be good too. You can also replace the sugar snaps and watercress with frozen peas or soya (edamame) beans.

For kids, don't add salt to the pasta as the smoked salmon has enough. Add a quarter of the horseradish, serve theirs, then season yours. Chop the watercress very finely or leave it out. The pasta is no good to purée but ok to chop finely and freeze for toddlers.

SERVES 2

Sides (pages 320–43)
Watercress and sugar snap salad, lemon dressing

Prep/cooking 30–35 mins

Active time 15–20 mins

1 medium onion, peeled and cut into 5mm–1cm dice

3 garlic cloves, peeled and finely sliced

20g butter

1 tbsp tomato purée

500ml vegetable stock

200g thin mezzanini penne, macaroni or other pasta

160g sugar snap peas, de-strung and cut into 3cm slices diagonally

50g cream cheese (or quark for a lower fat version)

4 tsp horseradish cream

120g packet smoked salmon trimmings, cut into 1cm pieces

40g watercress (½ small packet/bunch)

Salt and freshly ground black pepper

1. Boil your kettle.

2. Start with the pasta. Get a small saucepan. Add the onion, garlic and butter. Cover and put the pan on a medium heat. Sweat for 7–10 minutes until the onion is soft. Stir in the tomato purée. Add the vegetable stock and bring to the boil. Add the pasta and bring back to the boil. Stir. Boil furiously for 1 minute. Turn the heat to low. Cover and simmer gently for 12 minutes, stirring occasionally so it doesn't stick together.

3. Take the lid off the pan. Simmer and stir for 3 minutes. Take the pan off the heat. By now the pasta should have absorbed most of the liquid, be slightly creamy and just cooked through. Take the pan off the heat and taste the pasta to check. If it looks too dry, add hot water, 1 tbsp at a time, but remember you'll add cream cheese later. Cover and leave to sit for 2 minutes, to finish cooking the pasta.

4. While the pasta sits, fill a medium-sized saucepan with boiling water from your kettle. Add salt and bring back to the boil. Put a colander in your sink. Boil the sugar snaps for 3–4 minutes until tender. Don't worry if the pasta sits for a few minutes extra, it will be fine. Drain the sugar snaps in your colander.

5. Stir the cream cheese and horseradish cream into the pasta. Fold in the smoked salmon, sugar snaps and watercress. If you would like the consistency to be a bit saucier, add hot water, 1 tbsp at a time. Season to taste with salt and pepper. Serve from the pan into deep bowls.

Cook extra
Double the recipe and freeze half. The watercress and sugar snaps discolour when you reheat them, but it still tastes lovely.

3/ Pesto orzotto, sautéed vegetables & sunblush tomatoes

I started using orzo a few years ago and I now use it at least as often as risotto rice. In this recipe I move away from risotto's traditional technique. I don't toast anything, I don't add any wine and I don't stir nonstop. This takes about 10 minutes out of the recipe without taking out any of the taste. I particularly like the radishes, carrots and spring onions together – binding them with pesto gives their simple flavours extravagance. For an express version, replace the vegetables with 250g frozen peas.

For younger kids, chop the vegetables into smaller pieces and stir them into the orzo for a great way to introduce new tastes. To go one step better, use giant wholemeal couscous instead of orzo. No good to purée but good to chop and freeze.

SERVES 2

Sides (pages 320–43) None needed. Bean, radish and carrot salad, lemon dressing
Prep ahead Make pesto and cook vegetables, a day ahead
Prep/cooking 25–30 mins
Active time 15–20 mins

Leaves from 1 bunch of
    basil (25g)
5 tbsp extra virgin olive oil
4 tbsp grated Parmesan
100g small Chantenay
    carrots, tops trimmed,
    washed and halved
1 bunch of spring onions
    with fat bulbs, trimmed
12 radishes, halved,
    leaves kept
500ml vegetable stock
2 garlic cloves, peeled and
    finely chopped
200g orzo
½ x 400g tin flageolet or
    cannellini beans
10 sunblush tomatoes
Salt, freshly ground black
    pepper and sugar

1. Boil your kettle. Fill a large pot with boiling water. Put a bowl of cold water next to your cooker. Put a colander in your sink.

2. Start with the pesto. Add the basil leaves to the boiling water. Boil for 15 seconds. Using a sieve, scoop the leaves out and into the bowl of cold water; keep the boiling water for the vegetables. As soon as the basil leaves are cold, drain them and squeeze out any excess water. Put the basil into a small blender. Add 4 tbsp of the extra virgin olive oil and the Parmesan. Blend to a smooth purée. Put this pesto next to your cooker.

3. Bring the basil water to the boil. Add the carrots and boil for 7 minutes. Thinly slice the top third of the spring onions (the greenest part). Cut the remaining two-thirds in half lengthways. Add these halved spring onions and the radishes to the water and boil for 4 minutes or until tender. Drain the vegetables in your colander. Return them to the pan. Add the radish leaves. Sauté over a medium heat for 10–20 seconds. Turn off the heat.

4. While the carrots boil, get a medium-sized saucepan. Add the vegetable stock, garlic and remaining 1 tbsp of extra virgin olive oil. Add the orzo and bring back to the boil. Boil for 1 minute. Turn the heat to low. Cover and simmer gently, stirring occasionally, for 5 minutes. Take the lid off. Stir and simmer for 2–3 minutes until the orzo is tender.

5. Fold the beans and their liquid into the orzo. Bring to the boil. Turn off the heat. By now the orzo should have absorbed most of the liquid, be very creamy and just cooked through. Cover and leave to sit for 2 minutes. By this stage your vegetables should be ready too; don't worry if they're not, the orzo is fine to sit for a few minutes extra.

6. Add the sliced green spring onions and 6 tbsp of the pesto to the orzo. Gently fold them in. If you would like the consistency to be a bit saucier, add hot water, 1 tbsp at a time. Toss the vegetables with the sunblush tomatoes and remaining pesto. Season to taste with salt, pepper and sugar. Serve the vegetables on top of the orzo.

4/ Roast garlic, winter vegetable & sausage penne

This is food to wrap you up in warmth from the inside out. It's also a little beauty for when you've ended up with one parsnip, one carrot, one sweet potato and a bit of squash or pumpkin lurking in the fridge. Here I've used predominantly sweet potato and carrot, because I liked their orange colour with the pasta, but any combination is fine.

For younger kids, cut vegetables into smaller chunks to start with. Serve theirs before you add the sliced spring onions. The pasta is no good to purée. It can be frozen.

SERVES 2

Sides (pages 320–43)
None needed. For contrast, carrot salad
Prep ahead Simmer the sausages and vegetables and make the purée, a day ahead
Prep/cooking 30–35 mins
Active time 25–30 mins

500g mixed carrot, parsnip, sweet potato, squash and/or pumpkin, peeled and trimmed
4 medium pork sausages (about 300g)
6 spring onions, trimmed
4 large garlic cloves, peeled and thinly sliced
30g butter
400–500ml vegetable stock
1 tbsp tomato purée
200g plain or wholewheat penne or other pasta
2 tsp vegetable oil
Salt and cinnamon

1. Boil your kettle. Put a colander in your sink. Put the vegetable stock next to your cooker.

2. Start with the mixed vegetables. Fill a medium-sized pot two-thirds full with water from your kettle. Add salt and bring back to the boil. Cut the vegetables into 3cm chunks. Add to the water and bring back to the boil. Simmer gently for 6 minutes.

3. Cut the sausages into 3cm chunks. Thinly slice the top third of the spring onions (the greenest part). Cut the other two-thirds in half lengthways. Add these halved spring onions and the sausage chunks to the pan of vegetables. Simmer very gently for 5 minutes. Fill a mug with cooking water. Drain the vegetables and sausages in your colander.

4. While the vegetables simmer, get a small saucepan. Add the garlic and 15g of the butter. Cover and sweat over a medium heat for 2 minutes. Take the lid off. Fry, stirring, for 1–2 minutes until the garlic just turns golden. Quickly add the stock and bring to the boil. Whisk in the tomato purée. Add the pasta and bring back to the boil. Stir. Boil furiously for 1 minute. Turn the heat to low. Cover and simmer gently for 16 minutes; add an extra 2 minutes for wholewheat pasta. Take the lid off. Simmer and stir for 3 minutes. Cover and leave to sit for 2 minutes, to finish cooking the pasta.

5. Once the vegetables are cooked, get your blender. Add a third of the vegetables (but not the sausages or halved spring onions) and 6 tbsp of cooking water. Blend for 3–4 minutes until totally smooth; add more of the cooking water to help the blades move if you need to.

6. Get a medium-sized frying pan and put it on a high heat. Add the oil and get it hot. Add the remaining vegetables, sausages and spring onions. Fry over a medium-high heat for 2 minutes. Add the remaining 15g butter and the green spring onions. Fry for 15 seconds. Take the pan off the heat. Season to taste with salt and cinnamon.

7. Stir the vegetable purée into the pasta. Warm it though. Season to taste. If you would like the consistency to be a bit saucier, add hot water, 1 tbsp at a time. Serve the pasta with the vegetables and sausages on top.

5/ Spinach, onion & chorizo giant couscous pilaf

I first ate spinach and chorizo together in a tortilla in San Sebastian. The tortilla was firm and pretty, and it was sitting irresistibly alongside endless other flirtatious mouthfuls on the bar. We were expected to remember how many we'd eaten when it was time to pay. This honesty-based way of grazing on *pinchos* in the early evening was so social, so lovely. At one bar all the doors were open and we stood with one foot inside and the other out as we ate, while kids played around us. The rich spinach and spicy chorizo's marriage stayed with me. I hoped it would work as well with giant couscous or pasta as potatoes, and it did. The spinach gave me the opportunity to try another purée in place of cream too. If you don't want to purée the spinach, just stir it into the simmered and rested giant couscous for 30 seconds until it wilts, then add 4 tbsp of cream cheese.

This is a beauty for younger kids – a great way to get them to try spinach. Chorizo can be too tough, so slice it very thinly to serve alongside or eat it yourself. No good to purée.

SERVES 2

Sides (pages 320–43)
None needed. For contrast, spinach salad
Prep ahead Onion and chorizo mixture, a day ahead
Prep/cooking 35–40 mins
Active time 15–20 mins

150g chorizo sausage (dry or cooking chorizo, both work)
1 tbsp extra virgin olive oil
2 medium onions, peeled and cut into 1cm slices
500ml vegetable or chicken stock
2 garlic cloves, peeled and finely sliced
200g plain or wholewheat giant couscous or pasta
8 tbsp water
125g spinach
Salt, freshly ground black pepper and nutmeg

1. Start with the chorizo sausage. Cut 50g of it into 1cm dice; cut the other 100g into 5mm slices.

2. Get a medium-sized frying pan. Add the extra virgin olive oil and onions. Cover and sweat over a medium heat for 5 minutes. Add the sliced chorizo. Sweat for 2 minutes more until the onions are soft and reddish in colour from the chorizo. Take off the lid and fry gently for 2 minutes. Turn off the heat. Cover and keep warm.

3. While the onions sweat, get a small saucepan. Add the stock, garlic and 5 gratings of nutmeg. Put the pan on a high heat and bring to the boil. Add the giant couscous and the 50g diced chorizo. Bring back to the boil. Stir. Boil furiously for 1 minute. Turn the heat to low. Cover and simmer gently for 5 minutes; add an extra 2 minutes for wholewheat giant couscous. Take the lid off. Stir and simmer for 3 minutes. Cover and leave to sit for 2 minutes, to finish cooking the giant couscous.

4. Get a medium-large frying pan. Add 4 tbsp of the water. Put the pan on a high heat. Bring to the boil. Add the spinach. Cover the pan and wilt the spinach for 1½ minutes. Get your blender. Add the spinach and the remaining 4 tbsp of water. Blend for 2–3 minutes to a smooth purée; if the mixture is too thick to blend, add more water, 1 tbsp at a time.

5. Once the giant couscous is cooked, stir in the spinach purée. If you would like the consistency to be a bit saucier, add hot water, 1 tbsp at a time. Season to taste with salt, pepper and nutmeg. Serve scattered with the sliced chorizo and fried onions.

Cook extra
Double the recipe and freeze half. It will discolour slightly when you reheat it, but still taste lovely.

6/ Special occasion tiger prawn pasta

This pale beauty tastes like luxury. I've simmered my prawn stock thousands of times for risotto, to sauce fish, scallops, chicken and veal, and to make salad dressings. But each time I make it I marvel that I can find so much flavour, so easily, from bits that would usually go in the bin. To make it more economical, turn the prawns into two meals – make the pasta with the stock one day, then use the tail meat for the tagliatelle on page 204 or the broth on page 138 the next.

For younger kids, cooking pasta in prawn stock is a great way to introduce the taste of prawns without them having to struggle with the texture. Once they're happy with the taste, try adding the prawns, but take off their tail shells and chop them first. No good to purée, but can be chopped and frozen for toddlers.

SERVES 2

Sides (pages 320–43)
None needed. For contrast, crisp leaf or vegetable salad. Bread to mop up the sauce

Prep ahead Prawn stock, a day ahead; this can also be frozen

Prep/cooking 35–45 mins

Active time 15–20 mins

10 raw tiger prawns in shell, heads on (frozen are fine)
2 tbsp tomato purée
700ml water
1 medium onion, peeled and cut into 5mm–1cm dice
3 garlic cloves, peeled and finely sliced
30g butter
200g macaroni or other pasta
5 tbsp double cream
2 tsp vegetable oil
Salt and cayenne pepper

1. Start with the prawn stock. Pull the heads off the prawns and peel the shells away, but leave the tail end intact (purely because it looks nice). Keep all of the shells and heads for the stock. Halve the prawns lengthways and take out the black vein. Refrigerate the prawns.

2. Get a medium-sized saucepan. Add the tomato purée, the prawn shells and the prawn heads. Pour in the 700ml water. Bring to the boil and simmer rapidly for 10 minutes.

3. Meanwhile, boil your kettle. Get a small saucepan. Add the onion, garlic and butter. Cover and sweat over a medium heat for 7–10 minutes.

4. Strain the prawn stock into a measuring jug; you should have about 450ml. Put 150ml into a small saucepan to use for the sauce later.

5. Top the remaining stock up to 500ml with boiling water. Add to the onion and garlic. Bring to the boil. Add the pasta. Stir. Bring back to the boil and boil furiously for 1 minute. Turn the heat to low. Cover and simmer gently for 12 minutes. Take the lid off, simmer and stir for 3 minutes. Stir in 4 tbsp of the cream. Season to taste with salt and cayenne. Cover and leave to sit for 2 minutes, to finish cooking the pasta.

6. While the pasta simmers, bring the 150ml stock in the small pan to the boil. Boil to reduce by half. Whisk in the remaining 1 tbsp of cream. Take the pan off the heat.

7. Get a medium-sized frying pan. Add the oil and get it hot. Add the prawns. Fry them at a steady sizzle on a medium heat for 1 minute each side. The prawns are cooked when they turn pink.

8. Spoon the pasta onto your plates. Top with the prawns. Pour the stock into the frying pan the prawns were in and bring it to the boil. Spoon the sauce over the prawns and pasta.

BURGERS/MINCE STEAKS

Think of these burgers as tasty, juicy and cheap steak. They give you more goodies in the pan than a sirloin, and more flavourful fried beef pan gravy as a result. Mince is most often made with beef cuts that have tasty fat to baste the mince from within; I'd suggest 20–25 per cent; lean mince makes dry and chewy burgers. I've found mince for burgers to be better from my butcher's than supermarkets. None of the burger recipes are any good to heat up, so I don't recommend cooking extra.

For younger kids, use a ratio of 75 per cent meat to 25 per cent breadcrumbs to give the meat a softer texture. Good to purée or chop and freeze for babies and toddlers.

SERVES 2

Sides (pages 320–43)
Any you fancy
Prep/cooking 10 mins
Active time 10 mins

300–350g beef mince
2 tsp vegetable oil
Knob of butter (15g)
3 tbsp water
Salt
Freshly ground black
    pepper or other
    seasoning (see right)

1. Put a rack on a plate for resting the burgers and a bowl to drain the fat into next to your cooker.

2. Put the mince onto a plate. Flatten it to a 20cm circle. Add ¼ tsp of salt and ¼ tsp of pepper or other seasoning. Fold the seasonings into the mince. Don't season the mince more than 5 minutes ahead, don't overmix the mince and don't pack the burgers too tightly or they will become tough. Pat the mince into uniformly 2.5cm thick burgers. I like an oval shape. In the photo, the round burger weighs 150g and the oval 175g.

3. Get a frying pan big enough to fit the burgers easily. Put the pan on a high heat. Add the oil and get it really hot. Add the burgers. If they don't sizzle loudly, they won't brown so take them out again and wait. For medium-rare burgers, fry over a medium-high heat for 2 minutes. Turn and fry for 2 minutes on the other side. (Turn the heat to medium and add 1 minute each side for medium, or 1½ minutes each side for medium-well done.) For interior temperatures, see probe thermometer (page 35). Put the burgers on the rack. Drain the fat into the bowl. Put the burgers back into the pan. Put the pan on a medium heat. Add half the butter. Fry the burgers for 30 seconds. Turn. Fry for 30 seconds on the other side. Put the burgers back onto the rack to rest for 4 minutes. This allows the mince to settle and become more like one piece of meat.

4. Add the 3 tbsp of water to the pan. Bring to the boil. Stir vigorously. Take the pan off the heat. Stir in the remaining butter. This will give a few spoonfuls of concentrated fried beef gravy. Season to taste. Put the burgers and the resting juices that have dripped onto the plates into the pan. Turn the burgers in the juices until they are glossy and coated in their pan juices.

Instead of pepper
Try garlic, citrus zest, mustard or any herbs or spices you like.

Magic adventures
Serve the burgers with pesto, tapenade, tomato compote, garlic butter or soft, sweet, sticky onions.

1/ Glazed burger with sweet potato chips & cucumber relish

This is a sweet, sour and crunchy take on the typical burger with pickles, chips, onion and sweet sauce. I have my own barbecue sauce recipe, but I found that the bottled stuff was fine to give you a sticky, sweet and moreish exterior. Brown sauce works quite nicely too.

For younger kids, leave the raw onion and chilli out of their relish, serve theirs and then spice up your own. Get them to shape their own burgers, and then build their own buns with the relish at the table.

SERVES 2

Sides None needed. Burger buns for bulk

Prep ahead Relish and simmer sweet potatoes, up to 2 hours ahead

Prep/cooking 35–40 mins

Active time 25–30 mins

2 small sweet potatoes, about 150g, cut into quarters lengthways

2 tsp red wine vinegar

2 tsp extra virgin olive oil

8 tbsp plus 2 tsp orange juice (fresh or from a carton)

½ chilli, deseeded and finely chopped

1 small red onion, peeled and finely chopped

¼ cucumber, halved, deseeded and cut into 1cm slices

4 tsp vegetable oil

350g beef mince

Knob of butter (15g)

2 tbsp barbecue sauce

Salt, sugar and chilli powder

1. Preheat your grill to its highest setting. Boil your kettle.

2. Start with the sweet potatoes. Put a colander in your sink. Get a medium-sized saucepan. Fill it with boiling water and add salt. Cover and bring to the boil over a high heat. Add the sweet potatoes. Bring back to the boil. Lower the heat and simmer for 7 minutes or until the sweet potatoes are soft but not breaking up. Drain in the colander. Pat dry with kitchen paper.

3. While the sweet potatoes simmer, make the relish. Get a medium bowl. Add the wine vinegar, extra virgin olive oil, the 2 tsp of orange juice, the chilli and a quarter of the red onion. Whisk together. Add the cucumber. Season to taste with salt and sugar.

4. Put the sweet potato wedges on a baking tray. Brush with 2 tsp of the vegetable oil. Season with salt and chilli powder. Grill for 3–4 minutes until golden. Turn and grill for 3–4 minutes on the other side. (Grills vary, so keep an eye on them.) Turn off the grill. Keep the sweet potatoes warm.

5. Put a rack on a plate, a bowl, the rest of the chopped red onion, the 8 tbsp of orange juice and the barbecue sauce next to your cooker.

6. Season the mince with ¼ tsp of salt and a pinch of chilli powder (or more if you like). Pat into 2.5cm thick burgers. Get a medium-sized frying pan. Put it on a high heat. Add the remaining 2 tsp of vegetable oil and get it really hot. Add the burgers. For medium-rare burgers, fry over a medium-high heat for 2 minutes. Turn and fry for 2 minutes on the other side. (Turn the heat to medium and add 1 minute each side for medium; 1½ minutes each side for medium-well done.) Drain the fat. Add the butter to the pan. Fry the burgers on a medium heat for 30 seconds. Turn. Fry on the other side for 30 seconds. Put the burgers on the rack to rest for 2–4 minutes.

7. Add the remaining red onion to the pan. Fry for 2 minutes over a medium heat, stirring occasionally, until slightly browned. Add the 8 tbsp of orange juice. Bring to the boil and reduce by half. Stir in the barbecue sauce. Boil until it's thick enough to lightly coat the back of a spoon. Turn off the heat.

8. Put the burgers into the sauce and turn them in it to coat and glaze. Serve the burgers with the sweet potato chips, cucumber relish and sauce.

2/ Burger with red wine & onion sauce & sautéed potatoes

In 1991 I worked at a 2 star Michelin restaurant in Burgundy where we served this sauce with rib of beef and called it *Marchand de Vin*. My Chef Jean Crotet would be shocked that I've added soy sauce and balsamic vinegar, but if I gave him a taste I'm sure he would be convinced by the gloss and guts they add to the sauce. He'd certainly be surprised to see the glorious sauce that can be made with cranberry juice in place of the wine.

For younger kids, halve the mustard and finely chop rather than slice the onions. The alcohol is cooked out of the wine. Good to purée or chop and freeze for babies and toddlers.

SERVES 2

Sides (pages 320–43)
None needed. For contrast, beans, peas or a leafy salad. For bulk, bread

Prep ahead Sauce to end of step 2 and boil potatoes, up to a day ahead

Prep/cooking 30–35 mins

Active time 20–25 mins

60g butter
1 medium red onion, peeled and cut into 5mm slices
1 tbsp balsamic vinegar
1 tbsp dark soy sauce
3 tbsp water
250ml red wine, such as Cabernet Sauvignon, or cranberry juice
200ml beef or chicken stock
300–400g small waxy potatoes, such as Charlotte, halved
4 tsp vegetable oil
4 tbsp sliced flat-leaf parsley
350g beef mince
4 tsp Dijon mustard
Salt, salt flakes and sugar

1. Preheat your oven to 75°C/Gas low. Boil your kettle.

2. Start with the sauce. Get a medium-sized frying pan. Add 10g of the butter, the red onion, balsamic vinegar, soy sauce and the 3 tbsp of water. Cover and sweat over a medium heat, stirring often, for 8 minutes or until the onion is soft. Take the lid off. Turn the heat to high. Fry the onion for 1 minute until it is lightly browned. Add the wine and bring to the boil. Reduce over a high heat by three-quarters. Add the stock and reduce by two-thirds. It should lightly coat the back of a spoon. Turn off the heat.

3. While the sauce reduces, get a medium-sized saucepan. Fill it with boiling water from your kettle. Add salt to taste and bring to the boil. Add the potatoes. Simmer for 12 minutes or until tender. Put a colander in the sink. Drain the potatoes well and leave them to sit in the colander for 5 minutes.

4. Put a bowl next to your cooker to drain the fat into. Get a large frying pan. Put it on a high heat. Add 2 tsp of the oil and get it really hot. Add the potatoes, cut side down. Lower the heat to medium and fry, on the cut side only, for 5 minutes or until golden. Drain the fat. Add 10g of the remaining butter. Toss the potatoes with salt flakes over the heat for 30 seconds. Add the parsley. Put the pan in the oven to keep warm.

5. Season the mince with the mustard and ¼ tsp of salt. Pat into 2.5cm thick burgers. Get a medium-sized frying pan. Put it on a high heat. Add the remaining 2 tsp of oil and get it really hot. Add the burgers. For medium-rare burgers, fry over a medium-high heat for 2 minutes. Turn and fry for 2 minutes on the other side. (Turn the heat to medium and add 1 minute each side for medium; 1½ minutes each side for medium-well done.) Drain the fat. Add 10g of the remaining butter to the pan. Fry the burgers on a medium heat for 30 seconds. Turn. Fry on the other side for 30 seconds. Put the burgers on the rack to rest for 2–4 minutes.

6. Add the red wine sauce to the frying pan. Bring to the boil. Take the pan off the heat. Stir in the remaining 30g butter. Season to taste and balance the acidity with sugar. Add the burgers and their resting juices to the sauce. Serve the burgers with the sauce and sautéed potatoes.

3/ Chorizo burger with red pepper, Parmesan & fried egg

I love smoked paprika and a seemingly tiny twist completely transforms this burger. I seize the opportunity for extra flavour when I fry eggs in the meaty, chorizo-flavoured fat. Once broken, the yolk moistens the burger and caresses the saucy red pepper. This all serves as a dressing for the rocket that completes the dish. For a cheaper version, leave out the chorizo and season the mince with smoked paprika.

For younger kids, dice rather than slice the onion and pepper. Either try to find a very moist chorizo or leave it out of the burgers and serve a few very thin slices on the side for them to get acquainted with. Let your kids sprinkle their own cheese over the top. If the eggs are completely cooked through, this can be chopped or puréed and frozen for babies and toddlers.

SERVES 2

Sides (pages 320–43)
Toasted ciabatta, brioche or burger buns, or plain or tasty grains

Prep ahead Peppers, a day ahead

Prep/cooking 30 mins

Active time 25–30 mins

1 medium onion, peeled and cut into 1cm slices

2 garlic cloves, peeled and sliced

1 large red pepper, halved, deseeded and cut into 1cm slices

2 tbsp extra virgin olive oil

1 tbsp red wine vinegar

2 tbsp water

250g beef mince

100g chorizo sausage, cut into 5mm dice

2 tsp vegetable oil

Knob of butter (15g)

2 large eggs

40g rocket (½ small packet)

4 tbsp grated Parmesan

Salt, sugar and smoked paprika

1. Start with the red pepper. Get a medium-sized shallow pan. Add the onion, garlic, red pepper, extra virgin olive oil, wine vinegar, the 2 tbsp of water and ¼ tsp of smoked paprika. Put the pan on a high heat. Cover and bring to the boil. Lower the heat to medium. Simmer to soften the pepper without browning for 15 minutes. If the pepper gets too dry and starts to fry, add another 2 tbsp of water to the pan.

2. Take the lid off the pan and increase the heat to high. Fry, stirring occasionally, for 2–3 minutes, until the pepper and onion are just starting to caramelise around the edges. Turn off the heat. Season to taste with salt, sugar and smoked paprika.

3. While the pepper softens, make the burgers. Mix the mince with the diced chorizo, salt and 1 tsp of smoked paprika. Pat into 2.5cm thick burgers. Once the peppers are ready, get a medium-sized frying pan. Put it on a high heat. Add the vegetable oil and get it really hot. Add the burgers. For medium-rare burgers, fry over a medium-high heat for 2 minutes. Turn and fry for 2 minutes on the other side. (Turn the heat to medium and add 1 minute each side for medium; 1½ minutes each side for medium-well done.) Drain the fat. Add the butter to the pan. Fry the burgers on a medium heat for 30 seconds. Turn. Fry on the other side for 30 seconds. Put the burgers on the rack to rest for 2–4 minutes.

4. Break the eggs into the frying pan. Turn the heat to low. Cover the pan and gently fry the eggs for 2 minutes or until just set. Sprinkle with salt and smoked paprika.

5. While the eggs fry, put the pepper and onion and the rocket on your plates. Sprinkle with the Parmesan. Add the burgers. Serve the eggs on top of the pepper and onion.

4/ Ginger burger with mushroom 'buns' & Chinese coleslaw

Big mushrooms make marvellous buns. I first came across the idea when I read about Michel Trama's Cèpe Burger fifteen years ago and I've been waiting for a chance to use it since. The Chinese coleslaw is part of the fun – pak choi gives you a bright, juicy crunch. If you want a bit of 'cheese', a slice of silken tofu would be nice. These mushrooms could be adapted to suit my other burger recipes for anyone on a wheat-free diet.

For younger kids, finely dice the mushrooms. Give them the crunchy pak choi stalks rather than leaves. Leave out the sesame seeds, raw spring onion and chilli, grate lemon zest finely and use less ginger. Good to purée or chop and freeze for babies and toddlers.

SERVES 2

Sides (pages 320–43)
Prawn crackers or popcorn with hoisin or soy sauce
Prep/cooking 30 mins
Active time 20–25 mins

4 very large mushrooms
2 tbsp honey
2 tbsp hoisin sauce
1 tbsp plus 3 tsp sesame oil
Zested or grated zest of
    1 small lemon and
    2 tbsp juice
2 tbsp sesame seeds
6 spring onions, trimmed
1 medium carrot, peeled
    and grated
1 head of pak choi, leaves
    and stalks roughly cut
1 mild red chilli, deseeded
    and finely chopped
350g beef mince
2 tsp grated ginger
3 tbsp water
Salt and sugar

1. Preheat your oven to 220°C/Gas 7, position upper middle shelf.

2. Start with the mushrooms. Get a baking tray. Put the mushrooms on the tray. Get a small bowl. Add the honey, hoisin sauce, the 1 tbsp of sesame oil and 1 tbsp of the lemon juice. Whisk together. Brush the mushrooms all over with a third of this mixture. Season with salt. Turn the mushrooms rounded side up. Sprinkle with sesame seeds. Roast for 10 minutes. Turn off the oven and leave the mushrooms inside with the door slightly ajar, to keep warm without overcooking them.

3. While the mushrooms roast, thinly slice the white part of the spring onions and keep the slices for the burger sauce.

4. Next, make the Chinese coleslaw. Thinly slice the green spring onion tops diagonally and put the slices into a bowl. Add the grated carrot, pak choi, 1 tsp of sesame oil, the remaining 1 tbsp of lemon juice, half the chilli and half the lemon zest. Season lightly with salt and sugar. Toss together. Put the coleslaw onto one side of each plate.

5. Mix the mince with the ginger and ½ tsp of salt. Pat into 2.5cm thick burgers. Get a medium-sized frying pan. Put it on a high heat. Add the remaining 2 tsp of sesame oil and get it really hot. Add the burgers. For medium-rare burgers, fry over a medium-high heat for 2¼ minutes. Turn and fry for 2¼ minutes on the other side. Brush the burgers with enough of the honey and hoisin mixture to coat them. Turn off the heat. Turn the burgers in the pan until they are sticky and shiny. Put them on the tray in the oven with the mushrooms. Add the chopped white spring onions to the frying pan. Sweat over a medium heat for 30 seconds. Add the rest of the hoisin mixture and the 3 tbsp of water. Boil for 10 seconds or until the sauce is thick enough to coat the back of a spoon. Take the pan off the heat.

6. Put a mushroom onto each plate, rounded side down. Put a burger on top of each. Spoon the sauce over the burgers and around the mushrooms. Put a second mushroom, rounded side up, on top of each burger. Sprinkle the remaining lemon zest and chilli over the top.

5/ Pepper burger with glazed potatoes, carrots & onions

This burger is based on pepper steak but I take the tastier, easier and less bitter option of putting the pepper in the burger and sauce. Feel free to double the quantity if you like it really peppery. If you're more in the mood for a decadent version, you can add double cream; if not, the peppered pan juices are light in texture but a real flavour heavyweight.

For younger kids, put a tiny sprinkle of pepper into their sauce, serve theirs, then add the rest to yours. The vegetables are all lovely and soft, but slice the white spring onions finely before cooking them. Good to purée or chop and freeze for babies and toddlers.

SERVES 2

Sides None needed

Prep ahead Vegetables can be cooked and stock reduced, a day ahead

Prep/cooking 30–35 mins

Active time 20–25 mins

6 Chantenay carrots (about 150g), halved

6 small waxy potatoes (about 250g), such as Charlotte or Maris Peer, halved

40g butter

6 spring onions, trimmed

350g beef mince

1½ tsp coarsely cracked black pepper

2 tsp vegetable oil

250ml beef or chicken stock

6 tbsp double cream (for the decadent version)

Salt and sugar

1. Start with the vegetables. Get a medium-sized shallow pan. Add the carrots and potatoes. Add just enough water to cover the vegetables, 20g of the butter and a tiny pinch each of salt and sugar. Put the pan on a high heat. Bring to the boil.

2. Cut each spring onion into 3 lengths. Thinly slice the top third (green part) and keep to add later. Add the rest to the potatoes and carrots. Bring back to the boil. Lower the heat to medium. Cover and simmer rapidly for 10–12 minutes or until the potatoes and carrots are tender. Turn up the heat and remove the lid. Boil for 5 minutes or until almost all of the liquid has evaporated and the vegetables are glazed in a buttery sheen. Add the sliced green spring onions. Take the pan off the heat. Season to taste.

3. While the vegetables simmer, put a rack over a plate, the stock, cream if you're using it, and 1 tsp of cracked pepper next to your cooker.

4. Mix the mince with ¼ tsp of salt and ½ tsp of the cracked pepper. Pat it into 2.5cm thick burgers. When the vegetables are nearly ready, get a medium-sized frying pan. Put it on a high heat. Add the oil and get it really hot. Add the burgers. For medium-rare burgers, fry over a medium-high heat for 2 minutes. Turn and fry for 2 minutes on the other side. (Turn the heat to medium and add 1 minute each side for medium; 1½ minutes each side for medium-well done.) Drain the fat. Add 10g of the remaining butter to the pan. Fry the burgers over a medium heat for 30 seconds. Turn. Fry on the other side for 30 seconds. Put the burgers on the rack to rest for 2–4 minutes.

5. Add the stock and remaining 1 tsp of cracked pepper to the pan. Bring to the boil and boil until it has reduced by two-thirds. If using cream, add it now, bring back to the boil and boil for 30 seconds or until the sauce is thick enough to coat the back of a spoon. Take the pan off the heat. Stir in the remaining 10g butter. Season to taste.

6. Add the burgers and their resting juices to the pepper sauce. Brush the burgers with the sauce until they are well coated and glossy. Serve with the glazed vegetables.

6/ Provençal burger with orange zest, olives & basil

The bright burst of orange adds a lovely touch to this burger, as does its juice to the salsa. If there is to be bread, it has to be some sort of garlic bread, drenched with extra virgin olive oil. For an extra treat, serve the burger with garlic mayo.

For younger kids, separate their portions of the mince before you add the cayenne. Serve their salsa without the chopped chilli, and then add it to yours. Can be puréed or chopped and frozen for babies and toddlers.

SERVES 2

Sides Garlic bread or buns
Prep ahead Salsa, an hour ahead
Prep/cooking 25–30 mins
Active time 25 mins

Grated zest of ½ orange and 6 tbsp juice
2 tbsp extra virgin olive oil
125g baby plum tomatoes (½ punnet), halved
½ mild red chilli, deseeded and finely diced
12 black olives, pitted and halved
3 tsp vegetable oil
1 small firm courgette, halved lengthways and cut into 1cm slices
2 garlic cloves, peeled and finely chopped
350g beef mince
4 tbsp sliced basil
2 anchovies, very finely chopped (optional)
Knob of butter (15g)
4 tbsp water
1 mozzarella ball (about 125g), drained and cut into 10 slices
Salt, sugar and cayenne pepper

1. Start with the salsa. Get a small saucepan. Add the orange juice. Put the pan on a high heat. Bring to the boil and boil for 1 minute or until the juice is thick enough to lightly coat the back of a spoon. Add the extra virgin olive oil, baby plum tomatoes, chilli and olives. Warm for 1 minute to soften the tomatoes slightly and encourage their juice to bleed into the salsa. Take the pan off the heat.

2. Next, get a medium-sized frying pan. Add 1 tsp of the vegetable oil and get it hot. Add the courgette. Fry for 1 minute. Add half the garlic and fry for 30 seconds. Season to taste with salt and cayenne. Add the courgette to the salsa. Put a rack over the salsa pan to rest the burgers on and a bowl next to the cooker.

3. Next, make the burgers. Mix the mince with the orange zest, half the basil, the rest of the garlic, the anchovies if using, ½ tsp of salt and a pinch of cayenne. Pat it into 2.5cm thick burgers.

4. Wipe out the pan you used for the courgette. Put it on a high heat. Add the remaining 2 tsp of vegetable oil and get it really hot. Add the burgers. For medium-rare burgers, fry over a medium-high heat for 2 minutes. Turn and fry for 2 minutes on the other side. (Turn the heat to medium and add 1 minute each side for medium; 1½ minutes each side for medium-well done.) Drain the fat. Add the butter to the pan. Fry the burgers on a medium heat for 30 seconds. Turn. Fry on the other side for 30 seconds. Put the burgers on the rack over the salsa to rest for 2–4 minutes.

5. Add the 4 tbsp of water to the pan and bring to the boil. Stir to get every last bit of meaty goodness from the pan. Add these pan juices to the salsa. Add the remaining basil to the salsa.

6. Spread the mozzarella slices over your plates. Put the burgers in the middle. Spoon the salsa over the top.

2/
The Magic Fridge

Six saucy standbys, and six tricks
to turn each one into dinner

Delicious food, fast food, fresh food, easy food, real food and beautiful food. I want it and I want it now. So, when I'm in a rush, what can I cook that looks and tastes great? Well, just like cheating without the guilt, I get the 'magic fridge' to help me out. The magic fridge is full of goodies that burst with fast flavours that you can grab to give you a hand.

You put the magic in the fridge yourself. This begins with a trip to the shops and then takes you to the kitchen, where you start to fill the fridge with your tricks. Choose one or more from pesto, tapenade, sticky onions, tomato compote, garlic butter and green curry paste. These will keep, carefully stored in the fridge, for a week or in most cases much longer. They will also freeze, so you can make large quantities each time and have bags of instant flavour that you can add to an everyday meal to turn simple into sublime.

Now, whether you feel like fish, meat, vegetables, pasta or a baked potato, you have the means to make it magical. Come home, swing open your magic fridge door, choose tonight's trick and you're on your way to wonderful food.

My family and I ate these saucy standbys for weeks while I worked on the recipes and they stayed exciting, because each one was changed by what it was served with. This is part of the magic. When tomato compote takes on the flavour of curry, its character is transformed. It is entirely different from the paprika-spiced tomato that sits saucily beneath roast chorizo wrapped chipolatas. Each time you use the tomato compote, it becomes more familiar, and you further anticipate the way it welcomes one seasoning or another. Each transformational trick becomes your own magic.

If you think pesto works only with pasta, think again. Try it with fish, chicken, lamb, beef, risotto, roasted peppers, cheese on toast and more... The same applies to the other items in the magic fridge, and you can turn them into comfort food if that's what you fancy. Come home with a few sausages and make a gutsy onion gravy in minutes with the soft, sweet, sticky onions and a splosh of brown sauce. Return with some chicken breasts and make a feisty curry with my green curry paste. Bring back some cooked beetroot, grill goat's cheese over the top and turn the two into an irresistible feast of sweet, soft and salty with tapenade. I know the meals in this chapter so well and I've cooked them so often that they glow with warm familiarity. At the same time, I am always ready to taste something new, because each saucy standby is an invitation to endless possibility.

I would ask you to be careful about how you store your magic fridge preparations. Sometimes they will keep for longer than I suggest; I once tasted tomato compote that I had made 39 days earlier. It had kept because I'd used a sterilised jar, covered the compote with a thin layer of olive oil to keep the air out, and covered the jar with cling film and a lid. Once I dug into my compote, I had to use it within a couple of days.

Sterilising sounds intimidating. It's not. Put your jars and lids through your dishwasher on its hot cycle just before you're going to use them. If you don't have a dishwasher, stand the jars in a pan of water, bring it to the boil, boil for 10 minutes and then dry the jars in a low oven for 10 minutes or so. Boil the lids, too.

You can put the preparations in very clean plastic containers, which can be more practical because it's easier to find smaller ones. You can't sterilise plastic, but I tested pesto in plastic alongside pesto in jars and they kept, untouched, for the same length of time. The key thing is to put the preparation into a vessel that is the size of a single or at most double use, because it's when you dip into your sauce that air and bacteria find their way in and cause problems. Look at the individual introductions for any specific tips.

That's the technical bit over. I reckon the magic fridge speaks to our basic instinct for preservation, to take nature's bounty when it is plentiful and store it for later use. Today we need to preserve our precious time as well. Here's to a magical future filled with delicious, easy, fast, fresh, beautiful food… Magic.

P.S. Of course you can buy all of these preparations. Their colours and flavours will vary, but some are very good and they're getting better. If it'll help you cook, help yourself.

BASIL PESTO

If my happiness was a herb it would be basil, and if there was any preparation to make this happiness happier it would be my beautiful and beloved basil pesto. The scent and taste of pesto lift me in every way possible. I love pesto. I can't imagine life without pesto. Pesto is simple to make, easy to use, and hugely versatile. Good pesto makes everyday meals extraordinary.

I boil the basil and garlic briefly to make the garlic more gentle and keep the basil bright green. I like to think pesto tastes so much better when you can eat it with your eyes before you get caught up in its narcotic scent.

Younger kids will find pesto more tempting if it is very smooth.

MAKES 20-22 TBSP; AT LEAST 7 SERVINGS

Prep ahead Keeps in the fridge for up to a month (see storage)

Prep/cooking 15–20 mins

Active time 15–20 mins

100g basil (1 large or 4 small supermarket-sized bunches)

2 garlic cloves, peeled and thinly sliced

6–8 tbsp extra virgin olive oil, plus extra to cover

3 heaped tbsp pine nuts

5 heaped tbsp grated Parmesan

Salt and freshly ground black pepper

1. Boil your kettle. Get a large pot. Fill it two-thirds full with water from the kettle. Add salt. Bring to the boil. Fill a large bowl with cold water and put it next to your cooker. Put a colander or sieve in your sink.

2. Pick the basil leaves off their stalks.

3. Add the basil leaves and garlic to the boiling water, pushing the leaves down to submerge them. Count to 30. Quickly transfer the leaves and garlic to the cold water with a skimmer or sieve. As soon as they are cold, drain in your colander. Press the leaves lightly. Shake away any excess water. It will seem like a tiny amount of basil; don't worry, this is normal.

4. Get your blender or small processor (a blender works best). Put the basil, garlic, 6 tbsp of extra virgin olive oil, the pine nuts and Parmesan into the blender. Blend to a paste for 1–2 minutes. If the blades turn but the pesto doesn't, tap the side of the blender to release the trapped air at the bottom. Add more olive oil, 1 tbsp at a time, if the pesto is too thick. I like quite a smooth texture, just short of a purée. Season to taste with salt and pepper. Spoon the pesto into a jar and cover it with a layer of extra virgin olive oil.

Storage

Use small sterilised jars or clean plastic containers, ideally enough for a single use, so that once they are opened you use them up quickly. The key to storage is keeping air away from the pesto. Tap the bottoms of the jars to ensure there are no air bubbles and leave 2cm at the top of the jar for a good layer of olive oil. Pour the olive oil over the top of the pesto to seal it. Cover the jars first with cling film, then with a lid. Store in the fridge. If you use some but not all of the pesto, it's best to put the rest in a smaller jar. If you don't have one, clean the exposed sides of the jar with kitchen paper. Cover the remaining pesto with a fresh layer of oil. Unopened jars will keep for up to 1 month. Pesto can also be frozen. Once the jar is open, use the pesto within 2 days and cover it with oil after each use.

Simple Pesto Magic

Pesto gives me a magical multitude of options every time I open my fridge. The magic goes far beyond the recipes in this chapter and I will happily eat pesto every day without ever eating the same thing. I try to cook and eat with great generosity – and being generous with pesto is very simple. I take a fillet of fish, put it in the oven for a few minutes on top of halved baby plum tomatoes. I slide it all onto a plate, spoon over some pesto and serve it with a salad dressed with pesto and lemon. A chunk of bread to catch and carry any pesto that escapes will round off a delightful meal. The fillet of fish could just as easily be chicken, grilled goat's cheese, pork, roast red peppers, risotto, pasta or steak.

Pesto perks up toast and tins of anything savoury; it's a fresh-tasting dip or a delicious dash of flavour in gravy. In winter I spoon pesto over my stews and soups for a little sunshine, and broths finished with pesto are like a warm cloud of flavour that engulfs your insides. Whatever you put pesto on, or wherever you put it, please add it at the last minute to catch its fresh flavour – best of all, at the table just before you eat.

Pesto variations I sometimes use fresh walnuts when they are in season instead of pine nuts, but I never toast the nuts because they become overpowering. You can make pesto with coriander, parsley or rocket. I always make mine with basil.

Magic for everybody Sometimes I make a basil, garlic and olive oil purée with no nuts or cheese, so if you don't have or can't eat either of these you don't have to miss out.

Magic for kids Pesto is a great way to get kids involved with their food. From when Jake was about 18 months old I discovered that if he was losing interest halfway through his meal I could get him to the end of it by giving him things to add himself: grated cheese, olive oil, a pepper grinder that didn't work, or a little dish of pesto. Make sure it is a little dish though because the kids will add it all, just for the messy fun of it.

Magical adventures Any of the meat and fish 'hero' recipes from Adventures with Ingredients (pages 36–123) can be seasoned and served with pesto. The pasta pilaf/risotto can be finished with pesto.

Magical transformations You can use pesto for all of the green curry paste recipes (pages 209–223) except the basic curry and the salmon.

Slow cook magic Pesto can go on the side of, or into the gravy for, roast chicken (page 229), braised lamb (page 245) and roast belly pork (page 261); into the sauce for, and on top of, braised mackerel (page 293); or mixed into the braised lentils (page 307).

Instant snack Tortilla chips with ricotta, sunblush tomatoes and pesto.

Hot snack Mix freshly cooked popcorn with pesto and Parmesan.

Grilled snack Chop a tomato finely, mix it with pesto, spread it on toast, top with Cheddar and grill until melted and bubbling.

Frittata Mix wilted spinach, rocket or Swiss chard, sautéed courgettes or sunblush tomatoes with pesto and eggs. Fry and then bake in a non-stick ovenproof frying pan.

Salad Mix pesto with cucumber, olives, spring onions, cherry tomatoes and a tin each of pole-caught tuna and haricot beans.

Vegetable soup Add a whopping great spoonful to your soup at the table.

Special occasion brunch Spread pesto over baked potato slices or blinis. Top with cream cheese and smoked salmon.

Late night snack Cut a baguette in half lengthways. Toast. Spread generously with pesto.

Pasta with pesto I like fusilli (spiral pasta) best because the pesto gets caught in the spirals so that each piece of pasta is seasoned with pesto inside and out. I find that pesto slips off spaghetti and tagliatelle too easily and more of it ends up in the bottom of the plate than on the pasta.

Comfort treat Spoon pesto over the top of macaroni cheese.

Morning sunshine Boil an egg for 4½ minutes, cut open the top, spoon pesto over the yolk and dunk little toast soldiers.

Dip Serve a bowl of pesto with raw peppers, carrots, tender spring onions, fennel, cucumber and radishes.

Liven up boiled vegetables and potatoes Add a spoonful of pesto.

For a delightful melting pot Spoon pesto over Irish stew.

A decadent treat Find the ripest, fattest, most sun-drenched tomato you can. Put it in a bowl with a tomato vine (cheat's way to get the freshly picked flavour) and cover with foil. Leave it in the sunniest place you can at the sunniest part of the day. Cut the tomato in half just before the sun goes in. Spread it with pesto and eat it with the last of the sun's warmth on your face. Just for a moment, you'll be in heaven...

Magical cheats If you're stuck for time, there are some good commercial pestos available. Choose the greenest one you can find. The recipes might not be quite the same, but still worth doing if you get a good quality pesto.

1/ Braised sea bass fillets with beans, peas & pesto

I first fell for the fashion of serving spring vegetables *à la française* while working for Jean Crotet at his 2 star Michelin restaurant Hostellerie de Levernois in Burgundy – my first job in France as an enthusiastic nineteen-year-old chef. We made the base with chicken stock and it was served with roast Bresse pigeon. I cooked it so often that it feels like an old friend. For this recipe I use water rather than stock so that the cooking juices pick up the flavour of the fish as it braises and welcomes each individual taste before the pesto makes the dish whole. The sea bass fillets you are most likely to find are the small farmed ones; you can use sea bream or pollock instead.

    Sea bass is sweet-fleshed and great for kids. For younger kids, finely chop the onions and lettuce and be sure to remove any strings from the beans. It is often these stringy or tough bits and unexpected textures that put kids off their vegetables, rather than the taste. Good to purée or chop and freeze for babies and toddlers.

SERVES 2

Sides (pages 320–43)
None needed. For bulk, simmered potatoes

Prep ahead Onions and lettuce can be sweated up to 2 hours ahead

Prep/cooking 30–35 mins

Active time 20–25 mins

2 small onions, peeled and finely sliced
2 tbsp extra virgin olive oil
200ml water
1 baby gem lettuce, cut into 1.5cm slices
2–4 skinless farmed sea bass fillets, about 120g per portion
4 tbsp basil pesto (page 129)
200g mixed peas, broad beans and sliced French or runner beans, mangetout or sugar snap peas (or just one of these)
Salt and freshly ground black pepper

1. Preheat your oven to 200°C/Gas 6, position upper middle shelf. Boil your kettle.

2. Start with the onions. Get a medium-large ovenproof frying pan. Add the onions and extra virgin olive oil. Cover the pan and put it on a medium heat. Sweat for 7–10 minutes until the onions are soft; if the pan gets too hot, don't let the onions fry, just add a spoonful or two of water. Pour in 200ml water and bring to the boil. Add the lettuce. Bring back to the boil and boil furiously for 1 minute until the lettuce wilts. Season to taste with salt and pepper.

3. Season the sea bass fillets. Put them on top of the onion and lettuce mixture. Press the fillets down slightly to submerge them in the juices. Spread 1 tbsp of the pesto over the top of each fillet. Braise in the oven for 6 minutes or until the sea bass is just cooked through. Turn the oven off and let the sea bass rest inside for 2–4 minutes with the door slightly ajar.

4. While the sea bass braises, get a large saucepan. Fill it with boiling water from your kettle. Add salt, cover and bring to the boil. Put a colander in your sink.

5. Add the green vegetables to the boiling water. Cover, bring back to the boil and boil for 3–4 minutes or until tender. Drain in your colander. Put the vegetables back into the empty pot. Put the pot back on a medium heat for 10–30 seconds to dry them out.

6. Put the sea bass fillets into the middle of your plates. Add the green vegetables to the onion mixture. Stir in the remaining 2 tbsp of pesto. Season to taste. Spoon the vegetable and pesto mixture around the fish.

2/ Lamb chops with tomatoes, olives, fried potatoes & pesto

When I tested this recipe, I cooked it three times in a row when once would have done, because the combination of lamb, potatoes, baby tomatoes, black olives and basil pesto is outrageously good, even decadent. The lamb juices caress the potatoes to make them go slightly soft, the tomatoes burst with a taste like enthusiasm and the two combine to give you a rich, meaty mass. Pesto binds it beautifully and the olives are just salty enough to season everything. Lamb shoulder chops are the gloriously chewy cousin of a cutlet, cheaper than best end chops and shaped more like a steak.

The potatoes, tomatoes and pesto are a lovely combination for kids. Slice their lamb very thinly before serving. Good to purée or chop and freeze for babies and toddlers.

SERVES 2

Sides Bread and/or salad leaves to mop up the sauce
Prep ahead Potatoes can be boiled, a day ahead
Prep/cooking 35–40 mins
Active time 20–25 mins

300–400g small waxy potatoes (depending on your appetite), such as Anya or Charlotte, cut in half
1 tbsp vegetable oil
2 lamb shoulder chops, 175–200g each
250g baby plum tomatoes (1 punnet)
14 black olives, pitted
Grated zest of ¼ lemon and 2 tsp juice
4 tbsp basil pesto (page 129)
1 tbsp extra virgin olive oil
Salt, freshly ground black pepper and sugar

1. Preheat your oven to 50°C/lowest Gas, position middle shelf. Boil your kettle. Put a resting rack on top of a plate in the oven.

2. Start with the potatoes. Get a large pot. Fill it with boiling water from your kettle. Add salt, cover and bring to the boil. Put a colander in your sink. Add the potatoes to the boiling water. Bring back to the boil. Cover and simmer gently for 10 minutes or until tender. Drain in the colander. Dry the potatoes as well as possible so that they will fry better.

3. Once the potatoes are drained, get a large frying pan. Add the vegetable oil and get it really hot. Season the lamb chops with salt. When the pan is hot, add the chops. Fry over a very high heat for 2 minutes. Lower the heat to medium. Fry for 2 minutes. Turn the chops. Fry for 4 minutes on the other side. Depending on the position of the bone, the chops may curl a little when you turn them; don't worry if this happens, there is nothing you can do to stop it.

4. Transfer the chops to the rack over the plate in the oven and leave them to rest while you finish the potatoes. Add the potatoes, cut side down, to the pan. Fry over a medium heat for 2–3 minutes. Turn the potatoes. Fry them for 2–3 minutes on the other side, until they are golden. Add the tomatoes. Sauté for 1–2 minutes until the tomatoes just warm through and begin to burst. Add the olives. Turn off the heat.

5. To make the sauce, take 8 cooked tomatoes and 4 olives out of the pan. Chop these roughly and put them into a small bowl. Add the lemon zest and juice, 2 tbsp of the pesto, the extra virgin olive oil and the resting juices from the lamb. Season to taste with sugar, salt and pepper. The pesto will go a little brown; don't worry, this is because of the lemon.

6. Toss the potatoes, tomatoes and olives with the remaining 2 tbsp of pesto. Season to taste. Serve with the lamb chops and sauce.

3/ Jake's pesto meatballs with tomatoes & garlic

This dish heralded the first time Jake opened a tin by himself. It was, as befits a son of mine, tomatoes, and he had to open four tins before we got the dish right. Meatballs make a marvellous social occasion in the kitchen – it's amazing how much fun rolling a handful of mince with friends and family can be. The peppers and pesto give the meatballs lip-smacking glamour and the mozzarella keeps the mince moist and tender.

For younger kids, cut the pepper into very small pieces. I use very little cayenne in ours; if you'd like it spicier, dish up the kids' portions, then add more cayenne to yours. Good to purée or chop and freeze for babies and toddlers.

SERVES 2

Sides Soft polenta (page 340)
Prep ahead Meatballs and sauce, up to 2 days ahead
Prep/cooking 40–45 mins
Active time 25–30 mins

8 garlic cloves, peeled and sliced
2 tbsp vegetable oil
1 orange pepper, halved, deseeded and finely sliced
2 tbsp water
1 tbsp tomato purée
½ x 400g tin chopped tomatoes
200ml beef, chicken or vegetable stock
1 mozzarella ball (about 125g), drained
200g beef mince
Grated zest of ¼ orange
40g breadcrumbs
6 tbsp basil pesto (page 129)
Salt, sugar and cayenne pepper

1. Start with the garlic. Get a small saucepan. Add the sliced garlic, 1 tbsp of the oil, a pinch of salt and a pinch of sugar. Cover and sweat over a low heat, watching carefully, for 3–4 minutes until the garlic is soft. Turn the heat up to medium. Fry the garlic gently for 1 minute until it is pale golden; be careful as it will burn quickly. At this stage it will stick together a little; don't worry, once it cools it goes crisp. Transfer two-thirds of the garlic to a large bowl.

2. Add the orange pepper and the 2 tbsp of water to the remaining garlic in the saucepan. Cover and sweat over a medium heat for 10 minutes. Add the tomato purée, chopped tomatoes and stock. Bring to the boil. Lower the heat and simmer for 5 minutes.

3. Start the meatballs while the pepper sweats. Chop the mozzarella into 1cm cubes. Add half to the garlic in the bowl. Add the mince, orange zest, breadcrumbs and 3 tbsp of the pesto. Mix together, just enough to combine everything. Season with salt and cayenne. Divide the mince mixture into 12 even-sized morsels. Roll them between the palms of your hands, pressing lightly, into 12 firm balls.

4. Put a bowl next to your cooker to drain the fat into. Get a medium or medium-large frying pan. Add the remaining 1 tbsp of oil and get it really hot. Add the meatballs and fry over a medium heat for 1 minute. Turn them. Fry for 1 minute. Drain the fat into your bowl.

5. Add the pepper and tomato sauce to the frying pan. Lower the heat and simmer gently for 15 minutes, turning the meatballs once. Season to taste with salt, sugar and cayenne.

6. Divide the meatballs and sauce between deep plates or bowls. Scatter the remaining mozzarella over the top. Spoon a little pesto over each meatball.

Cook extra
Double the meatball and sauce recipe and freeze half.

4/ Prawn, carrot & noodle broth with ginger & pesto

I first made this one day after a sleepless night with the kids. I turned in tired circles while I cooked and made notes, trying to make sure I didn't forget anything. Then I added the pesto and tasted the broth. Bang, I was energised, excited. The incredible combination of fish sauce, ginger and pesto blazed through my body and brought me back to life. The broth is fragrant, fresh, delicious and deeply satisfying. I thought I'd try the combination for fun and it blew my socks off. I hope it does the same for you. If you are a vegetarian you could replace the prawns with tofu.

Kids love noodles and soup – just accept the mess while they have super slurpy fun. For younger kids, cut back on the ginger and leave out the chilli. Serve theirs, then add the chilli to yours. They may also find the texture of prawns difficult; if so, eat the prawns yourself for the time being.

SERVES 2

Sides None needed
Prep/cooking 20 mins
Active time 10–15 mins

800ml chicken or vegetable
   stock (or water plus an
   extra 1 tbsp fish sauce)
2 tbsp Thai fish sauce
2 tsp grated ginger
1 mild red chilli, deseeded
   and finely chopped
1 large carrot (at least
   150g), peeled and cut
   into 5mm slices
100g baby corn, cut in half
   lengthways
2 nests of egg noodles
100g mangetout, cut in
   half lengthways
200g raw prawns
   (defrosted if frozen)
4 tbsp basil pesto
   (page 129)
Salt

1. Boil your kettle.

2. Start with the broth. Get a medium-sized saucepan. Add the stock. Bring it to the boil. Once the stock boils, add the fish sauce, ginger, chilli, carrot and baby corn. Bring back to the boil. Lower the heat to medium and simmer for 5 minutes.

3. While the broth simmers, get a large pot. Fill it with boiling water from your kettle. Add salt, cover and bring to the boil. Put a colander in your sink. Add the noodles to the boiling water. Cover and bring back to the boil. Take the lid off and stir the noodles to separate them. Boil for 30 seconds. Add the mangetout. Cover, bring back to the boil and boil for 2 minutes or until the noodles and mangetout are just cooked through.

4. Once the broth has simmered for 5 minutes, add the prawns. Take the pan off the heat. Leave the prawns to poach in the residual heat for 2 minutes.

5. Drain the noodles and mangetout. Give the colander a shake to get out all of the water so it doesn't dilute the broth. Use tongs to transfer the noodles and mangetout to bowls.

6. Stir the pesto into the broth. Ladle the broth, vegetables and prawns over the noodles.

Cook extra
You could make double the broth (to the end of step 2), then freeze half ready for a quick meal another time. It doesn't have to have the prawns; the broth would be equally lovely with extra noodles.

5/ Rump steak with pesto, mustard, beetroot & pak choi

For all my love of Provence, I'm proud to say that the pesto dish that marked me the most was made by a New Zealander in New Zealand. The gifted trail blazer Peter Gordon was once to be found at a restaurant on Vivian Street in Wellington. The Sugar Club's Beef Pesto was legendary: an extraordinary beef fillet marinated in a tamari and mustard mixture, grilled and then served with raw beetroot, Swiss chard and pesto. My recipe is a respectful and nostalgic nod to his combination. The original can be found in the *Sugar Club Cookbook* by Peter Gordon. It is best to get 3cm thick rump steaks rather than two long thin slices. You could also make this with skirt, rib eye, sirloin or fillet.

This is a dish that I have yet to try on my kids. I will when they are a little older. For now it is our treat.

SERVES 2

Sides None needed, but egg noodles would be good
Prep ahead Marinate beef, up to 2 days ahead
Prep/cooking 30–35 mins
Active time 20–25 mins

4 tbsp tamari soy sauce
2 tbsp balsamic vinegar
2 garlic cloves, peeled and finely chopped
½ mild red chilli, deseeded and finely chopped
1 tbsp grain mustard
2 tbsp extra virgin olive oil
2 rump steaks, about 220g each
200g raw beetroot (2 small or 1 large), peeled
1 tbsp vegetable oil
15g butter
2 heads of baby pak choi, or 1 large one, cut into 3cm slices
4 tbsp basil pesto (page 129)
Salt

1. Boil your kettle.

2. Start with the marinade. Get a shallow bowl. Add the tamari, balsamic vinegar, garlic, chilli, mustard and extra virgin olive oil. Whisk everything together. Add the steaks and turn them in the marinade until they are well coated. Leave to marinate next to your cooker for at least 15 minutes.

3. While the steaks marinate, get a medium bowl and a grater. Grate the beetroot into the bowl. Put it next to your cooker.

4. Get a large pot. Fill it with boiling water. Add salt, cover and bring to the boil. Put a colander in your sink.

5. Get a medium-sized frying pan. Add the vegetable oil and get it really hot. Put a rack on top of a plate next to your cooker.

6. Lift the steaks out of the marinade, shake off any drips and add the steaks to the pan. Fry for 2 minutes. Lower the heat to medium. Drain off the fat. Add the butter to the pan. Fry the steaks for 1 minute. Turn and fry for another 3 minutes for pink beef. Don't worry if some of the marinade caramelises a little in the pan. Transfer the steaks to the rack and leave to rest for at least 5 minutes while you make the salad.

7. Boil the pak choi for 30 seconds. Drain it in your colander. Put it back in the pan for 30 seconds to dry out. Add it to the beetroot. Add the marinade to the pan. Put it back on the heat. Bring to the boil and boil for 30 seconds until it lightly coats a spoon. Add it to the grated beetroot and pak choi.

8. Add the steak resting juices to the salad. Spread 2 tbsp of pesto on top of each steak. Serve with the salad and warm marinade.

Cook extra
The steak and marinade are very good cold in a noodle salad.

6/ Spinach, crème fraîche, gnocchi, Parmesan & pesto bake

This creamy, cheesy tomato and basil gnocchi with an orange tang is an intensely flavoured pan full of fun. It's comfy and cosy, but also elegant and a touch fruity. I've sometimes dressed the gnocchi up differently by adding leftover ham, turkey, ratatouille or a tin of chickpeas or lentils. I've also replaced the gnocchi with penne (using half the weight) and the spinach with rocket.

This is a good meal for younger kids. Chop or slice the spinach rather than add it whole. Go easy on the cayenne, or just sprinkle a little over yours after dishing up theirs.

SERVES 2

Sides (pages 320–43)
Crisp leaf or vegetable salad and/or bread

Prep ahead To the end of step 6, up to a day ahead. Warm through in the microwave, then grill

Prep/cooking 25–30 mins

Active time 15–20 mins

500g gnocchi (1 packet)
125g crème fraîche (half fat if you prefer)
60g Cheddar, grated
5 tbsp basil pesto (page 129)
Grated zest and juice of ½ orange (2–3 tbsp)
½ x 400g tin chopped tomatoes
100–120g spinach
Salt, caster sugar and cayenne pepper

1. Preheat your grill to medium. Boil your kettle.

2. Start with the gnocchi. Get a large pot. Fill it with water from your kettle. Add salt, cover and bring to the boil. Add the gnocchi and boil it according to the instructions on the packet.

3. While the gnocchi boils, get a medium bowl. Add the crème fraîche, Cheddar and pesto. Stir them together. Season to taste with salt and cayenne. Put the bowl next to your cooker.

4. Drain the gnocchi into a colander. Add the orange zest and juice to the empty pan. Bring to the boil and boil for 1 minute until it is thick and sticky, almost dry. Add the tinned tomatoes. Bring back to the boil and boil for 2 minutes until there is almost no liquid left; if you pull your spoon through the mixture, the channel you make should remain.

5. Add the gnocchi and spinach to the pan. Stir for 30 seconds until the spinach just starts to wilt. Stir in two-thirds of the crème fraîche, Cheddar and pesto mixture.

6. Season to taste with salt, cayenne and sugar. Spoon the gnocchi into an ovenproof dish. Spread the final third of the crème fraîche, Cheddar and pesto mixture over the top.

7. Grill for 3–6 minutes until the top is pale gold over the green pesto cream. (Grills vary enormously, so start checking after 3 minutes and keep checking until your bake is golden.) Serve from the pan.

TAPENADE

I first tasted tapenade over twenty years ago in Wellington. I was working at an idyllic restaurant called Giverny and my chef Martin Bosley would use it to stuff salmon. I was hooked from the first fingerful on my teenage lips, because tapenade is something that grabs you, that gives you a salty thirst from its oily, black and beautiful depths. I was a long way from Provence, but I already had a taste for her classics. In Provence, tapenade always appears at aperitif time, on croûtons, with crudités or with eggs. There are notable exceptions. At Le Grain de Sel in Cogolin, chef Philippe Audibert serves warm roast peppers with tapenade in perfect simplicity, while further along the coast in Monte Carlo, Alain Ducasse spreads tapenade on red mullet, the dish that inspired my sardines.

To make your shopping as practical as possible, I've tested the recipes using very standard black olives, either à la grecque or in herbes de Provence. These are strongly flavoured and stored without any oil or brine. They'll be in bowls at your deli or in jars of 230g–270g at most supermarkets. The easiest way to remove the stones is to pinch the fat end of the olive and squeeze them out with your index finger and thumb. If you like the taste of a certain olive, use that. I love tiny Taggiasca olives, but they are easily overpowered by the capers that give tapenade its name, from *tapeno* in Old Provençal. I am loyal to the name and its provenance so I can't bear to leave them out, but whether the tapenade would miss them, I'm not so sure. Feel free to try.

I know it's because they're salty, but I've been quite amazed at how many kids like olives. More so when it is made into tapenade and mixed into meals like my fritters and filo pie. If you think your kids will find the tapenade too strong, try making it with milder olives – gentle little green ones or the tiny Niçoise olives.

**MAKES 21 TBSP;
AT LEAST 8 SERVINGS**

Prep ahead Keeps in the fridge for at least 6 months (see storage)

Prep/cooking 10–15 mins

Active time 10–15 mins

230–270g black olives, stones removed (about 200g stoned weight)

1 tbsp small salted capers, rinsed

2 salted anchovy fillets

1 garlic clove, peeled and crushed

4–6 tbsp extra virgin olive oil, plus extra to cover

1. Put all of the ingredients into a blender. Now blend together for as long or as little as you like, depending on whether you prefer a chunky or smooth texture.

2. Spoon the tapenade into jars. Cover the top completely with a thin layer of extra virgin olive oil. Seal the jars with lids.

Storage

Use small sterilised jars or clean plastic containers. The key to storage is keeping air away from the tapenade. Tap the bottoms of the jars to ensure there are no air bubbles and leave 1cm at the top of the jar for a good layer of olive oil. Pour the olive oil over the top of the tapenade to seal it. Cover the jars first with cling film, then with a lid. Store in the fridge. If you use some but not all of the tapenade, it's best to put the rest in a smaller jar. If you don't have one, clean around the exposed sides of the jar with kitchen paper. Cover the remaining tapenade with a fresh layer of oil. Unopened jars will keep for at least 6 months. Once a jar is opened, it will still keep well in the fridge for several weeks.

Simple Tapenade Magic

I know my tapenade well, and I've taken the recipe with me on my travels from one side of the world to the other. While I've cooked the recipes for this chapter and many more, I've found it to be incredibly versatile, equally happy to be the flavour that dominates, as it is to be part of a trilogy.

You'll notice a harmonious theme to the ingredient combinations in this section, something creamy, something salty and something sweet. The sweet contrasts with, then complements the tapenade, and the cream smooths it all over. This is a theme that I love in the kitchen and I've enjoyed for a long time. Keep it in mind when you're after a simple magic snack from your fridge. It could be tapenade with sweet boiled beetroot, sunblush peppers or poached prawns; it could with ricotta, mozzarella or cream cheese; it could be with a baked sweet potato and soured cream. Or it could be with hot toast, cold wine, the couch and closed eyes.

Can I hook you? I hope so. But beware of the late night cravings that lurk in the dark, salty side of your Magic Fridge.

Seasoning transformations You can make tapenade with half olives and half rehydrated sun-dried tomatoes. Or add mint, basil, rosemary or thyme. Or add roast garlic, prepared as for the sweet baked garlic butter on page 194. Or add chilli or harissa to heat it up, or ras-el-hanout to soften it a little. For a fruity touch, try sumac or lemon, grapefruit or orange zest.

Magical adventures The meat, salmon and aubergine recipes from Adventures with Ingredients can be served with tapenade. You can also use it as a condiment for the macaroni.

Slow cook magic Use a little tapenade to season the braised lentils (page 307). Try it as a condiment for the braised lamb (page 245), roast belly pork (page 261) or roast chicken (page 229); I particularly like it with roast potatoes and crème fraîche. Mix tapenade with lemon zest and spread it over the braised mackerel (page 293). If you ever have leftover roast gravy, mix it with tapenade and spread it on toast.

Simple snack Dip croûtons, freshly cooked popcorn or breadsticks into your tapenade.

Dips Surround a bowl of tapenade with crisp raw vegetables, boiled eggs, simmered new potatoes, and anything else you would like to dip into it. A tapenade-enhanced hummus is also lovely. Purée a 400g tin of chickpeas with enough of their liquid for the blades to turn for 2–3 minutes until it is smooth. Stir in tapenade to taste, season with lemon zest for freshness and chilli or cayenne pepper for a little bite. I mix tapenade with garlic mayonnaise too; try this with hot chips.

Bruschetta Spread tapenade onto toasted baguette and top it with fresh goat's cheese.

Sweet and salty bliss Cut a couple of figs in half, spoon 1 tsp of honey and 1 tsp of olive oil over each half. Roast at 190°C/Gas 5 for 8–12 minutes depending on their ripeness until the figs are soft. Spread chunky toast thinly with tapenade and thickly with ricotta. Put the figs on top. Good served with watercress and Parma ham.

Pita Spread tapenade onto pita and top with sunblush tomatoes and cream cheese. Sprinkle with grated Cheddar and grill for 3–4 minutes until golden.

Sandwich Mix tapenade with soft-boiled eggs, spring onions and a little mayonnaise to fill a buttered, warm wholemeal bun.

Baked potatoes Bake potatoes until they are tender, cut them open, then top with soured cream and tapenade. Scatter over some chopped smoked salmon or crisp grilled bacon.

Eggs Chop 2 ripe tomatoes. Simmer them in a shallow pan with 2 tbsp of tomato juice, 2 tbsp of olive oil, 1 tsp of capers and a pinch of cayenne. Poach 2 eggs on top of the tomatoes, then top them with tapenade and Parmesan.

Tasty tapenade tart Lay two 12cm puff pastry squares on a non-stick baking tray. Spread them with tapenade. Put 5 tinned artichoke halves on each pastry base. Put 1 tsp mascarpone in between each artichoke half. Press a sunblush tomato into each spoonful of mascarpone. Drizzle with olive oil. Bake at 190°C/Gas 5 for 20 minutes. Scatter with basil.

Salad Slice 4 peeled, cooked beetroot thinly. Flavour 2 tbsp of tapenade with lemon zest. Brush it over the beetroot, then scatter goat's cheese and rocket over the top.

Barbecue Tapenade combines beautifully with the smoky taste of grilled food, especially sardines, beef and lamb.

Spaghetti Toss boiled spaghetti with tapenade and lemon zest. Stir in butter, olive oil or cream if you like. Scatter grated Parmesan over the top.

Prawns Fry small tiger prawns for 1 minute each side, then add a good knob of butter and 1 tbsp of tapenade. Toss until the prawns are well coated. Serve with a salad dressed with lemon, olive oil and the pan juices.

Fish Chop 2 ripe tomatoes. Simmer them in a shallow ovenproof pan with 2 tbsp of water, 2 tbsp of olive oil, 1 tsp of capers and a pinch of cayenne. Put a sea bass, bream, mackerel or red mullet fillet on top and spread it with tapenade. Bake at 200°C/Gas 6 for 6–8 minutes.

1/ Grilled sardines with tomato tapenade sauce & beans

So simple and so deeply delicious, this recipe is incredibly satisfying to cook. You want to brown the courgette and beans quickly on one side in the pan to give their flavour a concentrated, almost barbecued edge. The tomato juice is a particularly good way to get this flavour from the pan into the tapenade sauce. As for all fish, choose the freshest on the counter. The sardines can be replaced with herring, mackerel, red mullet, sea bass, sea bream or even salmon.

Sardine fillets are great for kids. For younger ones, pick out any tiny bones once the sardines are cooked. The long green beans are fun finger food. Add a tiny touch of the tapenade to the tomato juice, serve theirs, then add the rest to yours. If the French beans are cooked until they are soft, then everything can be puréed or chopped and frozen for babies and toddlers.

SERVES 2

Sides (pages 320–43)
Mash of the remaining tinned beans and liquid (see page 341) or tomato and basil salad
Prep/cooking 20 mins
Active time 20 mins

3 tsp vegetable oil
8–10 small or 6 large
    sardine fillets, skin on
100g French beans, tail end
    removed
1 medium courgette, cut
    into 1cm slices
½ x 400g tin cannellini
    beans, drained
    (liquid kept for the side
    dish)
125g baby plum tomatoes
    (½ punnet), halved
1 garlic clove, peeled and
    finely chopped
2 tbsp plus 2 tsp extra
    virgin olive oil
6 tbsp tomato juice
2 tbsp tapenade (page 145)
Salt and freshly ground
    black pepper

1. Preheat your grill to its highest setting. Boil your kettle.

2. Start with the sardines. Line your grill tray with foil and brush it with 1 tsp of the vegetable oil. Lay the sardines on the foil, skin side up. Brush them lightly with 1 tsp oil. Season with salt and pepper.

3. Get a large saucepan. Fill it with boiling water from your kettle. Add salt, cover and bring to the boil. Put a colander in your sink. Boil the French beans for 3–4 minutes or until tender. Drain in the colander.

4. Grill the sardines for about 3 minutes (grills vary enormously so keep an eye on them). If the sardines are cooked before you're ready, just turn off the grill, lower the tray and leave the door open.

5. While the sardines are grilling, get a large frying pan. Add the remaining 1 tsp of vegetable oil and get it really hot. Add the sliced courgettes. Sauté for 1 minute. Add the French and cannellini beans. Sauté for 1 minute or until they begin to brown slightly. Add the tomatoes, garlic and the 2 tsp of extra virgin olive oil. Season to taste with salt and pepper. Sauté for 30 seconds. Spoon the vegetables onto plates.

6. Add the tomato juice to the pan. Bring to the boil and boil for 10 seconds. Take the pan off the heat. Stir in the 2 tbsp of extra virgin olive oil followed by the tapenade.

7. Put the sardine fillets on top of the vegetables. Spoon the tomato tapenade sauce over everything.

Cook extra

I love to eat sardines cold and I will happily eat this whole meal as a cold salad the next day. It would also be lovely in a baguette drenched with the sauce.

2/ Sea bream with tapenade, artichokes & sunblush tomatoes

Every mouthful of this meal is a memory of Provence; it excites, invigorates and refreshes. The sugar in the dressing plays an important part, balancing the acidity and bringing in the artichokes and sunblush tomatoes to make them irresistible accomplices to the bold tapenade. The recipe also works well with sea bass, herring, mackerel, salmon or, best of all, red mullet. You could also do a vegetarian version with the roast aubergine (page 69).

For younger kids, the leafy part of the artichoke hearts can be tricky, but try them on the soft lower part. Finely chop this along with the sunblush tomatoes, and make sure the dressing isn't too acidic. Can be puréed or chopped and frozen for babies and toddlers.

SERVES 2

Sides (pages 320–43)
Sautéed potatoes or pulses or plain grains and/or tomato salad
Prep ahead Dressing, except basil, up to 6 hours ahead
Prep/cooking 15–25 mins
Active time 10–15 mins

2 large or 4 small farmed sea bream fillets, about 120g per portion, skinned
400g tin artichoke hearts, well drained
4 tbsp extra virgin olive oil
Zested or grated zest and juice of ½ lemon (1½ tbsp)
12 sunblush tomatoes, halved
2 heaped tbsp sliced basil
2 heaped tbsp tapenade (page 145)
Salt, caster sugar and cayenne pepper

1. Preheat your grill to its highest setting.

2. Start with the sea bream. Get an oven tray. Line it with foil. Lay the bream fillets on it. Cut the artichoke hearts in half lengthways and pat dry with kitchen paper. Lay the artichoke halves, cut side up, on the tray next to the bream. Put 1 tbsp of the extra virgin olive oil into a little bowl.

3. Brush the oil evenly over the bream and artichokes. Season with salt and pepper. Grill for up to 5 minutes until the fish is just cooked through and the artichokes are a bit brown around the edges. If the fish is cooked before you're ready, just turn off the grill, lower the tray and leave the door open.

4. While the bream grills, get a medium bowl. Add the lemon zest, lemon juice, remaining 3 tbsp of extra virgin olive oil and ½ tsp of sugar. Whisk together. Stir in the sunblush tomatoes and basil. Season to taste with salt and enough cayenne to give the dressing a gentle bite.

5. Brush the bream with a little of the dressing. Spread 1 tbsp of tapenade over each fillet. Put a bream fillet on each of your plates. Put the artichoke hearts around the bream fillets. Spoon the sunblush tomato and basil dressing over everything.

3/ Rib-eye steak with tapenade, red pepper & broad beans

Meaty, sweet, succulent and salty, this combination catches fire when the orange picks up the steak's caramelised juice in the pan. This beefy juice moistens the tapenade in turn to make it more than just a sauce – it comes closer to the steak, becomes part of the meat. To get the best of this meal, eat a bit of everything in every mouthful. I'm still salivating at the memory of this steak that stunned me into silence.

For younger kids, I find cooking steaks medium rare then resting them to medium is best, because the meat is tender and juicy but not at all bloody. Slice it thinly and against the grain. Chop the zest very finely to mix in with the tapenade, then serve it on the side for them to add if they like. Chop the pepper and onion more finely and peel the skins from the broad beans. Good to purée or chop and freeze for babies and toddlers.

SERVES 2

Sides (pages 320–43)
Toasted baguette or olive oil glazed potatoes or couscous
Prep/cooking 30 mins
Active time 25–30 mins

1 medium red pepper, halved, deseeded and cut into 2cm dice
1 medium red onion, peeled and cut into 2cm dice
2 tbsp extra virgin olive oil
3 tbsp water
3 tbsp pine nuts
2 tsp vegetable oil
2 rib-eye steaks, about 200–250g each
Zested or grated zest and juice of 1 orange (120ml)
100ml beef stock
2 tbsp tapenade (page 145)
2 tbsp sliced basil
300g broad beans, shelled (150g podded weight), boiled and refreshed (and peeled if large)
Salt, sugar and cayenne pepper

1. Start with the red pepper and onion. Get a medium-sized shallow pan. Add the red pepper, onion, a pinch of salt, 1 tbsp of the extra virgin olive oil and the 3 tbsp of water. Cover and sweat the pepper and onion over a medium heat, stirring occasionally, for 10 minutes or until soft. Add the pine nuts. Turn up the heat. Fry for 2 minutes until the vegetables and nuts start to go brown around the edges. Take the pan off the heat.

2. Put this mixture, the orange juice, a resting rack on top of a plate and a bowl for hot fat next to your cooker.

3. Get a medium-large frying pan. Add the vegetable oil and get it really hot. Add the steaks; they should really sizzle, if not take them back out and get the pan hotter. Fry the steaks over a high heat for 2 minutes each side for medium rare; fry over a medium heat for 3 minutes each side for medium or 4 minutes for well done. Put the steaks onto the resting rack to rest while you finish everything else.

4. Drain half the fat into your bowl. Add the orange juice to the pan and boil it until only 2 tbsp remains. Add the beef stock and boil until it reduces by half. Take the pan off the heat. Stir in the remaining 1 tbsp of extra virgin olive oil, the tapenade, orange zest and basil. Season to taste with salt, sugar and cayenne.

5. Add the broad beans to the pepper and pine nut mixture and warm it through. Season to taste.

6. Put the steaks on plates and brush them vigorously with their resting juices. Spread the tapenade mixture over the top of the steaks. Spoon the vegetables alongside.

Cook extra

For a steak *pan bagnat*, cut a small baguette in half, hollow out the bottom, fill it with sliced steak, tapenade and the pepper mix. Press the top down.

4/ Roast chestnut, squash & kale penne with tapenade

This penne is rich, gently sweet and receptive to tapenade. I roast the squash and chestnuts, then use some of them to make a purée to flavour, coat and caress the pasta. I serve the tapenade and half the ricotta on top because I love the way it looks, then I mix it all together as I eat. You can replace butternut squash with sweet potato or pumpkin, and the kale with spinach.

   This is an ideal dish for kids as the squash and chestnuts are slightly sweet. For younger kids, slice the kale very thinly and cook it thoroughly. Let them mix in their own tapenade and ricotta. No good to purée, but can be chopped and frozen for toddlers.

SERVES 2

Sides None needed
Prep/cooking 40 mins
Active time 25–30 mins

½ large butternut squash (about 500g), use the top half
1 tbsp vegetable oil
100g cooked and peeled chestnuts (page 21)
1 medium onion, peeled and finely diced
2 garlic cloves, peeled and finely chopped
½ tsp ground cumin
8 tbsp hot water
1 heaped tbsp tomato purée
500ml vegetable stock
200g penne
100g kale
125g ricotta
3 tbsp tapenade (page 145)
Salt, sugar and ground cumin

1. Preheat your oven to 220°C/Gas 7, position upper middle shelf.

2. Start with the squash. Peel it with a speed peeler. Cut the flesh into 3cm dice. Get a baking tray. Put the squash on it. Spoon on the oil and toss the squash until it is well coated. Season with salt, sugar and cumin. Roast for 20 minutes, turning the squash halfway through. Add the chestnuts. Roast for another 5 minutes or until the squash is soft. Turn the oven off.

3. While the squash roasts, get a medium-sized saucepan. Add the onion, garlic, cumin and 4 tbsp of hot water. Cover and sweat over a medium heat for 5 minutes. Stir in the tomato purée. Pour on the vegetable stock and bring to the boil.

4. Add the penne, bring back to the boil and boil for 1 minute. Cover and turn the heat to low. Simmer for 16 minutes, stirring occasionally. Add more water from the kettle if the penne begins to dry out; it should always be a little soupy. Take the lid off. Simmer and stir for 3 minutes. Taste to see if the penne is cooked. Turn off the heat. Cover and leave to sit for 2 minutes.

5. While the penne simmers, boil your kettle. Get a medium-sized saucepan. Fill it with boiling water from the kettle. Add salt, cover and bring to the boil. Put a colander in your sink. Boil the kale for 3–4 minutes or until tender. Drain in the colander.

6. Take the squash and chestnuts out of the oven. Put one-third of each (using any broken chestnut pieces) into a blender. Add half the ricotta and 4 tbsp of hot water. Blend until it is completely smooth and the consistency of yoghurt. If you need to, add more hot water.

7. Stir the purée into the penne. Fold in the kale, chestnuts and squash. Season to taste. Spoon into bowls or deep plates. Dot with the tapenade and remaining ricotta.

Cook extra

To use the whole squash, double up the recipe to the point where you add the tapenade and the rest of the ricotta, and freeze half.

5/ Mushroom, tapenade, beetroot & goat's cheese pie

Beetroot, goat's cheese and olives are a culinary love triangle so suited that they rival conventional couples like strawberries and cream, or steak and chips. It was with this recipe that I found one of my best solutions for filo pastry. Rather than try and wrap the mushroom and creamy filling to make a parcel, I sit the filo roughly on top. This makes the pies easier to prepare, the end result crisper, and gives the pies a ruffled charm.

For younger kids, cut the goat's cheese into little dice and instead of layering it, mix all of the filling ingredients together. The pies are very easy, so get the kids to make their own in smaller mushrooms. Good to purée or freeze without the pastry.

SERVES 2

Sides (pages 320–43)
Dark green salad. For bulk, baguette or garlic bread

Prep ahead To the end of step 5, up to 6 hours ahead

Prep/cooking 25–30 mins

Active time 20 mins

3 ½ tbsp tapenade
    (page 145)
1½ tbsp honey
2 tbsp plus 2½ tsp extra
    virgin olive oil
1 tbsp chopped rosemary
300g cooked beetroot
    (see page 327)
4 tbsp crème fraîche
2 large mushrooms,
    10–12cm across
150g creamy goat's cheese
    with rind
4 sheets of filo pastry,
    trimmed to 24 x 22cm
2 tsp balsamic vinegar
Freshly ground black
    pepper

1. Preheat your oven to 200°C/Gas 6, position upper middle shelf.

2. Start with the dressing. Get a small bowl. Add 2 tbsp of the tapenade, the honey, the 2 tbsp of extra virgin olive oil and half the rosemary. Set aside.

3. Next, grate half the beetroot. Put the grated beetroot into a medium bowl. Add the remaining 1½ tbsp of tapenade, the crème fraîche and remaining rosemary. Mix together. Season with pepper. Cut the remaining beetroot into 10–12 wedges, 2cm thick. Toss them with 1 tsp of extra virgin olive oil. Spread the beetroot wedges over one half of a baking sheet.

4. Put the mushrooms, rounded side down, on the baking sheet in front of the beetroot wedges. Brush 1 tsp of the dressing all over each mushroom.

5. Spoon the grated beetroot mixture into the mushroom cups. Cut the goat's cheese into 3 pieces. Flatten 2 pieces with the heels of your hands into circles just smaller than the mushroom cups. Put the flattened cheese on top of the grated beetroot mixture.

6. Put 2 sheets of filo pasty flat on your worktop. Brush each sheet with a very thin layer of dressing. Put a second filo sheet on top of each. Brush with the dressing again. Drape the filo, brushed side down, over the top of the cheese; try to keep it from sitting directly on the cheese. Push the excess pastry around the base of the mushroom so that it just sticks. Brush the filo on each pie all over with 1 tsp of extra virgin olive oil. Make sure the pies are at least 5cm apart on the tray.

7. Put the tray in the oven with the pies towards the back (the hottest part). Bake for 10–12 minutes or until the pastry is golden all over, turning the beetroot wedges halfway through.

8. While the pies bake, cut the remaining goat's cheese into 10 chunks. Add the balsamic vinegar to the dressing. Once the pies are ready, take them out of the oven and brush each pie with ¼ tsp of extra virgin olive oil. Put a pie in the middle of each plate. Toss the roasted beetroot in the dressing. Spoon it around the pies and put the goat's cheese in between.

6/ Sweet potato, bacon & tapenade tart

This is an elegant comfort dish on top of a tart. The long, slim tarts are practical – because you don't have to cut individual tarts when they are hot, you can just serve them from the oven – and they're very pretty. The size of pre-rolled pastry sheets varies, so the first time you make this, cut all the pastry into portions, lay the ones you don't use in a single layer on a cling film lined tray and freeze them. Once frozen, wrap the individual portions in cling film, then store them in the freezer in a plastic box ready for the next time you want to bake one of these tarts. Any trimmings can be folded together and frozen for another use.

Sweet potatoes are great for kids. They can make their own tarts, cutting the pastry to a size that suits, or slice the cooked tarts into soldiers. For younger kids, leave out the bacon, use less tapenade and undercook the pastry slightly. No good to chop or freeze.

SERVES 2

Sides (pages 320–43)
Crisp vegetable or leaf salad
Prep ahead To the end of
step 6, a day ahead
Prep/cooking 40-45 mins
Active time 20-25 mins

1 pre-rolled sheet of puff
    pastry, 40 x 20cm
2 small sweet potatoes
    (300g), washed (or
    ½ large one, halved
    lengthways)
5 rashers of streaky bacon,
    halved widthways
5 tbsp tapenade (page 145)
Knob of very soft butter
    (15g)
1 tbsp honey
½ tsp red wine vinegar
½ mild red chilli, deseeded
    and finely diced
4 tbsp crème fraîche
Salt

1. Preheat your oven to 200°C/Gas 6, position upper middle shelf. Boil your kettle.

2. Start with the puff pastry. Unroll it; turn it over onto a small board and pull away the plastic. Put the pastry in the freezer for 15 minutes. Get a baking tray with slightly raised sides. Line it with a non-stick mat or baking paper. With a sharp knife, cut the pastry into 2 rectangles, each 20 x 8cm. Put the rectangles on the baking tray.

3. While the pastry is in the freezer, get a medium-sized saucepan. Fill it with boiling water from the kettle. Add salt, cover and bring to the boil. Put a colander in your sink. Cut the sweet potatoes into 1cm thick slices; you need 10 slices per tart. Cook any extra to serve on the side. Add the sweet potato slices to the boiling water. Turn the heat to low and simmer gently for 6 minutes. Add the bacon. Simmer for 1 minute more or until the sweet potato slices are just soft enough to push the point of a knife through easily. Drain in the colander. Pat dry with kitchen paper.

4. Spread 1 tbsp of the tapenade across the centre of each pastry rectangle, leaving a 1cm margin at the sides. Put a piece of bacon at the top of each tart, then 2 side-by-side overlapping slices of sweet potato. Continue overlapping with the remaining sweet potatoes and bacon.

5. Mix together the butter, honey, wine vinegar and diced chilli. Brush two-thirds of this mixture over the top of the sweet potatoes, bacon and pastry. Bake for 15 minutes.

6. Get the tray out of the oven. Turn the oven down to 180°C/Gas 4. Brush the tarts with the remaining glaze. Bake for 5 minutes or until they are glazed and golden. Serve the tarts hot or warm, with the crème fraîche and remaining tapenade on the side to dot on top.

SOFT, SWEET, STICKY ONIONS

Peel, slice, soften and fry a bag of onions and you have the cheapest luxury ingredient that money can buy. A soft, sticky, sweet and savoury mass of infinite potential.

You'll see soft onions under my braised lamb, around my roast chicken, in my mackerel sauce, on my pasta and almost everywhere else. Onions are the mothers of good food. They will never do quite the same thing or taste the same twice. They will happily sit in the background, do the hard work, absorb the flavours of those around them and let the others take the credit. Not here. In this section the onions lead the way and their taste is worth the tears.

I've cooked this recipe with 1.2kg onions, because that was the maximum I could fit comfortably in one domestic-sized pan. I buy the cheapest bags of onions, which are cheap only because they're all different sizes, but firm and not too big. The quantity you finish with will always vary a little, depending on the water content of the onions, but it will be roughly half the weight of the unpeeled raw onions. If you end up with a little more or less, don't worry, I've never found the difference to be more than 10 per cent and the recipes will all work with 10 per cent more or less sticky onions.

These onions are great for kids and good to mix with other things. For younger kids, chop the cooked onions. Good to purée or chop and freeze for babies and toddlers.

MAKES 600g;
ABOUT 6 SERVINGS

Prep ahead The onions keep in the fridge for up to a week (see storage)

Prep/cooking 45–50 mins

Active time 30–35 mins

1.2kg firm onions, peeled and cut into 5mm slices (with a food processor if you prefer)
1½ tbsp vegetable oil
2 tbsp water
Salt, freshly ground black pepper and sugar
Olive oil to cover (if storing in a jar)

1. Get a medium-large sauté pan with lid (or a similar sized saucepan, but this will take longer to brown the onions because the evaporation will be slower). Add the onions, oil, the 2 tbsp of water, and ½ tsp each of salt, sugar and pepper. Cover the pan and put it on a medium heat. Sweat the onions, without browning, for 8 minutes or until they are soft but not mushy, stirring 3 or 4 times to make sure the onions don't stick.

2. Take off the lid. Turn the heat to high. Fry the onions, stirring frequently, for 5–10 minutes, depending on their water content, until they are golden brown and most of their liquid has evaporated. Add more oil if they start to stick. When the onions are ready they will be soft and sticky, and there should be no water in the pan. Turn off the heat. If, as often happens, some onion is stuck to the bottom of the pan, put the lid back on for 2 minutes to sweat the stickiness off. Give the onions a good stir and the softened bits on the bottom of the pan will mix together with the rest. Season to taste.

Storage

Use small sterilised jars or clean plastic containers, ideally enough for a single use. The key to storage is keeping air away from the onions. Tap the bottoms of the jars to ensure there are no air bubbles and leave 1–2cm at the top of the jar for a good layer of olive oil. Use within a week. If the recipe doesn't need it, you can use this olive oil for a salad dressing. Alternatively you can freeze the onions in little bags, in the quantities you will use for the recipes; they can be defrosted quickly.

Simple Soft, Sweet, Sticky Onion Magic

Sweet and sticky onions are as comfortable in great dishes at grand restaurants as they are tucked into a microwave baked potato. They have no favourites when it comes to cheese; they'll nestle into blue, charm the rind off a Camembert and make Cheddar melt. I add them to yesterday's roast meat to moisten it and make it go further in hot and cold sandwiches, wraps, samosas and stuffed vegetables, in pastas and pies, or mixed through rice, couscous and quinoa.

Soft, sweet, sticky onions also make the most beautiful and portable tarts, which are based on the pissaladière that introduced me to them. This bread-based beauty from the streets of Nice, with her wrinkled bed of onions and raunchy lines of anchovies and olives, is tattooed in my memory. I was seventeen when I first tasted this tart and I've used her onions with magical abandon ever since. In my search for more simple magic, I've discovered that you can use part-baked baguettes as the base to save you making the dough. These baguettes, in combination with my magic onions, give you endless and almost instant possibilities for tarts on toast.

Seasoning transformations Try flavouring soft, sweet, sticky onions with ras-el-hanout, curry powder, smoked paprika, jerk spice, fresh mint, grated orange zest and thyme, cumin, cinnamon, fennel seeds, ginger, grated horseradish, capers or balsamic syrup.

Magical adventures Any of the meat and fish 'hero' recipes from Adventures with Ingredients can be seasoned and then served with the sticky onions as a sauce, gravy, dressing or chutney (see below). You can also spread the onions onto the roast aubergine (page 69), then top it with olives and anchovies to make an aubergine pissaladière.

Sticky onion sauce, gravy and dressing Add stock and cream to the sticky onions for a cream sauce. Add stock and butter to the onions for gravy. Add herbs to either of these if you like. Add olive oil, vinegar, chopped tomato and basil for a dressing.

Quick chutney Season the sticky onions to taste with wine vinegar and brown sugar. Add raisins and/or chopped dried figs and/or grated apple. Serve with cheese.

Tarts on toast Toast half a baguette and spread it with the sticky onions. Top with anchovies and olives, or tomato and mozzarella, or pre-cooked beetroot and goat's cheese, or cream cheese and bacon, or blue cheese and pears, or any of the toppings on page 168.

Cheese on toast The sticky onions go under the cheese. Serve with Worcestershire sauce.

French onion soup Add beef or chicken stock to the sticky onions. Bring to the boil. Season to taste. Serve with cheese on toast.

Baked potatoes Cut a baked potato in half. Push one-sixth of a Camembert into the middle of each half. Spread the sticky onions over the top. Put the potato back in a hot oven for 10 minutes. Wow.

Baked fish Spread the onions in an ovenproof dish. Add a little white wine or stock. Put white fish fillets, like pollock, on top. Brush with butter. Season. Bake at 200°C/Gas 6 for 8 minutes. Sprinkle with chopped parsley.

Hot dogs and burgers These love sticky onions.

Omelette, pancake or hot wrap Make a stuffing with the sticky onions, cheese, crème fraîche, ham or fried mushrooms.

Pasta or risotto Mix the onions into pasta with cream or cream cheese and bacon or porcini, or broad beans and ham.

Filo parcels or samosas Mix the onions with cooked meat, vegetables or fish. Add the spice you fancy, and/or sliced mint. Stuff filo or samosa pastry sheets and bake. (This is intentionally vague because the combinations are endless and you can vary the quantities.) A great way to use up leftovers.

Courgette and tomato tians Spread sticky onions over the base of a gratin dish. Cover generously with overlapping layers of courgette and tomato. Brush with olive oil. Season. Cover tightly with foil. Bake at 160°C/Gas 3 for 45 minutes. Uncover and bake for up to a further hour until the tomatoes and courgettes are dark and dry on top. Brush with olive oil to serve. To turn your tian into a filling meal, mix a cooked pulse like lentils or chickpeas into the sticky onions.

Autumn tians Spread sticky onions over the base of a gratin dish. Cover with sliced butternut squash, pumpkin, sweet potatoes or potatoes. Bake as above, making sure that the vegetable is cooked enough to easily pierce with the tip of a knife when you take off the foil. You can change the seasoning to suit each ingredient: curry, cumin and nutmeg are all very good with the sweetness of the squash and sweet potatoes; black olives, black pepper, fennel and caraway seeds are all good with the potatoes.

Stuffed tomatoes Cut large ripe tomatoes in half. Scoop out the pulp and seeds. Mix these with sticky onions and oregano. Fill the tomato halves with this mixture. Put them into an ovenproof pan. Cover with foil and bake at 220°C/Gas 7 for 10 minutes. Take off the foil. Sprinkle oregano, breadcrumbs and Parmesan over the top. Bake, uncovered, for another 15–20 minutes until the tomatoes are soft and the tops are golden.

1/ Chicken with jerk spice, sticky onions & sweet potatoes

I call this 'The Magic Fridge Mackay One Pan Roast and Braise'. Catchy, don't you think? It's a new technique that I've discovered. I roast the chicken legs on foil over the sticky onions and sweet potatoes that braise in the pan underneath. This means that the chicken is dry enough to roast and crisp, while the potatoes below are moist enough to cook through. I remove the foil between them for the last 10 minutes so that the two can get to know each other and become a couple rather than a pair of legs with spuds on the side. Their happy union manages to be warm and sunny at the same time as being comforting.

For younger kids, leave most of the spice rub off the chicken, but keep it in the potatoes. Sweet potatoes are great for kids. Use them in combination to introduce less sweet vegetables, like turnips and swedes. Can be puréed or chopped and frozen for babies and toddlers.

SERVES 2

Sides (pages 320–43) None needed. For something fresh, a leaf salad, peas or beans

Prep ahead The whole thing can be made a day ahead

Prep/cooking 45–50 mins

Active time 15–20 mins

450g sweet potatoes (2 medium), washed and cut into 1cm slices

2 tsp jerk spice, or more to taste

200g soft, sweet, sticky onions (page 161)

150ml chicken stock

2 chicken legs, about 200g each

1 tsp vegetable oil

1 tbsp thyme leaves

Zested or grated zest of ½ orange

½ mild red chilli, deseeded and finely chopped

Salt

1. Preheat your oven to 220°C/Gas 7, position upper middle shelf.

2. Start with the sweet potatoes. Spread the slices out on your chopping board. Sprinkle them with 1 tsp of the jerk spice and ⅛ tsp of salt.

3. Get a medium-sized ovenproof frying or sauté pan. Spread half of the sweet potatoes over the base. Spread the sticky onions over the sweet potatoes. Spread the rest of the sweet potatoes over the onions; don't worry if you can still see some of the onions. Pour the chicken stock over the top. Cover the pan tightly with foil. Put the pan on a high heat. Bring to the boil. You'll be able to hear it boiling under the foil; if in doubt, set a timer: it takes about 1½ minutes. Take the pan off the heat.

4. Brush the chicken legs with the oil. Brush each chicken leg with a pinch of salt and ½ tsp of jerk spice, or more if you like it hot. Lay the chicken legs, skin side up, on the foil that covers the pan. Bake for 20 minutes.

5. Take the pan out of the oven. Put the chicken legs on a plate. Cut a hole in the foil. Drain the chicken cooking juices and fat through the hole into the pan. Discard the foil. Put the chicken legs, skin side up, on top of the potatoes and onions. Bake for 10 minutes.

6. Brush the chicken legs with the cooking juices in the pan. Mix the thyme leaves, orange zest and chilli together. Sprinkle this mixture over the chicken and sweet potatoes. Serve straight from the pan.

Cook extra

Double the recipe and freeze half.

2/ Sesame glazed herrings with sticky onions & beetroot

A month before I first cooked this recipe I spent a week in Tokyo. It was the first time I'd eaten real Japanese food and my senses were battered by its brilliance. The flavours were so clear that they sparkled and the contrasts in textures delighted and inspired me.

This fish flakes under its crisp sesame sheet, the beetroot leads to the oozing onions and there's the crunch of the cucumber salad all around. With contrasting tastes and textures, it's food that blazes with colour, bursts with flavour and manages to be fresh and comforting at the same time. The hoisin sauce hugs the onions, gives depth of flavour to the salad, seasons, sweetens, glazes and sticks the sesame seeds to the herrings.

I've learnt that younger kids like the sweetness of hoisin sauce with oily fish. If they won't eat the diced cucumber and peppers, try giving them sticks that they can pick up.

SERVES 2

Sides (pages 320–43)
None needed. For bulk, plain grains or egg noodles

Prep ahead Dressing and vegetables, except mint, a few hours ahead

Prep/cooking 25–30 mins

Active time 25–30 mins

2 tsp vegetable oil

1 tsp sesame oil

2 tbsp hoisin sauce

Zested or grated zest and juice of 1 lime (2 tbsp)

200g soft, sweet, sticky onions (page 161)

150g cooked beetroot (see page 327), cut into 10 slices

6 herring or sardine fillets, about 120g per portion

2 tbsp sesame seeds

¼ cucumber, deseeded and cut into 2cm pieces

½ red pepper, deseeded and cut into 2cm dice

1 tbsp soy sauce

2 tbsp sliced mint

4 tbsp plain yoghurt

1. Start with the dressing. Get a medium bowl. Add the vegetable and sesame oils, hoisin sauce, lime zest and 1 tbsp of the juice. Stir to combine. There's no need for salt. Put 2 tbsp of the dressing in a cup ready to brush onto the herrings.

2. Preheat your grill to its medium setting.

3. Cut two 20cm squares of non-stick baking paper. Put these on a baking sheet (without a lip). Put half the onions onto each piece of paper. Flatten each pile of onions into a 10cm circle. Lay the beetroot slices over the onions in a single layer. Brush the herring fillets with 1 tbsp of dressing from the cup on each side.

4. Put the herring fillets, skin side up, on top of the beetroot. Sprinkle 1 tbsp of the sesame seeds over each portion. Grill for 5–7 minutes until the sesame seeds are golden and the fish fillets are just cooked through. Grills vary enormously so keep a close eye on the herring fillets and take them out from under the grill as soon as they are ready.

5. Next make the salad. Add the cucumber and red pepper to the dressing. Stir in the soy sauce, the remaining 1 tbsp of lime juice and the mint.

6. Slide one piece of paper with everything on top onto each plate. Put a fish slice flat against the side of the herrings, then pull out the paper like a magic tablecloth trick. Spoon the cucumber and red pepper salad around the edge of your plates. Serve the yoghurt on the side.

Cook extra
Try this combination in a rice paper or lettuce wrap, or in a cold noodle salad. Leave out the beetroot if you are taking it to eat at work.

3/ Creamy onion & smoked salmon tart with horseradish

This recipe serves 4 to use all of the packet of puff pastry. It also gives you the opportunity to make 4 different toppings on the same base. They're all yummy and once you have the sticky onions the tart takes only 10 minutes to put together. If you like, you can make a single portion on a pita bread base, or 2–3 on large wraps. If someone can't eat wheat, use a thin polenta base (see page 340), or the roast aubergine pizza base (on page 80).

These tarts are great for kids. Get them to put their own toppings on. Top a large base with the onions, show them which is their section and offer them toppings: ham, smoked mackerel, trout, bacon, favourite cheeses, grapes, cherry tomatoes. A mixture of what they want to eat and what you'd like them to eat is ideal. No good to purée or freeze.

SERVES 4

Sides (pages 320–43) Any raw vegetable or leaf salad, potato salad or grain salad

Prep ahead The tart can be made a day ahead. Warm up in a hot oven for 5 minutes

Prep/cooking 35 mins

Active time 10 mins

320–375g packet ready-rolled puff pastry (about 35 x 23cm), out of the fridge for 5 minutes, unrolled

400g soft, sweet, sticky onions (page 161)

250g tub mascarpone

1 tbsp grated horseradish or 2 tbsp horseradish cream

100g hot-smoked salmon

Salt and freshly ground black pepper

1. Preheat your oven to 220°C/Gas 7, position upper middle shelf.

2. Line a 30 x 20cm shallow baking tray (Swiss roll tin) with lightly oiled non-stick baking paper, leaving a long overlap to help you remove the tart once it is cooked. Lay the pastry over the top. Press the excess pastry inwards to make a small lip. Prick the pastry all over with a fork.

3. In a bowl, mix together the onions, mascarpone and horseradish. Season to taste with salt and pepper. Spread the mixture over the pastry. Flake the smoked salmon over the top. Push it gently into the onions. Bake for 20–25 minutes until crisp and golden. Don't worry if the tart balloons up in the centre; this always happens to me – just pop it with a knife.

4. Take the tart out of the oven and leave it to sit for 2 minutes. Use the overhanging paper to pull the tart off the tray and onto your chopping board. Cut into 4 portions to serve.

Variations (all serve 4)
These alternative toppings all use the same amount of soft, sticky onions and cook for the same length of time. Horseradish is optional.

Chorizo Cut 120g chorizo in half lengthways and then into 1cm slices. Stir 1 heaped tsp of smoked paprika into the onions and mascarpone. Scatter the half-slices of chorizo on top of the onions.

Artichoke Mix 3 tbsp sliced basil into the onions and mascarpone. Drain a 400g tin of artichoke hearts. Cut each into 6 wedges. Scatter the artichoke wedges, 16 sunblush tomatoes and 20 pitted olives on top of the onions.

Red pepper and Gorgonzola Quarter and deseed a red pepper, then cut into 5mm thick slices. Mix the pepper slices with the onions and only 125g mascarpone. Dot 120g Gorgonzola over the top.

Cook extra
Make 2 tarts. A delicious and easily portable lunch.

4/ Bangers with brown sauce & onion gravy

As well as transforming themselves into flamboyant tarts, my onions can give you a good old culinary cuddle – a meal as cosy as an easy novel you've read before. My wife introduced me to brown sauce and my (now mostly cured) cheffiness made me resist it until late one night when we formed an exciting new relationship over half a loaf and a packet of bacon. Now I can't eat a bacon sandwich without a salty brown slick melting into the butter and bacon fat. The sauce teams up with my onions to make an intentionally slightly synthetic tasting gravy. I resisted the urge to add anything that could be considered sophisticated.

For younger kids, use half the quantity of vinegar. This is a great meal to serve with mashed vegetables or pulses that they haven't tried before; it's how I introduced my kids to polenta, which they now eat all the time. Can be puréed or chopped and frozen for babies and toddlers.

SERVES 2

Sides Mashed potato
(page 338)
Prep/cooking 25–30 mins
Active time 20–25 mins

2 tsp vegetable oil
4–6 sausages (300–400g)
1 tbsp malt or balsamic
    vinegar
200ml beef stock
150g soft, sweet, sticky
    onions (page 161)
2 tbsp brown sauce
½ tsp cornflour
2 tbsp water
Salt and freshly ground
    black pepper

1. Preheat your oven to 200°C/Gas 6, position upper middle shelf.

2. Put a bowl next to your cooker to drain fat into. Make sure you have all of the ingredients close to hand, ready to add. You need to go quickly once you add the vinegar so it doesn't burn.

3. Start by frying the sausages. Get a medium-sized ovenproof frying pan. Add the oil and get it really hot. Add the sausages. Fry and turn the sausages over a medium heat for 3 minutes until they are golden all over. If the pan gets too hot, take it off the heat for a few seconds. If you fry sausages for too long over too high a heat, they harden unpleasantly on the outside and they can burst.

4. Turn off the heat. Put the sausages on a plate. Drain the fat from the pan. Standing well back, add the vinegar to the pan. It will sizzle and reduce to almost nothing. Quickly add the beef stock, onions and brown sauce. Bring to the boil. Take the pan off the heat.

5. Put the cornflour into a small bowl. Add the 2 tbsp of water and stir with until the cornflour is completely dissolved. Off the heat, stir the dissolved cornflour into the onion gravy. Put the pan back on a medium-high heat. Stirring constantly, bring the gravy back to the boil and boil for 10 seconds until it is thick enough to coat the back of a spoon. Season to taste with salt and pepper. Add the sausages to the pan.

6. Put the pan into the oven to finish cooking the sausages in the gravy for 8 minutes. Turn off the oven and leave the pan inside to sit for 2 minutes with the door ajar. Serve the sausages and gravy with mash.

Cook extra
Double the recipe and freeze half.

5/ Lamb's liver with sticky onions, bacon, apples & sage

It's impossible to ignore liver in the context of onions. Lamb's liver, often coming (hooray) from New Zealand, is excellent value and delicious when it isn't overcooked. Liver, onions, apple and sage are like a happy little family playing on a plate. Although you don't usually find them all together, I thought this was my opportunity for a good old shindig.

Now, controversially, I have suggested serving this with soft polenta as my first preference. I just love the stuff, cooked in stock and finished with butter. I also love the colour. Of course you can have your mash, or sweet roast vegetables.

Younger kids may find liver too strong, but give it a go. Fry the liver, rest it, then cut the slices thinly. The apples will go down well. Chop the onions before you add them to the reduced juice. Can be puréed or chopped and frozen for babies and toddlers.

SERVES 2

Sides (pages 320–43) Soft polenta or mashed potato and/or broccoli, cabbage or roast sweet vegetables

Prep ahead Stock and apple juice can be reduced, a day ahead

Prep/cooking 20–25 mins

Active time 20–25 mins

300ml apple juice

2 tsp vegetable oil

4 rashers of streaky bacon

1 large Braeburn apple, cored and cut into 2cm dice

8 large sage leaves

150g soft, sweet, sticky onions (page 161)

300g lamb's liver, cut into 4 slices, 2cm thick

3 tbsp plain flour

2 knobs of butter (30g)

Salt and cinnamon

1. Start with the sauce. Get a small saucepan. Pour in the apple juice. Put the pan on a high heat. Bring to the boil and boil until the juice has reduced by two-thirds.

2. Heat a medium-large frying pan with 1 tsp of the oil. Add the bacon. Fry for 1 minute. Turn the bacon. Add the apples and sage. Fry for 2 minutes. Transfer everything in the pan to a plate.

3. Add the reduced apple juice to the frying pan. Scrape up all the goodies. Pour the juice back into the saucepan. Add the onions to the juice and warm them through. Wash out your frying pan.

4. Season the liver with salt and cinnamon. Put the flour onto a plate. Heat the frying pan. Add the remaining 1 tsp of oil and get it really hot. Dip each side of the liver in the flour, just enough to coat it thinly. Shake off the excess flour. Fry the liver over a medium-high heat for 1½ minutes. Turn the liver. Fry for 1 minute. Turn down the heat. Add half of the butter in little pieces near each slice of liver. Return the apples, bacon and sage to the pan. Warm through for 30 seconds over a medium heat. Put the apple mixture on one side of your plates and the liver on the other side.

5. Add the apple juice and onions to the frying pan. Stir to get all of the caramelised goodies off the bottom of the pan. Stir in the remaining knob of butter. Season to taste. The sauce will be more like a compote. Spoon it around the side of the liver, rather than over the top of it, so you don't soften the crisp surface.

6/ My salute to the tartiflette of my youth

This recipe is based on the great tartiflette, a creamy potato and wine affair topped with a whole Reblochon. It comes by way of my days in the snow at Courchevel 1850 where I worked in a 2 star Michelin restaurant called The Drunken Boat. We worked every day of the week, skied most afternoons and went out most nights after service. There is a saying in the French Alps, 'In tartiflette we trust', and we would often trust a tartiflette to soak up the beer and help us through the late nights. I've changed the cheese to Camembert, because it's cheaper and easier to find, and I've changed the wine to stock.

Kids may find Camembert too strong, but you could do a section topped with grated Cheddar, then next time try half Cheddar, half Camembert. Or just peel the skin off the Camembert. For younger kids, leave out the bacon and chop the onions finely.

If you do not have a suitable baking dish, you could bake the tartiflette in a 20cm ovenproof frying pan.

SERVES 2

Sides None needed

Prep ahead To the point of baking, up to a day ahead

Prep/cooking 50–55 mins

Active time 15–20 mins

600g waxy potatoes, such as Charlotte or Maris Peer, peeled and cut into 1cm slices

1 tsp vegetable oil

100–125g bacon lardons or streaky bacon, cut into 1–2cm chunks

200g soft, sweet, sticky onions (page 161)

100ml chicken or vegetable stock

150ml whipping cream

½ Camembert (125g)

Salt, freshly ground black pepper and nutmeg

1. Preheat your oven to 200°C/Gas 6, position upper middle shelf. Boil your kettle. Get an 18 x 23cm baking dish, 4–5cm deep.

2. Start with the potatoes. Fill a medium-sized saucepan two-thirds full with boiling water. Add salt and bring to the boil. Add the sliced potatoes. Bring back to the boil. Turn down the heat and simmer the potatoes gently for 12–15 minutes or until tender.

3. While the potatoes simmer, get a medium-sized frying pan. Add the oil and get it really hot. Add the bacon and fry for 2 minutes until pale golden. Stir in the onions. Take the pan off the heat.

4. When the potatoes are tender, drain them in a metal colander. Put the colander into the oven for 5 minutes to dry the potatoes out.

5. Cover the bottom of your dish with half of the potatoes. Season with salt, pepper and nutmeg. Spread the onion and bacon mixture over the top. Cover with the second half of the potatoes. Season again. Mix the stock and cream together. Pour this mixture over the potatoes.

6. Slice the half Camembert in half horizontally through the centre. Slice each piece into 3 wedges. Lay the cheese wedges, rind side up, over the potatoes. Bake for 30 minutes or until the tartiflette is pale golden on top and the cream bubbles around the edges.

TOMATO COMPOTE

It was August in the south of Italy and the sun shone all month. The tomatoes were ripe, they smelt like their vines, and they were soft and warm in your hand. At the end of that month in 1996 four tonnes of San Marzano tomatoes arrived on a truck at Don Alfonso's restaurant. We boiled them with basil and olive oil in giant pans, then strained the sauce and funnelled it into empty water bottles that we sealed and boiled to sterilise their precious liquid. The local staff brought their families to help, making the day feel like a festival. The sauce would be served at the restaurant long after I had left. I think perhaps the idea for The Magic Fridge was planted in that sunny setting.

To concentrate the tomato compote's flavour and consistency, the liquid in the tomatoes needs to evaporate almost entirely. This means that if you make the tomato compote with only tinned tomatoes it becomes too strong, too much like tomato purée. If you can get ripe, soft and heavily scented tomatoes, use all fresh; if you can't, or if you make the compote out of season, use half tinned and half fresh. Tomatoes vary, as does the amount of water they hold, so the cooking time can change accordingly.

For younger kids, use your tomato compote as an introduction to vegetables such as turnips, carrots, courgettes, leeks, aubergines (peel the skin), swede, cabbage, mushrooms, celeriac and runner beans. Gradually mix the vegetables with less of the tomato compote.

MAKES 920G–1KG; ABOUT 8 SERVINGS

Prep ahead Keeps in the fridge for up to 2 weeks (see storage)

Prep/cooking 45–50 mins

Active time 15 mins

2 medium onions, peeled and cut into 5mm dice

8 garlic cloves, peeled and thinly sliced

4 dried or 8 fresh orange zest strips

3 tbsp extra virgin olive oil, plus extra to cover

1.8kg very ripe tomatoes (18 average), dark tops removed, cut into 2cm dice (in a food processor if you prefer)

4 tbsp tomato purée

Salt, cayenne pepper and sugar (ideally brown)

1. Get a large, preferably quite shallow saucepan. Add the onions, garlic, orange zest and 2 tbsp of the olive oil. Cover and sweat for 7–10 minutes, stirring occasionally.

2. Add the chopped tomatoes and tomato purée to the pan. Bring to the boil over a high heat; it should be bubbling all over. Lower the heat to medium-high. Simmer for 32–35 minutes or longer if necessary, stirring frequently. The tomato compote is ready when you can pull a wooden spoon through the centre and it leaves a channel that fills in seconds later. Take out and discard the orange zest.

3. Stir in the remaining 1 tbsp of extra virgin olive oil. Season to taste with salt, cayenne and sugar. Spoon the tomato compote into sterilised jars in the amount that you will use for the recipes. Pour a layer of extra virgin olive oil on top of the tomato compote to exclude air. Seal with cling film, then put the lids on.

Storage

Make more compote than you need, at least twice the recipe, as it freezes well, and keeps unopened for a couple of weeks in the fridge. Use small sterilised jars or clean plastic containers, ideally enough for a single use, so that once they are opened you use them up quickly. Seal and store in the fridge or freezer. Once the container is opened, use the tomato compote within 2 days.

Simple Tomato Compote Magic

Tomato sauce of one sort or another is one of the things that many of us cook with most often, but tomato compote has more uses when it comes to simple magic. A sauce becomes a compote when you simmer it for longer to make the mixture drier and to concentrate its flavour. This means that tomato compote can be a tomato stock cube and a tomato spread, a trendy tomato marmalade or 'fondue' (melted tomato). If you want a sauce, simply add water or fruit juice, stock or coconut milk, or let the mussels on page 23 add their salty sauce for you.

Along with the simple magic ideas, five of the recipes on the following pages offer great scope for variation. Look to the pollock for a way to braise fish into almost any international flavour by adding different liquids, herbs and spices; serve the sauce for the duck with beef, lamb or pork; make the spaghetti with any type of mollusc; serve anything you fancy in the tomato under your eggs. I suppose I've been making simple magic with tomato compote since I first picked up a pan, and I'll keep cooking with it until the pan drops.

Seasoning transformations Try flavouring tomato compote with smoked paprika, harissa, curry powder, ginger, chilli, ras-el-hanout, citrus zest and juice, rosemary, star anise, jerk spice, cumin, caraway, cardamom or coriander seeds. Or flavour the compote with any herb: cook hard herbs in the compote; add soft herbs at the last second.

Magical adventures Any of the meat and fish and aubergine 'hero' recipes from Adventures with Ingredients can be seasoned and then served with tomato compote. You can also use tomato compote as the sauce for the tomato pasta pilaf.

Magical transformations Exchange tomato compote for the soft, sticky onions but use half the amount of mascarpone to make the tart on page 168. Use tomato compote instead of the onions for the herrings on page 166, or you could also use half tomato compote and half sticky onions. You can stir garlic butter (page 193), basil pesto (page 129), green curry paste (page 209) or tapenade (page 145) into the tomato compote to serve as a sauce.

Tomato sauce Add 4 tbsp water, tomato juice or vegetable stock to 230g tomato compote. Either leave the tomato sauce chunky or purée it in a blender for 2 minutes and strain it through a sieve for a smooth sauce.

Quick tomato chutney Add vinegar and sugar or honey to the compote to taste. You can also spice it up with chilli for a quick tomato chilli jam. If you want a glossy chutney, boil the compote with the vinegar and sugar for 1–2 minutes, stirring constantly. Serve with cheese, anything deep-fried or barbecued, pan-fried liver or sausages, prawns or squid.

Tomato and blue cheese pastry parcel Put a large triangle of blue cheese on a double sheet of filo pastry. Put a spoonful of the quick tomato chutney (see left) on top. Brush the filo pastry with melted butter or beaten egg and then wrap up the blue cheese and chutney. Bake at 200°C/Gas 6 for 12–15 minutes. Serve with more of the chutney and watercress or rocket on the side. Cooked beetroot is good with this.

Pita or wrap pizzas Spread the tomato compote over pita bread, top with grated Cheddar, goat's cheese, mozzarella or any other cheese (tomato compote loves cheese), and grill as you would cheese on toast. Or you can just make cheese and tomato compote on toast – I love it on baguettes but any bread will do. Sprinkle with sliced basil.

Tomato tortillas Season tomato compote with chilli. Stir in kidney beans, cheese, cooked pork or chicken. Wrap in tortillas. Bake or grill. Serve with soured cream and avocado.

Tomato and goat's cheese gratin Cover the base of an ovenproof dish or pan with tomato compote. Sprinkle with thyme. Cover with sliced plum tomatoes. Scatter over some olives. Spread more tomato compote over the top and then cover with sliced goat's cheese. Bake at 200°C/Gas 6 for 10 minutes. Grill for 3–4 minutes until brown and bubbling.

Tomato, gnocchi, ham and mascarpone 'lasagne' Open a packet of ready-made gnocchi, boil and drain well. Mix the gnocchi with enough tomato compote to make it as saucy as you like. Put it into a baking dish or ovenproof pan. Cover the gnocchi with slices of ham. Smooth a mixture of mascarpone, Parmesan and sliced basil over the ham. Bake at 200°C/Gas 6 for 12–15 minutes until the top is golden.

Meatball sauce for pasta Roll well seasoned pork sausage meat into meatballs. Simmer them in equal amounts of tomato compote and chicken or vegetable stock for 15 minutes or until cooked through.

Tomato garlic prawns Spread tomato compote in an ovenproof dish. Top with prawns, basil, garlic and butter (or use garlic butter or pesto). Bake at 200°C/Gas 6 for 6–10 minutes until the prawns turn pink.

Fish en papillote with tomato compote Spread tomato compote on one half of a large piece of foil. Put a 2–3cm thick fillet of fish on top. Add 2 tbsp of white wine or water and 1 tbsp of extra virgin olive oil. Fold the foil over, seal the edges tightly. Bake at 220°C/Gas 7 for 14 minutes.

Magical cheats For all of the recipes you can substitute a good quality, thick tomato sauce. You may need to boil and reduce it slightly to get the texture you need for these recipes.

1/ Chipolata & chorizo skewers, tomato compote & polenta

One Christmas, my friend Chris Pope taught me a way of preparing multiple wrapped chipolatas that I loved so much I had to include it here. As you roast the chipolatas over the tomato, you get the same sort of taste that you would with a hot pot, even better maybe. The chipolatas are not the tiny ones, but more the size of a slim sausage. You can replace the chorizo with salami or streaky bacon. You'll need 4 long wooden skewers.

Kids can help wrap and spear the chipolatas – a fun thing to do together (carefully). For younger kids, use slightly less smoked paprika in the sauce, serve theirs, then add more to yours to taste. Good to purée or chop and freeze for babies and toddlers.

SERVES 2

Sides (pages 320–43)
None needed. A rocket, spinach or watercress salad would be good for contrast

Prep ahead Wrap the chipolatas in chorizo, up to a day ahead

Prep/cooking 15–20 mins

Active time 15–20 mins

10 slices of chorizo sausage, 5cm in diameter (pre-sliced is fine)
10 chipolatas, 30–40g each
225–250g tomato compote (page 177)
450ml plus 2 tbsp water
2 garlic cloves, peeled and finely chopped
80g one-minute polenta
50g Cheddar, grated
25g butter
Salt and smoked paprika

1. Preheat your oven to 220°C/Gas 7, position upper middle shelf. Boil your kettle.

2. Lay a chorizo slice on your chopping board. Put a chipolata in the centre. Wrap the chipolata tightly, overlapping the chorizo slightly. Do this with the rest of the chipolatas and chorizo. Make 2 lines of 5 chorizo-wrapped chipolatas. Push 2 skewers through each line a third of the way from the ends of the chipolatas. Pull the chipolatas apart so that there is about 2cm between each one. Make sure there is enough of the skewer at each end to suspend the chipolatas over the pan.

3. Get a medium-sized ovenproof frying pan or dish. Add the tomato compote, the 2 tbsp of water and ½ tsp of smoked paprika. Stir them together. Put the chipolata skewers over the top. Brush the chipolatas with tomato compote. Roast in the oven for 10 minutes. If you're not quite ready when they are, turn off the oven and leave the pan inside with the door slightly ajar to keep everything warm until you are ready to dish up.

4. After 5 minutes' roasting, get a medium-sized saucepan. Add the 450ml water and the garlic. Bring to the boil. Take the pan off the heat. Add the polenta in a slow steady stream, whisking constantly until there are no lumps. Put the pan on a medium-high heat. Bring the polenta to the boil, stirring. Stir for 1 minute. Be careful as it will boil volcanically. Take the pan off the heat. Stir in the Cheddar and butter. The polenta should be quite soupy, like very soft porridge; it will firm up as it cools. If it gets firmer than you'd like before you are ready to serve it, add boiling water, 1 tbsp at a time. Season to taste with salt.

5. Brush the chipolatas with tomato compote, which should be the texture of a chunky tomato sauce; if it's too thick, add 1–2 tbsp of boiling water. Serve the chipolatas on the tomato compote with the polenta alongside.

Cook extra
I like these wrapped chipolatas cold in a sandwich with some of the tomato compote, or dipped in mayonnaise.

2/ Curried pollock with coconut milk & tomato compote

The pollock I bought for this came in magnificent thick fillets. If you'd asked me what it was I would have sworn it was cod. Braising fish is an under-used and outstanding technique that always excites me. Along with the tomato compote that you have ready, this pollock could have enough variations for a chapter all of its own.

For the following ideas, you leave out the curry and swap the coconut milk for 6 tbsp of water or vegetable stock: add olives, capers and parsley; or ras-el-hanout, raisins, dried apricots and mint; or bits of bacon, tinned haricot beans and sage. Alternatively, you can braise the pollock on the compote, then spread pesto or tapenade over the top, or change the butter to garlic butter. Add cooked mushrooms, peppers, courgettes, aubergines, potatoes, carrots, sweet potatoes, squash, parsnips or corn to the compote if you like.

Braising pollock on tomato compote is an excellent way to cook it for kids. For younger kids, put less curry in the compote, only a tiny amount on their fillets and then add as much curry as you like to yours. You can cut their fillets to the size they'll eat before you bake them. If it helps, sprinkle a few breadcrumbs over their fish. Good to purée or chop and freeze for babies and toddlers.

SERVES 2

Sides (pages 320–43)
Rice, chickpeas or lentils
Prep/cooking 20–25 mins
Active time 5 mins

225–250g tomato compote
   (page 177)
8 tbsp coconut milk
   (see page 21)
4 tbsp water
2 skinless pollock fillets,
   120–150g each
20g butter
Salt, mild curry powder
   and sugar

1. Preheat your oven to 200°C/Gas 6, position middle shelf. Boil your kettle.

2. Get a roasting tin, baking dish or ovenproof frying pan with raised sides. Add the tomato compote, ½ tsp of curry powder, the coconut milk and the 4 tbsp of water. Stir together until the ingredients are well combined.

3. Season each pollock fillet with salt and ½ tsp of curry powder, more if you like it hot. Put the pollock in the sauce. Turn each fillet in the sauce until it is well coated.

4. Dot the butter over the top of the pollock fillets. Bake for 12 minutes. Turn off the oven and leave the pollock to rest inside for 2–3 minutes with the door slightly ajar.

5. Put the pollock onto your plates. Season the tomato compote with salt, sugar and curry powder to taste. It should be the texture of a chunky tomato sauce; if it's too thick, add 1–2 tbsp of boiling water. Spoon the curried tomato compote over the top of the pollock.

3/ My last meal mussels with tomato compote

I spent the summer of 1996 working for the wise and wonderful Don Alfonso in St Agata in the south of Italy. This great man taught me a great deal about respect for people, respect for food and generosity with both. One night around midnight when the village was having a party, he gently ordered four of his cooks away from our bar under the stars. '*Ragazzi*,' he said, 'Let's give everyone some food.' We cooked spaghetti with olive oil, garlic and chilli in great stockpots, we carried them to the square and we fed hundreds of happy people. Don Alfonso brought wine from his cellar and stood talking to people while they ate. He had this way of holding his pipe next to his heart when he was happy, stroking the base.

Don Alfonso asked me what I'd like for a last meal the day before my brief summer was over. I asked for spaghetti with little clams. There were no clams at the market that day so he made it with mussels and the tomato sauce we'd bottled a few weeks before. The sauce was seasoned by the sea and the taste is a memory like my children's laughter.

Give younger kids a go with mussels. At a time when I couldn't get my youngest to eat much, he would eat mussels.

SERVES 2

Sides Bread

Prep/cooking 20–25 mins

Active time 15–20 mins

200g spaghetti

230–250g tomato compote
   (page 177)

2 tbsp extra virgin olive oil

2 tbsp water

500g–1kg mussels, cleaned
   (see page 23)

2 heaped tbsp sliced basil

1. Put your serving bowls in the oven. Turn it to the lowest setting. Boil your kettle. Fill a large pot with boiling water. Add salt and bring back to the boil. Put a colander in your sink.

2. Add the spaghetti to the boiling water. Cover and bring back to the boil. Take the lid off. Boil the spaghetti until it is just tender but firm; check the packet for a guide to the cooking time. Set a timer to let you know when the spaghetti has 5 minutes to go and you can start steaming your mussels.

3. While the spaghetti boils, get a large shallow pan. Add the tomato compote, extra virgin olive oil and the 2 tbsp of water. When the timer goes off, put the pan on your highest heat. Bring to the boil. Add the mussels in an even layer. Put the lid on. Boil for 1–2 minutes or until the mussels start to open – enough for you to see the flesh inside. As they do, they will release their liquid and the compote will become thinner, more like tomato sauce.

4. When the spaghetti is ready, drain it in the colander. Add the spaghetti to the mussels. Toss together. Boil for 30 seconds to 1 minute until all of the mussels are open; discard any that stay closed. The spaghetti wants to soak up and be coated by the tomato, mussel juice and olive oil. Add the basil and toss it through. The mussels give the sauce all the salt it needs. Use tongs to divide the spaghetti, mussels and sauce evenly between your serving bowls.

4/ Duck breast with tomato, olive, fennel seeds & orange

Here the duck's pan juices emulsify with the tomato compote to make it meaty and gorgeous, while the sunblush tomatoes and fresh orange echo and enhance the cooked tomato and dried orange zest in the compote. The same ingredients, prepared differently, make each flavour more intense, like a delicious magic trick.

For younger kids, once the duck breasts have cooked and rested, remove the tender little fillets from their undersides. Chop these and the sunblush tomatoes, then mix them with the beans and sauce (leave out the fennel seeds). Can be puréed or chopped and frozen for babies and toddlers.

SERVES 2

Sides None needed

Prep/cooking 30–35 mins

Active time 25 mins

2 duck breast fillets (with skin), about 200–230g each

225–250g tomato compote (page 177)

1 tsp fennel seeds

Zested or grated zest of 1 orange and 4 tbsp juice

2 tbsp water

½ x 400g tin haricot beans

12 sunblush tomatoes

10 pitted black olives

100g soya beans, broad beans or peas

Salt, sugar and salt flakes

1. Preheat your oven to 200°C/Gas 6, position upper middle shelf. Put a resting rack on top of a plate and a bowl for hot fat next to your cooker. Boil your kettle. Put a colander in your sink.

2. Get a medium-sized ovenproof frying pan. Lay the duck breasts in the pan, skin side down. Put the pan on a medium heat. Fry the duck breasts for 10 minutes. Drain the fat. Put the pan in the oven. Roast for 6 minutes for duck that is perfectly pink (don't turn the duck breasts). Remove the pan from the oven. Turn the oven off. Put the duck breasts, skin side up, on the resting rack over the plate. Put the plate in the oven.

3. Next, make the sauce. Drain all but 2 tbsp of fat from the frying pan. Add the tomato compote, fennel seeds, orange juice and the 2 tbsp of water to the pan. Bring to the boil. Add the haricot beans and their liquid, sunblush tomatoes and olives.

4. Put the duck on the rack over the top of the sauce. Put the pan back in the oven, leaving the door slightly ajar. Let the duck rest for 6 minutes.

5. Boil your kettle again. Fill a small pan with boiling water. Add salt and bring back to the boil. Add the soya beans and boil for 2 minutes. Drain. Put the beans back into the pan.

6. When you are ready to serve, transfer the duck to a board. Turn each duck breast, flesh side up, on your board. (Slicing from the flesh side makes the job easier, more pleasant and the resulting slices neater.) Carve each duck breast as thickly or thinly as you prefer, against the grain. I like to season the duck slices with salt flakes once I've carved them.

7. Add the soya beans to the sauce. Put the pan on a high heat. Bring to the boil. Season to taste with salt and sugar. The consistency needs to be that of a chunky tomato sauce; if it is too thick, add 1–2 tbsp of water.

8. Spoon the sauce into deep plates. Put the duck slices on top and push them into the sauce. Sprinkle orange zest over everything.

5/ Eggs, ham & potatoes baked in tomato compote

I've snuck in a cured pork and eggs number again, one that is rich and oh-so-tasty. The hot broken yolks enrich the sauce and enrobe the potatoes, while the tomato compote holds everything together. My eggs are loosely based on *huevos rancheros* with potatoes instead of beans providing the bulk. If you're out of potatoes, you can replace them with a drained tin of kidney beans. If you're cooking for a vegetarian, leave out the ham or replace it with bits of cheese.

This is a fun recipe for kids and you can bake it in individual dishes. They can choose their own (cooled) vegetables to layer in the dishes, spoon in the tomato compote and break an egg on top. Cook the eggs completely and it is then good to purée for babies, or pulse in the food processor for toddlers (it's messy to chop by hand). Both can be frozen.

SERVES 2

Sides (pages 320–43)
None needed. Green salad would be good for contrast

Prep/cooking 25 mins
Active time 10–15 mins

300g waxy potatoes, such as
  Maris Peer or Charlotte,
  washed and cut into
  1.5cm slices
1 tbsp plus 2–4 tsp extra
  virgin olive oil
120g spinach
225–250g tomato compote
  (page 177)
100ml chicken stock
120g cooked ham (2 large
  slices), cut into 1cm
  ribbons
2–4 large eggs
Salt, sugar and cayenne
  pepper

1. Preheat your oven to 200°C/Gas 6, position upper middle shelf. Boil your kettle. Fill a large pot with boiling water. Add salt and bring back to the boil. Put a colander in your sink.

2. Add the potatoes to the boiling water and bring back to the boil. Turn down the heat and lift the lid so it sits slightly ajar. Simmer on a low heat for 10 minutes or until the potatoes are tender. They want to be cooked through, not partially cooked. Drain the potatoes and shake them to get as much of the water out as you can.

3. Get a medium-sized frying pan. Add the 1 tbsp of extra virgin olive oil and get it really hot. Add the potatoes; be careful if they are wet as the oil will spit. Sauté for 2 minutes over a medium heat. They should be barely golden; you're not looking to fry them really, just dry them out. Add the spinach. (It will seem a lot for the pan, but don't worry, it'll wilt down to very little.) Stir the spinach for 30 seconds or until it is slightly wilted. Season with salt and cayenne pepper – I like it to be a little spicy.

4. Add the tomato compote and chicken stock to the pan. Bring to the boil. Season to taste with salt and sugar. Scatter the ham ribbons over the top. Turn off the heat.

5. Make 2–4 gaps in the tomato and potato mixture for the eggs. Break the eggs into the gaps. Bake for 7–8 minutes until the eggs are just set. Spoon 1 tsp of extra virgin olive oil over each egg.

6/ Ricotta & spinach dumpling with tomato compote

This divine dumpling is light and delightful, but heavy on flavour. If you have time to chill the mixture, it will become firmer and easier to shape into spoonfuls. If not, you will have flat rather than pert dumplings, but they'll still taste as good. The quantity of spinach needs to be exact so if you buy a large bag, serve a spinach salad on the side and add any leftover ricotta to it. Or devour the dumpling and then split a hot baguette, drench it with the sauce on your plate, spread the ricotta over it, trickle with olive oil and grind over some pepper.

The dumpling is wonderful for kids – nothing needs changing. It's an excellent way of getting kids to eat spinach purée while they struggle with the texture of cooked and raw leaves. Good to purée or chop and freeze for babies and toddlers.

SERVES 2

Sides (pages 320–43)
Spinach salad. Hot baguette
Prep ahead Dumplings, ready to bake, a day ahead
Prep/cooking 45–50 mins
Active time 15–20 mins

1 tbsp water
120g spinach
1 large egg
30g self-raising flour
50g Parmesan, grated
175g ricotta, drained
225–250g tomato compote (page 177)
150ml vegetable stock
2 tbsp plus 2 tsp extra virgin olive oil
Salt, freshly ground black pepper and nutmeg

1. Preheat your oven to 170°C/Gas 3–4, position middle shelf. Boil your kettle.

2. Start with the spinach. Put a colander in your sink. Get a large shallow pan. Add the 1 tbsp of water. Bring to the boil. Add the spinach. Cover and wilt over a high heat for 1 minute. Remove the lid. Stir-fry for 1 minute to remove as much moisture as possible without browning the spinach. Transfer to the colander. Press out any remaining liquid. It will seem like a tiny amount of spinach; this is normal.

3. Put the spinach into your food processor. Blend for 30 seconds until it is roughly chopped. Add the egg. Blend for 1 minute until the spinach is finely chopped, nearly a purée. Add the flour and Parmesan. Blend for 30 seconds. It will look quite liquid at this stage. Add the ricotta. Use the pulse button to incorporate the ricotta, just enough to combine with the other ingredients. Season to taste with salt, pepper and nutmeg. The mixture will be the texture of thick yoghurt. Chill it if you have time.

4. Get a 24 x 18cm, 6cm deep baking dish or a 20cm ovenproof pan. Spread the tomato compote in it. Stir in the vegetable stock. Fill a pot or jug with boiling water. Put a large kitchen spoon in the boiling water. Use it to scoop 2 large spoonfuls of the mixture into grapefruit-sized ovals on top of the sauce.

5. Trickle 1 tbsp of extra virgin olive oil over each dumpling (they are too soft to brush). Cover tightly with foil. Bake for 30 minutes. Take the foil off. Bake for a further 5–7 minutes until the dumplings are just firm to the touch. Puff out your cheeks and push one with your finger; this is the texture you're after. Spoon 1 tsp of extra virgin olive oil over each dumpling. Serve straight from the dish.

GARLIC BUTTER

Garlic is glorious. Give me a garlic-scented kiss any day. I grow garlic, I hang garlic, I chop garlic, I poach and I fry and I roast garlic, I like garlic with oil and in gravy. I love garlic bread and garlic pasta and garlic prawns and garlic curry, and I like it in restaurants when it's called *ail* or *aglio*. I enjoy the texture of garlic's papery skin and I like the way it feels between my palms when I push and the bulb explodes into a pile of dancing cloves.

Garlic bulbs and cloves vary greatly in size, so I decided that the best way to give you this recipe would be to use spoonfuls of chopped garlic; please feel free to add as much more as you like. Parsley is garlic's regular sidekick in compound butter, so I've given it as an option, but Jess and I prefer basil, and I cooked the six subsidiary recipes with basil. The quantities I've given you are so that you can buy a bulb of garlic, a pack of butter, and a supermarket-sized herb bunch. But feel free to leave the herb out altogether.

This is my standard recipe for garlic butter. Turn the page to discover gentle garlic butter, sweet baked garlic butter and nut brown garlic butter.

SERVES 2

Prep ahead Keeps in the fridge for up to 2 weeks (see storage). The butter can also be frozen

Prep/cooking 10–15 mins

Active time 10–15 mins

¾ average head of garlic (to yield 2 tbsp chopped, see method)

1 bunch of curly parsley or basil (25g), leaves only (optional)

250g soft butter

Salt and freshly ground black pepper

1. Boil your kettle. Get a medium bowl. Put the garlic cloves in it. Pour the boiling water over them. Leave for 5 minutes. Drain.

2. Start peeling the garlic as soon as it is cool enough to handle. Chop the garlic and parsley leaves finely. This can be done by hand or in a small food processor/mini chopper.

3. Get a large bowl. Add the butter, garlic, parsley, ¼ tsp of salt and ¼ tsp of pepper. Mix together well.

4. Put a roll of cling film behind your chopping board to hold the roll steady. Pull out enough cling film to cover your board. Scoop the butter out of your bowl with a spatula. Spread it across the cling film in a rough line, 20cm long. Lift the edge of the cling film over the butter. Roll the butter in the cling film, pulling it tight and smoothing it into a cylinder after each roll. Once you've rolled the butter about 4 times, cut the cling film. Twist the ends in opposite directions like a sweetie wrapper until you have a tight round log, about 15cm long.

Storage

Refrigerate the garlic butter and cut off slices as required. Or freeze for up to 3 months. A good way to freeze garlic butter is to cut it into 25g slices first, then put the slices into a sealed plastic box so that you can get a portion out easily when you need it without having to hack into the log.

Simple Garlic Butter Magic

Before you start your simple magic I'd like to offer you a few options. Garlic can be brash, but I'll show you how it can be subtle too. It can be supportive – look at almost any recipe in this book. It can be gentle or sweet or even a little nutty. I'll introduce you to these last three because if you don't fancy it raw, you may like one of them more. The gentle and sweet variations are good ways for kids to get to know garlic butter.

Gentle garlic butter Put the garlic into a medium-sized saucepan. Cover with 1.5 litres water. Bring to the boil and boil for 5 minutes. If you want a very delicate flavour, do this twice. Drain. Peel the garlic cloves. Continue as for the main recipe.

Sweet baked garlic butter The garlic becomes very sweet and delicate which means you need more of it to make an impact; I use two full heads. Preheat your oven to 200°C/Gas 6, position upper middle shelf. Rub each head with 10g soft butter. Sprinkle them with salt. Wrap the heads tightly in foil. Bake for 15 minutes. Pull the foil away from the side of the garlic but leave it under the base. Put the garlic back into the oven for 5 minutes to roast. Take the garlic out of the oven. Leave it to cool. Separate the cloves. Inside the skin, the garlic is the squashy texture of sticky soft butter. Squeeze the soft garlic out of each clove into a bowl; it won't need chopping. Continue as for the main recipe with 230g butter.

Nut brown garlic butter Get a very small saucepan. Put a bowl next to your cooker. Add the chopped garlic, 50g butter and a pinch of salt. Sweat over your lowest heat, stirring all the time, and watching carefully, for 4 minutes until the garlic is soft. Turn the heat up to medium. Fry the garlic gently for 1 minute until the garlic is pale gold and the butter foams and smells nutty. The heat in the pan will now be enough to burn the garlic, so transfer it quickly to the bowl. The smell at this point is so incredible that it would be worth making for this alone. Let the garlic and butter cool, then continue as for the main recipe with 200g soft butter.

Seasoning transformations Try flavouring garlic butter with horseradish and dill; orange zest and fennel seed; smoked paprika or harissa; curry powder and Calvados (really!); lime, ginger and coriander; tarragon and mustard; or rosemary, chilli, ras-el-hanout, lemon zest and finely chopped dried apricots.

Magical adventures Any of the meat and fish 'hero' recipes from Adventures with Ingredients can be seasoned and served with garlic butter. The pasta pilaf/risotto can be finished with garlic butter.

Magical transformations All of the garlic butter dishes can be made with pesto and vice-versa, except the gnocchi (page 142) .

Snack Flavour freshly cooked popcorn with melted garlic butter.

Garlic bread Slice a baguette in half lengthways. Spread the insides of both halves with garlic butter. Stick them back together. Wrap the baguette in foil then bake it. Or just toast an old crust or halved muffin and spread it with garlic butter. Bacon and egg on top would be nice.

Garlic mushrooms Turn large mushrooms upside down on a baking tray and fill their cups with garlic butter. Roast the mushrooms at 220°C/Gas 7 for 10 minutes or until the garlic butter sizzles and the mushrooms are cooked through.

Soups and broths Stir garlic butter into broths to make them richer and into soups to make them silky. I particularly like stirring nut brown garlic butter into chicken broth and raw garlic butter into potato soup.

Baked potatoes Cut a baked potato or sweet potato in half. Cut a cross in the flesh and insert as much butter as you fancy. Top with Parma ham and eat at once, or top the potato with ham and grated Cheddar and then bake it. Alternatively, scoop out the flesh, mix it with garlic butter, cheese, sweetcorn and curry powder. Put the mixture back into the potato skins and bake until they are hot and golden.

Scrambled eggs Stir garlic butter into the eggs just as they thicken. Spread toast with garlic butter and serve the eggs on top.

Kippers and eggs Smother kippers with garlic butter and grill them until they are golden. Serve with eggs fried very slowly in garlic butter.

Baked fish Put white fish fillets, like pollock, into an ovenproof dish. Spoon 3 tbsp of water or white wine over each one. Slice the garlic butter very thinly. Spread it over the top of the fish. Bake at 200°C/Gas 6 for 8 minutes. The butter will glaze the fish and combine with the cooking juices to make a light and luscious sauce.

Garlicky vegetables Toss hot boiled, roasted or fried vegetables and potatoes with garlic butter. Replace the butter in glazed vegetables with garlic butter.

Barbecues When the sun shines, put a bowl of iced water with slices of garlic butter next to your barbecue. It will go on top of anything.

Gravy There is a French term, *monter au beurre* that refers to adding butter to a sauce to thicken it and make it shine. Next time you make a gravy that needs some guts, stir in a slice of garlic butter.

1/ Chicken, bacon, tomato & watercress salad

Smoky bacon, juicy chicken, spicy watercress, sweet tomatoes, very little labour and very few dishes. The butter bastes the breasts from the inside and the bacon moistens the outer skin. And this juicy beauty also provides a rich mixture in the pan which you'll turn into roast gravy that has all that's best from a bacon breakfast, a Sunday roast chicken and my glorious garlic.

For younger kids, leave out the chilli, cut the onion very finely and leave it in a bit less salt and sugar for longer to soften its flavours. Or just leave the onion out, serve theirs, then add it to yours. The watercress leaves will be hard work for younger kids, but try them on the crisp stalks. Good to chop for toddlers, but not to purée or freeze.

SERVES 2

Sides (pages 320–43)
Pasta or plain or tasty grains, olive oil glazed potatoes, bread or garlic bread

Prep/cooking 30–35 mins
Active time 25–30 mins

2 skinless, boneless
   chicken breasts,
   160–180g each
50g garlic butter (page 193),
   cut into 6 slices
6 rashers of smoked streaky
   bacon
3 tsp balsamic vinegar
½ medium red onion,
   peeled, cut in half and
   thinly sliced
½ mild red chilli, deseeded
   and finely chopped
2 tbsp extra virgin olive oil
2 large ripe tomatoes
   (about 200g)
4 tbsp tomato or orange
   juice
40g watercress or rocket
   (½ small packet)
Salt, sugar and cayenne
   pepper

1. Preheat your oven to 200°C/Gas 6, position upper middle shelf.

2. Start with the chicken. Season each breast with a little cayenne. Lay them flat on your board. Cut the breasts horizontally from the side, through the middle, but not all the way through, so you can open each one out like a book. Put 2 slices of garlic butter inside each. Close them up. Wrap each chicken breast in 3 rashers of streaky bacon. Put the chicken breasts in an ovenproof frying pan just large enough to hold them, with the overlapping ends of the bacon on the underside.

3. Brush each chicken breast all over with ½ tsp of balsamic vinegar. Bake for 20 minutes. Turn off the oven and leave the chicken to rest inside for 5 minutes with the door slightly ajar.

4. While the chicken bakes, make the tomato salad. Get a large shallow bowl. Add the sliced red onion, then ¼ tsp of salt and ¼ tsp of sugar. Add the remaining 2 tsp of balsamic vinegar, the chopped chilli and the extra virgin olive oil. Stir well. Using a serrated knife, cut the tomatoes in half and cut each half into 3 wedges. Sprinkle these with salt and cayenne. Put them on top of the onion.

5. Get the chicken breasts out of the oven. Turn them in their cooking juices. Put the chicken on your chopping board. Add the tomato juice to the pan. Bring it to the boil. Stir vigorously to mix the tomato juice with the cooking juices. Stir in the remaining 2 slices of garlic butter. Turn off the heat. Season to taste.

6. Mix the tomatoes and onion together. Put them on plates. Scatter the watercress over the top. I like to slice the chicken but you don't have to. Put the chicken on top of the salad. Spoon the pan juices over everything.

Cook extra
This chicken is delicious cold. Slice the breasts and mix with the tomato and onions for a salad, sandwich or wrap.

Chickpea fritters with garlic butter, spinach, olives & pita

The garlic butter moistens the inside and slowly bubbles out to baste these fritters as they fry, giving them a taste like roast garlic peanut butter. In this recipe I use more oil than I usually do to shallow fry, so that it can reach around the outsides of the fritters. The oil needs to be very hot; if it isn't hot enough the fritters will soak it up. Make sure you get a loud sizzle as you put the first fritter in the pan; if you don't, lift it out again and wait.

My kids loved these and the onion went unnoticed. The fritters will open up any number of opportunities to introduce new vegetables. Let them add their own yoghurt at the table. For younger kids, finely chop the spinach. Can be puréed and frozen for babies.

SERVES 2

Sides None needed

Prep ahead Fritters can be shaped ready to cook, a day ahead

Prep/cooking 25–30 mins

Active time 20–25 mins

400g tin chickpeas, well drained

½ tsp ground cumin

½ tsp ground coriander

½ medium onion, peeled and cut into 3cm dice

50g garlic butter (page 193)

1 medium egg

2 pita breads

1 large tomato, cut into 6 slices

4 tbsp vegetable oil

10 black olives, finely chopped

Zested or grated zest of ½ lemon and 4 tsp juice

6 tbsp plain yoghurt

2 tbsp sliced mint

80g baby spinach (1 small packet)

50g feta, crumbled

Salt, sugar and ground cumin

1. Preheat your oven to 200°C/Gas 6, position upper middle shelf.

2. Start with the chickpea mixture. Get your food processor. Add the chickpeas, cumin, coriander and onion. Blend to a coarse purée; it should look like rough breadcrumbs. Add half the garlic butter and the egg. Blend to combine. Season with salt, sugar and cumin to taste.

3. Using a spatula, scrape the mixture onto a large plate. It will be sticky and slightly moist, but should hold together well. Divide the mixture into 6 equal-sized pieces. Squeeze each piece into a ball then flatten it into a fritter, about 1.5cm thick and 5cm in diameter.

4. Next, get a baking tray. Put the pita breads on the tray. Split them by cutting through one side and around the ends. Open them out. Put 3 slices of tomato on one side of each pita. Season with salt and cumin.

5. Get a fish slice and a medium-large frying pan. Add the oil and get it really hot. Add the fritters. Fry over a high heat for 2 minutes. Turn the fritters carefully; this is when they are at their most delicate. Fry on the other side for 2 minutes until they are deep golden brown. Take the pan off the heat.

6. Lift the fritters onto the tomatoes. Cut the remaining garlic butter into 6 slices. Put a slice on top of each fritter. Brush the uncovered side of the pita with oil from the pan. Put the tray in the oven. Bake for 6 minutes.

7. While the tray is in the oven, make the dressing. Get a large shallow bowl. Add the olives, lemon zest, lemon juice, yoghurt and mint. Mix together. Season to taste. Put half the yoghurt dressing into a small bowl to serve on the side. Toss the spinach in the large bowl with the remaining yoghurt dressing and the feta.

8. Put the uncovered pita and salad on your plates. Use a fish slice to lift the pita topped with the tomato slices and chickpea fritters onto your plates.

3/ James's pasta butterflies with peas & garlic butter

I'm often asked how I come up with recipes. Sometimes it's an idea from something I've seen or eaten, other times it's seasonal, but mostly it's just about what I want to eat. Here I've used pasta butterflies because they enchant my kids. This recipe is also a way to make good vegetables taste great. I braise the onion, lettuce and stock mixture to emulsify with the butter and coat the pasta, to give it warmth and intensity so the sweet peas can play amongst the butterflies without any responsibility. For a speedier version simply boil the vegetables with the pasta, then stir in the garlic butter.

This is great for kids, and a very good way to get them acquainted with the garlic and herbs in the butter. It's also a good meal to help you introduce new vegetables. Good to purée or chop and freeze for babies and toddlers.

SERVES 2

<u>Sides</u> None needed

<u>Prep/cooking</u> 25–30 mins

<u>Active time</u> 25–30 mins

200g butterfly pasta
   (farfalle)
1 medium onion (100g),
   peeled and cut into
   1cm dice
6 tbsp water
200ml vegetable stock
1 baby gem lettuce or 120g
   Romaine, baby gem or
   other lettuce leaves, cut
   into 1cm slices
250g mixed peas, sliced
   mangetout and sliced
   French or runner beans
   (or just one of these)
8 radishes, halved
   lengthways
60g garlic butter (page 193),
   cut into 6 slices
4 tbsp grated Parmesan
   (optional)
Salt and freshly ground
   black pepper

1. Start with the butterfly pasta. Boil your kettle. Fill a medium-sized saucepan with boiling water. Add salt and bring back to the boil. Add the butterfly pasta. Bring back to the boil and boil rapidly for 8 minutes. Put a colander in your sink.

2. While the pasta boils, get a large sauté pan. Add the onion and the 6 tbsp of water. Cover the pan and put it on a medium heat. Sweat for 7–10 minutes until soft, checking the onion halfway through and adding 2–3 tbsp of water if it starts to dry out. Once the onion is soft, add the vegetable stock. Bring to the boil. Add the lettuce. Bring back to the boil and boil rapidly for 2 minutes; the liquid will have reduced by about half and the lettuce should be soft. Turn off the heat.

3. Once the pasta has boiled for 8 minutes, add the peas, beans and radishes. Bring back to the boil and boil for 3–4 minutes or until just tender. Drain the pasta and vegetables in the colander.

4. Add the garlic butter to the onion and lettuce in the sauté pan. Bring to the boil. Add the pasta and vegetables. Stir until everything is well coated with butter. Season to taste. Put the pan on the table. Serve with the Parmesan on the side.

4

North Norfolk mackerel & mussel boil 'n' braise

This is my memory stew; a combination of seafood stories that light up my meals at my wife Jess's cottage in Wells-Next-The-Sea in Norfolk. I go beach fishing often but I've only ever caught one mackerel and I did so while an old man 5 metres to my left caught thirty. I buy the mussels down a little lane between Wells and Cley where they leave bags on a rickety shelf and you pay into an honesty box. In summer they have lobster, crab and samphire. The neighbours have two boats, and they gave me a big bag of brown shrimp one year, but these are tricky to get hold of so I've left them out. If you can get some, pop them in on top of the mackerel and you have another step towards a Norfolk bouillabaisse.

Mussels are worth a try for younger kids as they are tender, sweet and fun to eat. Show kids how to use a spare shell as a pair of tongs to pull the flesh out. Can be puréed or chopped for babies and toddlers.

SERVES 2

Sides Bread, toast or garlic toast

Prep/cooking 25–35 mins
Active time 20–30 mins

400g waxy potatoes, such as Charlotte or Maris Peer, washed and cut into 2cm slices
1 medium onion, peeled and cut into 3mm slices
1 large carrot (150g), peeled and cut into 3mm slices
200ml plus 4 tbsp water
2 tsp tomato purée
500g mussels, cleaned (see page 23)
2 mackerel fillets, each cut into 5 pieces, or 4 herring fillets, each cut into 3 pieces
50g garlic butter (page 193)
Salt and freshly ground black pepper

1. Start with the potatoes. Boil your kettle. Put a colander in your sink. Fill a medium-sized saucepan with boiling water. Add salt and bring back to the boil. Add the sliced potatoes. Bring back to the boil. Turn the heat to medium. Lift the lid so that it sits slightly ajar. Simmer for 11 minutes or until the potatoes are tender. Drain them in the colander.

2. While the potatoes simmer, get a large shallow pan. Add the onion, carrot and the 4 tbsp of water. Cover and sweat over a medium heat for 7–10 minutes until tender, checking twice and adding a little more water if the pan starts to dry out. Add the tomato purée. Stir it in well. Add the 200ml water. Bring to the boil and boil for 30 seconds.

3. Add the potatoes in a single layer. Scatter the mussels over the top in a single layer. Cover, bring to the boil and boil for 1–2 minutes or until the mussels open enough for you to see the flesh inside.

4. Push the mussels to the edges of the pan but don't move the potatoes. Season the mackerel. Put the mackerel on top of the potatoes in a single layer. Dab the garlic butter over everything. Cover and bring to the boil. Turn the heat down low the second it boils. Poach for 3 minutes, making sure the liquid never boils. The mackerel should be just cooked through. Discard any unopened mussels. Cover the pan and turn off the heat. Leave to sit for 2 minutes to allow the mackerel to finish cooking.

5. Take the boil 'n' braise to your table and lift the lid off to catch the scent of the sea.

5/ Prawns, bacon & fresh pasta tossed in garlic butter

I ate prawn and Parma ham pasta sitting at Justin North's kitchen pass at Becasse restaurant in Sydney. I heard the fat prawns as they hit the hot pan and I smelt them as they caramelised around the edges. I saw the head chef Monty glaze the fresh fettuccine with prawn stock and butter. And I could taste the Parma ham he added just before passing me my plate, still raw but warmed with a whisper of heat. It was a triumph of soaring flavour. This is my everyday adaptation for you. It's not as elegant as Justin's, but the bacon, prawns and garlic butter make up for it through sheer brazen flavour.

My boys loved this pasta dish, but younger kids may find the texture of prawns tricky. Try chopping the prawns, or just eat them yourself. No good to purée or freeze.

SERVES 2

Sides Bread to mop up the buttery juices

Prep/cooking 15–20 mins

Active time 15–20 mins

250g fresh tagliatelle
100g soya beans or peas
50g garlic butter (page 193)
1 tsp vegetable oil
6 rashers of smoked bacon, cut into 4cm chunks
10 medium or 14 small raw prawns
80g sunblush or tinned roast peppers, cut into 1cm slices
Salt and cayenne pepper

1. You will need to cook the tagliatelle and prawns at the same time, so have everything ready next to your cooker. Don't worry if one is ready before the other; both are fine to wait for a minute or two. Boil your kettle. Fill a large pot with boiling water. Add salt and bring back to the boil. Put a colander in your sink.

2. Add the tagliatelle to the boiling water. Boil for 2 minutes. Add the soya beans. Boil for 2 minutes. Fill a mug with pasta water; keep it next to your cooker. Drain the pasta and beans. Put them back in the pan. Add 4 tbsp of the pasta water and half of the garlic butter. Boil for 30 seconds. The water and butter will emulsify and glaze the pasta and beans. Turn off the heat. Season with salt and cayenne to taste.

3. While the pasta boils, put a large frying pan on a medium-high heat. Add the oil and get it really hot. Add the bacon. Fry for 1 minute, turning the bacon halfway through. Add the prawns to the pan in a single layer. Fry for 30 seconds. Turn the prawns and fry for another 30 seconds.

4. Add the sunblush peppers and the remaining garlic butter to the frying pan. Fry for 30 seconds. The prawns should be cooked by this stage; they will have turned pink. Turn off the heat. Add 2 tbsp of the pasta water from your mug to the pan. It will bubble and spit, so be careful. Stir and coat everything with the buttery pan juices. Season to taste.

5. Mix the bacon, prawns, peppers and pan juices with the pasta and beans. Use a pair of tongs to dish up into pasta bowls and make sure you add every last bit of buttery juice in the pan.

6/ My perfect steak with hot, soft & hard garlic butter

I found my first steak under a slab of *maître d'hôtel* butter. The steak's sizzling brown surface melted the cold butter in my mouth. But a cold slab is no longer enough. Part of my butter needs to melt and mingle with the steak's meaty secretions in the pan, and part of it needs to soften and flow across the glistening flesh but stay a little hard in its heart. Sometimes I get sucked in by the smoky kisses of a charcoal-grilled steak, but a frying pan is the best place to catch the juices that fry to a meaty treasure. You release this bounty with water then add a knob of butter. Once your steak has had a rest – not too long, just a nap – turn it slowly in these juices until it glows with incandescent goodness. This makes the difference between a steak that is nice and a steak that is sublime. The less cooked you like your steak, the hotter the pan should be.

Very approximate cooking times for these steaks are: 2 minutes each side for medium-rare; 3 minutes each side for medium; 4 minutes each side for well done.

If you're willing to share, slice the steak quite thinly for younger kids. It doesn't seem right to purée or freeze a steak, but you probably can.

SERVES 2

Sides (pages 320–43)
Sautéed potatoes or chips.
Beans, peas or a leafy salad

Prep/cooking 10 mins
(but factor time for potatoes)

Active time 10 mins

1 tbsp vegetable oil
2 rib-eye steaks, 200–250g
  each
10g butter
6 tbsp water
50g garlic butter (page 193),
  cut into 8 slices, plus an
  optional extra 20g, cut
  into 2 slices to serve
Salt, freshly ground black
  pepper and salt flakes

1. Get everything ready before you start frying. Put a bowl to pour the fat into and a plate with a resting rack over the top next to your cooker.

2. Get a medium-sized frying pan; it needs to be just large enough to hold the steaks comfortably but not have too much space around them. (If the pan is too large, the butter will burn around the outside of the steaks.) Add the oil and get it really hot.

3. Season the rib-eye steaks on both sides with salt and pepper. Add them to the pan. Fry over a high heat for 2 minutes. Don't worry if the pan smokes, it needs to be this hot. Turn the steaks. Fry for 2 minutes. Drain the fat. Turn the heat to low. Add the 10g of butter to the pan. Fry the steaks for another 15 seconds on each side; the butter will go brown and smell nutty, but it shouldn't burn.

4. Put the steaks on your resting rack for 2 minutes. Add the 6 tbsp of water to the pan and stir vigorously. Bring to the boil and boil for 30 seconds until there is about 2 tbsp of liquid left. Take the pan off the heat. Stir in 4 slices of the garlic butter.

5. Put the steaks back into the pan. Add any juices from the plate under the rack. Turn the steaks over in the buttery pan juices until the surfaces are well coated. Top with the remaining 4 slices of garlic butter. Serve with every last bit of juice in the pan. As you put the steaks onto your plates, top each one with a slice of cold butter and a sprinkling of salt flakes... optional but wonderful.

MY GREEN CURRY PASTE

I took my time to get to know green curry paste. We don't have the history that I enjoy with pesto and the others. I wasn't worried about being authentic, I just wanted it to explode with flavour and freshness. The time and energy I spent were vital. I've found a vibrant curry paste that captures the vigour of each ingredient, and I'll show you how to make the flavours sparkle by adding fresh paste to the cooked food just before serving.

I left the lime juice out of the paste, because lime is best as a fresh burst, added as a squeeze when you serve and eat. The lime's acidity dulls the curry paste after a day or two, giving it a muddy colour and stewed taste. I prefer the coriander boiled first so that it combines with, rather than overpowers, the other ingredients. The amount of lemongrass, ginger/galangal, garlic and shallots in the recipe are roughly those you will get if you buy a little supermarket bag of Thai ingredients. You will need to adjust the quantity of chillies according to how hot you want your dishes to be. This is my curry paste. But it's all yours now: heat it up, cool it down, make it your recipe.

MAKES 26 TBSP

Prep ahead Keeps in the fridge for up to a month (see storage)

Prep/cooking 20 mins

Active time 15 mins

100g coriander (1 large or 4 small supermarket-sized bunches)

4 spring onions, trimmed, or 2 shallots, peeled

3 lemongrass stalks, trimmed and sliced

2–6 green chillies, to taste

4 garlic cloves, peeled

2 thumbs of galangal or ginger, peeled and chopped (4 tsp chopped)

1 tsp ground cumin

1 tsp ground black pepper

1 tsp ground coriander

4 heaped tbsp brown sugar

3 tbsp fish sauce, or 4 tbsp light soy for vegetarians

7 tbsp coconut milk

Vegetable oil to cover

1. Start by boiling your kettle. Get a large pan. Fill it with boiling water. Add salt and bring to the boil. Fill a large bowl with cold water.

2. Roughly chop the coriander. Slice the onions. Add the coriander and onions to the boiling water. Count to 30. Transfer the coriander and onions to the cold water, using a skimmer or a sieve. As soon as they are cold, drain them in a sieve. Squeeze out the excess water.

3. Get a small blender. Add the lemongrass, green chillies, garlic and galangal or ginger. Blend for 1½–2 minutes until they are very finely chopped. (You need to blend the hard ingredients first to get them as small as possible; once you add the liquid this is more difficult to do.)

4. Add the coriander, onions, cumin, pepper, ground coriander, brown sugar, fish sauce and 4 tbsp of coconut milk. Blend for 1–2 minutes until smooth. Add more coconut milk if the mixture looks too dry. (You can freeze any coconut milk you have left, see page 21.)

5. Spoon the curry paste into small, preferably sterilised, jars and pour over a layer of oil to cover the surface. Cover the top of the jar tightly with cling film and screw on the lid.

Storage

Use small sterilised jars or clean plastic containers, ideally enough for a single use, so that once they are opened you use them up quickly. Cover the jars first with cling film, then with a lid. Store in the fridge. If you use some but not all of the curry paste, it's best to put the rest in a smaller jar. If you don't have one, clean the exposed sides of the jar with kitchen paper. Cover the remaining curry paste with a layer of oil. Unopened jars will keep for up to 1 month. Once the jar is open, use within 2 days.

Simple Green Curry Paste Magic

Rather than give you lots of smaller suggestions, I thought my green curry paste would be most magical for you in the form of a few simple, reviving, fresh, feisty and quick green curries. They are not, nor are they intended to be, traditional. I don't fry the paste or the main ingredient. I don't add another lot of chopped ingredients that are already in the curry paste. And I cook the curry for only the length of time necessary to cook the chicken, fish or vegetables through. The choice of either coconut cream or light coconut milk is up to you and is purely a question of richness and thickness.

Many of the recipes I've seen speak of the importance of frying the paste before making the curry. I'm not so sure about this. What I think is more important is to add a little curry paste to refresh each recipe just before serving. The paste is about freshness and fragrance. Adding it at the end of the cooking time reinforces this and brings back the original ingredients with interest.

My green chicken curry

Serves 2

Cut two 150-175g chicken breasts into 2.5cm dice. Put the chicken into a bowl. Add 2 tsp of green curry paste and ¼ tsp of salt. Mix them together until the chicken is well coated with the paste. Get a small saucepan. Add 200ml coconut cream, 100ml chicken stock and 4 tsp of green curry paste. Bring to the boil. Lower the heat to medium. Simmer for 1 minute. Add the chicken. Cover, but leave the lid slightly ajar. Poach over a low heat, making sure the liquid never boils, for 8 minutes or until the chicken is just cooked through. Take off the heat. Cover and leave to rest for 2–3 minutes.

Boil your kettle. Get a large pot. Fill it with boiling water. Add salt and bring to the boil. Add 160g French beans, sliced runner beans or peas. Bring back to the boil and boil for 3–4 minutes or until tender. Drain the beans or peas and put them back into the pan. Sauté for 20 seconds. Turn off the heat. Add 1 tsp of green curry paste. Toss the vegetables until they are coated with the paste. Season to taste with salt and pepper.

Stir 2 tsp of curry paste into the chicken. Season with salt to taste. Put the vegetables on top. Serve from the pan.

Variations

Prawn curry

Simmer the coconut milk, stock and curry paste for 5 minutes. Replace the chicken with 10 small or 5 large raw prawns per person. Poach for 2–4 minutes depending on the size of the prawns, just until they change colour from clear to pink; make sure the liquid doesn't boil. Take the pan off the heat. Cover and leave to rest for 2 minutes. Continue as for the chicken curry (above).

Pollock curry

Follow the method and cooking time for the prawn curry (left), replacing the prawns with 300g pollock, cut into 5cm pieces.

Green vegetable and tofu curry

Replace the chicken with 200g tofu, cut into 2cm dice; mix this very gently with the curry paste. Simmer the coconut milk, stock and curry paste for 7 minutes. Add the tofu to the coconut milk and poach for 2 minutes, making sure the liquid doesn't boil or the tofu will break up. Continue as for the chicken curry (left), increasing the quantity of green vegetables to 200g. I like to add 50–80g watercress at the end and stir until it wilts.

Sweet potato, pepper and lentil curry

Replace the chicken with 350g sweet potatoes and 1 red pepper. Peel the sweet potatoes. Halve and deseed the pepper. Chop both into 3cm chunks. Put them into a roasting tray and toss with 1 tbsp vegetable oil. Roast at 200°C/Gas 6 for 20–30 minutes or until golden and soft. Simmer the coconut milk, stock and curry paste for 4 minutes. Stir in 250g cooked lentils (a drained 400g tin or pouch). Simmer for 1 minute. Season to taste. Toss the sweet potatoes and peppers with 2 tbsp of curry paste. Season. Put them on top of the lentils. Sprinkle sliced spring onion over the top.

Green curry on the barbie

This is my ideal way to add green curry to ingredients on the barbecue because I don't like to burn the paste. Once your ingredient is nearly cooked, brush the surface with green curry paste, turn it onto the barbecue grid for 20 seconds, then do the same with the other side. This is just enough to gently singe and grill the curry paste but not enough to make it bitter. You can also serve a little dish of green curry paste on the side. Try brushing steaks, lamb and pork chops, burgers, salmon, tuna, mackerel, sardines, sliced aubergine, peppers and haloumi.

Magical transformations The green curry paste recipes can be done with pesto and vice versa, except for the salmon on page 220.

Magic for kids I have found lightly spiced green vegetable and chicken curries to be a great success with kids. If you prefer your own more spicy, just add a minimum of curry paste at the start, serve your kids, then add more paste to yours. If the curry is still too spicy for your kids, give them a little jug of coconut cream to mix in. Curries are a great way to introduce new tastes, such as pumpkin, squash, sweet potatoes, parsnips and onions. The different curries are good to purée or chop and freeze for babies and toddlers.

Magical cheats There are a lot of good curry pastes on the market which will taste great but you might not find one as vibrant a green as mine.

1/ Beef, vegetable & noodle broth with green curry paste

This broth hits a spot in the soul that only good flavours find. The fact that it's healthy is good fortune. I'd be perfectly happy if this intense nourishment was a naughty treat. The texture and taste of the steak is much better when it is poached whole and then sliced than it would be the other way around. The beef takes flavour from the broth and noodles and gives its own back generously. The steak can be replaced with fish, prawns, chicken or tofu, or you could just add a few more vegetables.

This is ideal for younger kids who enjoy slurping broth and sucking up noodles. Leave out three-quarters of the curry paste, serve theirs, then add the rest to yours. Slice the steak very thinly. No good to purée for babies, but can be finely chopped for toddlers.

SERVES 2

Sides None needed

Prep/cooking 20–25 mins

Active time 15–20 mins

800ml beef stock

1 tbsp soy sauce

1 red pepper, quartered, deseeded and cut into 5mm slices

1 sirloin steak, 250g

3 tbsp plus 3 tsp green curry paste (page 209)

2 nests of medium egg noodles (or more depending on your appetite)

150g broccoli (¼–½ head), cut into about 10 small florets, stalk sliced

2 medium heads of pak choi, each cut lengthways into 6 slices

2 lime quarters

Salt

1. Preheat your oven to its lowest setting. Boil your kettle.

2. Start with the broth. Get a medium-sized saucepan. Add the beef stock and soy sauce. Bring to the boil. Add the red pepper and bring back to the boil. Lower the heat and simmer for 5–7 minutes until the pepper is soft. Put the pan on your lowest possible heat. Put serving bowls and a rack on a plate for resting the steak on in the oven to heat.

3. Season the steak with salt. Brush each side with 1½ tsp of green curry paste. Once the pepper is soft, add the steak to the broth, making sure it is completely submerged. Poach for 5 minutes, making sure the liquid never boils; turn the heat off if you need to. Lift out the steak with tongs and put it on the rack in the oven. Leave to rest for at least 5 minutes. Don't worry that the steak looks grey on the outside; it will taste wonderful and be pink in the middle.

4. While the steak poaches, get a large pot. Fill it three-quarters full with boiling water from your kettle. Add salt, cover and bring to the boil. Put a colander in your sink. While the steak rests, add the noodles to the boiling water. Cover and bring back to the boil. Stir to separate the noodles and boil for 1½ minutes. Add the broccoli. Cover, bring back to the boil and boil for 2 minutes. Add the pak choi. Boil for 1 minute. Drain in your colander, shaking out as much water as possible. Return the noodles and vegetables to the pan.

5. Bring the broth back to the boil. Stir in 2 tbsp of the curry paste. Season to taste with salt. Slice the steak thinly across the grain. Put the noodles and vegetables into your heated serving bowls. Add the steak slices. Ladle the broth over everything. Serve really hot with the lime quarters to squeeze over and the remaining 1 tbsp of curry paste in a little bowl alongside to dip the beef slices into.

2/ Chicken legs with fennel, tomatoes & green curry paste

In contrast to the simple magic recipe (page 210), I wanted a rich, saucy chicken curry with no cream. I wanted a bone to chew, the curry and chicken fried, and a sparklingly fresh finish. All along I wondered if the tomatoes and fennel would get on better with pesto than paste, but they flourished in green curry's company.

For younger kids, use less curry paste when you fry the chicken. Serve theirs once the chicken is cooked, then add as much paste as you like to your own. Good to purée or chop and freeze for babies and toddlers.

SERVES 2

Sides (pages 320–43)
Rice or noodles
Prep ahead To end of step 5, a day ahead. Reheat slowly for 10 minutes, then finish
Prep/cooking 50–55 mins
Active time 20–25 mins

2 chicken legs, 200–250g each
4 tbsp plus 2 tsp green curry paste (page 209)
1 tsp vegetable oil
1 large onion (160–200g), peeled and cut into 1.5cm slices
1 small fennel bulb, cut into 1.5cm slices
2 ripe tomatoes, cut into 5mm dice
1 tbsp tomato purée
½ mild red chilli, deseeded and finely chopped
2 tbsp water
250ml chicken stock
2 lime quarters
Salt

1. Put a bowl next to your cooker to drain fat into.

2. Start with the chicken legs. Put them on a plate. Brush each leg all over with 1 tbsp of curry paste and sprinkle with salt. Get a medium-sized shallow pan. Add the oil and get it really hot. Add the chicken legs, skin side down. Fry over a low to medium heat for 4–5 minutes until they are golden; be careful not to burn the paste. Put the chicken legs back on your plate. Drain half the fat into the bowl.

3. Add the onion, fennel, tomatoes, tomato purée, chilli and the 2 tbsp of water to the pan. Cover and sweat over a medium heat for 7–10 minutes until the vegetables have softened.

4. Tuck the chicken legs, skin side down, under the vegetables. Pour the chicken stock over the top. Stir in 1 tbsp of curry paste. Put the pan on a high heat and bring to the boil. Lower the heat to medium; the liquid should barely simmer. Put the lid on but leave it slightly ajar so that steam can escape. Simmer gently for 10 minutes. Turn the chicken legs skin side up. Simmer for 10 minutes. Remove the lid and simmer for 5 minutes.

5. Turn off the heat and put the lid back on the pan. Leave the chicken to rest for 5 minutes. It can happily sit until you are ready to serve.

6. When you're ready, heat the chicken curry until it starts to boil. Stir 1 tbsp of curry paste into the sauce and vegetables. The top of the sauce will look slightly oily; don't worry, this is as it should be. Brush each chicken leg with 1 tsp of curry paste. Season to taste with salt. Serve straight from the pan with the lime wedges for squeezing.

Cook extra

To make an excellent salad, cook extra portion(s) of the whole recipe. Strain three-quarters of the sauce to dress hot rice or noodles. Chop the chicken and vegetables to mix with an equal quantity of warm rice, dress with the remaining sauce and season with fresh lime and mint. Or make double and freeze half.

3/ Braised sea bream with prawn & green curry broth

I've probably demonstrated how to make prawn stock more often than anything else. I get so overexcited at how much flavour I get, with so little effort, from prawn parts that usually get chucked away, that I just have to show everyone. I use the stock in all sorts of things but rarely has it been as happy as it is in this light and spicy broth.

For younger kids, prawns can be too chewy, so you may prefer to chop them finely or leave them out. Use less curry paste for kids and make sure they have plenty of rice to soak up the sauce. Fine to chop for toddlers, but no good to purée or freeze.

SERVES 2

Sides (pages 320–43)
None needed. For bulk, rice
Prep ahead Stock and pepper mixture, up to a day ahead
Prep/cooking 40–45 mins
Active time 30–35 mins

6 raw tiger prawns in shell, heads on
2 tsp tomato purée
400ml plus 5 tbsp water
1½ tsp grated ginger
1 red pepper, halved, deseeded and cut into 1cm slices
1 tbsp plus 2 tsp green curry paste (page 209)
2 skinless farmed sea bream fillets, about 120g each
4 heads of baby pak choi or 2 large ones, halved
4 spring onions, trimmed and finely sliced diagonally
2 lime quarters
Salt and freshly ground black pepper

1. Preheat your oven to 200°C/Gas 6, position upper middle shelf. Boil your kettle.

2. Start with the prawns. Pull off the heads and shells. Remove the dark vein running down the back of each prawn with a sharp knife. Put the heads and shells into a small saucepan. Add the tomato purée and the 400ml water. Bring to the boil and simmer rapidly for 10 minutes.

3. While the stock simmers, get a medium-large shallow ovenproof pan. Add the ginger, red pepper and the 5 tbsp of water. Cover and sweat over a medium heat for 10 minutes until the pepper is soft.

4. Get a large pot. Fill it with boiling water. Put it on the heat. Put a colander in your sink.

5. Strain the prawn stock through a sieve into a measuring jug. You should have about 180ml; top it up with more water if you need to. Pour it over the red pepper. Stir in 1 tsp of green curry paste. Bring to the boil. Turn off the heat.

6. Brush each sea bream fillet with ½ tsp of green curry paste. Put the fillets on top of the pepper. Put the prawns around the outside. Submerge them in the liquid. Braise in the oven for 6–7 minutes or until the fish and prawns are just cooked through.

7. While the fish braises, add the pak choi to the boiling water. Bring back to the boil and boil for 1 minute. Drain in your colander. Put the pak choi onto your plates. Put the sea bream and prawns on top.

8. Stir the spring onions into the broth. Bring back to the boil. Stir in the 1 tbsp of curry paste. Season with salt and pepper to taste. Spoon the broth and vegetables over the sea bream, pak choi and prawns. Serve with the lime quarters.

4/ Mussels with green curry paste, rice noodles & apple juice

This idea came from a Normandy recipe called Marmite Dieppoise, a great dish that starts from a base of mussels cooked in cider. I liked the place where the apple and mussels met and I wanted to go beyond the typical bowlful of Thai mussels. Along the testing tightrope, I found that adding even the most ordinary vegetables interfered with the clear flavours. Only rice noodles, which imbibe the sea, coconut and spice without being too outspoken, made it into the final recipe. I use light coconut cream because it is less cloying than full fat, but you can leave out the cream entirely for a lighter version; just add 100ml more apple juice at the start.

For younger kids, add 1 tbsp curry paste, stir it in, dish theirs up, and then add the remainder to yours. Try cooking the mussels in a pan with a glass lid and getting your kids to watch them open; this is incredibly exciting and enticing.

SERVES 2

Sides (pages 320–43)
None needed. For something fresh, stir-fried steamed leaves or mangetout salad or green salad, lemon dressing
Prep/cooking 15 mins
Active time 10 mins

250ml apple juice
1kg mussels, cleaned
   (see page 23)
150g rice noodles or 300g
   straight-to-wok rice
   noodles
200ml light coconut cream
3 tbsp green curry paste
   (page 209)
2 lime quarters
Salt

1. Boil your kettle. Get a large saucepan. Fill it with water, add salt and bring to the boil. Put a colander in your sink.

2. Start with the mussels. Get a large sauté or saucepan with a lid. Add the apple juice. Bring to the boil. Add the mussels and cover the pan. Bring to the boil over a high heat. Boil as fast as you can for 2–3 minutes or until all of the mussels open. Discard any that don't. Turn off the heat. Cover the pan but leave the lid slightly ajar; the mussels can wait for the noodles if you need them to.

3. While the mussels steam open, add the rice noodles to the boiling water. Bring back to the boil and boil for 3–4 minutes; it is best to undercook these noodles slightly because they quickly turn soft. Drain. (If you are using straight-to-wok noodles just stir them into the cooked mussels and warm them through for 1 minute.)

4. Add the rice noodles to the mussels. Add the coconut cream and curry paste. Bring to the boil and boil for 10 seconds. Serve straight from the pan, with the lime quarters.

5/ Salmon with chickpeas, tomatoes & green curry paste

When I worked for Raymond Blanc I learnt to hunt for opportunities to enhance flavours that are already in a dish. It is this glimmer of Raymond's genius that keeps me searching for a chance to improve on every recipe I cook. As this salmon cooks in foil, the flavours are all bound up with nowhere to go. The opportunity to enhance comes as you open the foil parcel and it comes with a flicker of zest, a flash of juice and a soothing spoonful of coconut cream. These don't so much add something new as reinvigorate and refresh the ingredients that are already there. Be sure to slice the onions as thinly as you can. Use strong foil, or double it up.

Tinned chickpeas are good for kids as they are softer than those you cook yourself. For younger kids, don't put the curry paste on top of the salmon, and finely chop rather than slice the onions. Depending on how used your kids are to spice, you could leave half of the paste out of the vegetables. Good to purée or chop and freeze for babies and toddlers.

SERVES 2

Sides (pages 320–43)
None needed. For bulk, rice
Prep/cooking 25 mins
Active time 10 mins

400g tin chickpeas, drained
½ small red onion, peeled
   and very thinly sliced
125g ripe cherry tomatoes,
   halved
2 tbsp plus 4 tsp green
   curry paste (page 209)
10 tbsp (150ml) thick
   coconut cream
2 tbsp water
2 skinless farmed salmon
   fillets, 120–140g each
1 lime
Salt and sugar

1. Preheat your oven to 200°C/Gas 6, position upper middle shelf.

2. Start with the chickpea mixture. Get a large bowl. Add the chickpeas, red onion, cherry tomatoes, the 2 tbsp of curry paste, a pinch of salt and a pinch of sugar. Mix it all together.

3. Tear two 45cm pieces of foil. Put them on a baking tray so that they meet in the middle with half of the foil overhanging the tray. Spread half the chickpea mixture on each piece of foil in a thin layer, large enough for the salmon fillet to sit on. Fold the edges of the foil slightly upwards so that the liquid can't escape.

4. Spoon 4 tbsp of the coconut cream and 1 tbsp of the water over the chickpeas in each parcel. Put the salmon fillets in the centre. Season with salt. Spoon 1 tsp of curry paste on top of each fillet and brush all over the surface. Close the foil parcels. Fold the edges inwards a couple of times to seal them tightly and to stop any air from escaping.

5. Bake for 14 minutes. Put the parcels onto plates. Cut them open at the table and spoon the remaining 1 tbsp of coconut cream and 1 tsp of curry paste into each. Zest or grate the zest of ¼ lime over the top. Squeeze the juice of ¼ lime over each portion as you eat.

6/ Pork with green curry paste, orange, radish & carrot salad

This is a great way to serve belly pork. I brush the pork with green curry paste twice – the first time to grill the goodness into the pork, the second to finish it with a freshness that's like lighting a flavour flare. The ideal way to buy the belly pork is to get your butcher to slice it for you, but most supermarkets have a version, either called belly pork slices or rashers. The size of these slices varies. Don't worry if you get the total weight with two slices instead of three, as long as they are the same thickness, it won't affect the cooking time. You can squash the pork slices if you need to make them thinner.

For younger kids, halve the amount of curry paste on their pork. Leave the chilli out of their salad, then add it to yours. The pak choi stalks make good crunchy finger food. This recipe is no good to purée or chop and freeze.

SERVES 2

Sides (pages 320–43)
None needed. For bulk,
tasty or plain grains
Prep/cooking 30–35 mins
Active time 20–25 mins

6 slices of rindless belly
    pork, each 1.5cm thick,
    about 225g per portion
3 tbsp plus 2 tsp green
    curry paste (page 209)
4 spring onions, trimmed
½ small red chilli, deseeded
    and finely chopped
1 large orange
8 radishes, halved
    lengthways
2 tsp lemon juice
2 tsp extra virgin olive oil
1 medium carrot, peeled
2 medium heads of pak choi
Salt and sugar

1. Preheat your grill to high, position middle shelf.

2. Start with the pork. Line your grill tray with foil. Turn the edges upwards to catch the juice that will escape from the pork as it grills. Season the pork with salt. Brush each side of each portion with ½ tbsp of curry paste. Grill for 5 minutes on each side (be careful as grills vary enormously; raise the pork if it's not browning). Once the pork is cooked, brush the top of each portion with ½ tbsp of curry paste.

3. While the pork grills, get a large shallow bowl for the salad. Thinly slice the spring onions, keeping the green and white parts separate. Add the green spring onions and the chilli to the bowl. Zest or grate the orange zest into the bowl. Mix it all together. Put one-third of this mixture into a small dish ready to sprinkle over the pork just before you serve it.

4. Add the white part of the spring onions, the radishes, lemon juice, olive oil, a pinch of salt and a pinch of sugar to the salad bowl. Slice the carrot lengthways into ribbons with a speed peeler. Add the ribbons to the bowl.

5. Next prepare the orange. Cut off the top and bottom. Cut away the peel and white pith in strips. Cut the orange in half. Put each half flat on your board and cut across into 6 slices.

6. Put 3 large outer leaves from the pak choi onto your plates. Cut the little interior leaves into strips. Toss the pak choi strips, orange slices and the 2 tsp of curry paste with the other salad ingredients. Spread the salad on top of the leaves. Put the pork on top. Sprinkle the final third of the orange zest, spring onion and chilli mixture over the pork.

Cook extra

Make extra portion(s) of pork, the salad and dressing as they are good cold. Toss the salad with a plain grain for bulk and add a little extra dressing.

3/
Slow Cook Sorcery

Six fantastic feasts, and six wizardly
ways to transform their leftovers

The aroma of a chicken roasting in the oven fills your house with warmth and makes your mouth water. Lamb begins to melt and baste on a bed of soft onions and potatoes. Joy floats though your kitchen on the scent of pork roasting, with the expectation of crunchy crackling and succulent, irresistibly chewy, tasty flesh. Ginger and brown sugar burnish duck skin and sweeten the air. Rich mackerel braises into a savoury mass of tomato, orange and garlic. A heavy pot of lentils and wine gently murmurs in your oven, ready to explode into flavour. Slow-cooked meals give great pleasure in their anticipation – just being in the kitchen as they take shape is its own reward.

But how, when there's no time to cook these dishes from scratch, can you get these flavours every day? The answer is in this chapter. I'll show you six slow-cooked 'hero' recipes, then six subsidiary meals you can make with each one once they are cooked. These recipes will have all the slow-cooked flavour, but they are fast because you've already done the long cooking for the first meal. This 'slow cook sorcery' means you can savour the intense flavours from a glorious first feast of chicken, lamb, pork, duck, mackerel or lentils another day, because you have created the leftovers on purpose.

There is no point in taking shortcuts for the sake of it. If you want something in a flash, cook a dish that is designed to be quick from Adventures with Ingredients (pages 36–123) or The Magic Fridge (pages 124–223). Roast belly pork takes almost no work at all to prepare, but a while to roast. What makes great roast pork is not just the roasting, but slowly crisping the crackling first and resting the pork afterwards. If you take this time away you'll have tough meat with tough skin. Braised lamb takes a long time to braise, but without this lengthy cooking time it won't be meltingly tender. The food in this chapter is special because it is given the time it needs to be as good as it can be.

I love cooking with leftovers. I always have. I find the satisfaction overwhelming, but once my leftover dishes are made, they certainly don't feel like leftovers. At times I've gone for glamour – salads and salsas with great blasts of flavour and bright colours. Other times I've gone for comfort – pies and bakes and bundles of fun. They are all delights in their own right; they are simply recipes that require cooked rather than raw main ingredients.

Most of the 'hero' recipes will take little or no more time if you cook double the quantity. Once you've had your first meal, the rest can be frozen in portions with their sauce or gravy so they are ready for an evening when you don't want to cook at all, or when you'd prefer just to cook a little bit. I worked hard on these ideas to make it practical and economical for one person, two people, or families with young kids who need only three portions, to roast a chicken or braise a shoulder of lamb.

The recipes that follow each 'hero' roast or braise are all given in quantities for two portions and can be scaled up or down easily to serve more or less. Wherever I can, I'll give you options that will enable you to make a variation of the recipe even if you hadn't made the slow-cooked treat in the first place.

And we'll talk gravy. I love gravy and I'm often asked how to get more of it. Whatever else I give you, when there is gravy, there will be lots of it. Enough so that you can have gravy left over to sauce the 'heroes' from Adventures with Ingredients, pour over a plate of mash or onto a heavily buttered slice of bread.

Heavenly aromas of braising and sounds of roasting await you in this chapter. There will be scents that might already be familiar and others that can become so. Cooking a recipe you know well is all about warm and familiar smells, tastes and textures. It is about knowing how to make the best of what you have, and how to keep things special long after the excitement of the first meal fades.

ROAST CHICKEN

My roast chicken has golden, tasty, sticky skin, juicy flesh, tons of gravy, soft onions and lots of spuds. Now, this is how I get the best from my bird. First, I cut out the wishbone to make the chicken easier to carve. The wishbone's removal opens a pocket in the centre of each breast that I stuff butter into, to baste the bird from within. I like my spuds roasted with chicken, but not at the expense of gravy. For roast gravy you need the roast goodies in the tray; potatoes suck them up, onions give them back. To get potatoes flavoured with roast chicken, but keep the roasting juices I need for glorious gravy, I roast the spuds in a few spoonfuls of the chicken's tasty fat on a separate tray. To make my gravy more flavourful, I add the wings to the tray. I add thickened stock instead of water to get more gravy, and I boil it very briefly to keep it tasting freshly roasted.

To roast different sized chickens using this recipe, allow 17½ minutes per 500g, followed by 15 minutes' resting time for the chicken's fibres to relax and the juices to settle. The interior temperature needs to be 74–76°C in the thickest part of the breast (check with your probe), but it is often slightly higher. Don't worry if it is.

I have never met a kid who doesn't like roast chicken and potatoes.

SERVES 4–6

Sides (pages 320–43) Green vegetable and/or a leaf salad

Prep ahead Remove wishbone and stuff chicken with butter, a day ahead

Prep/cooking 1½ hours

Active time 30 mins

1 chicken, about 2kg
50g hard butter, in 2 sticks (optional)
2–3 tbsp plus 2 tsp vegetable oil
6 small-medium onions, peeled and halved
1kg floury potatoes, such as King Edward, in 4–5cm chunks
600ml chicken stock
1 tbsp dark soy sauce
1 tbsp cornflour
3 tbsp water
Salt

1. Preheat your oven to 200°C/Gas 6, position upper middle and lower middle shelves. Put a plate big enough to rest the chicken on next to your cooker.

2. Take off the string if there is one and prepare the chicken for roasting (optional, see overleaf). If you do this, put the wings and wishbone into your roasting tray with the chicken. Season the chicken inside and out with salt. Brush the 2 tsp of oil over the chicken's skin. Add the onions to the tray. Toss with 2 tbsp of oil. Turn the onions cut side up and tuck them around the chicken. Roast on the upper middle shelf for 35 minutes.

3. Get the chicken out of the oven. Put a baking tray with raised sides on the lower middle shelf of the oven to heat. Put the potatoes in a shallow bowl. Spoon 3 tbsp of fat from around the chicken onto the potatoes; if there isn't enough, add vegetable oil to make up the difference. Add a pinch of salt. Toss the potatoes until they are well coated in the fat.

4. Baste the chicken with its cooking juices. Turn the onions cut side down. Brush their rounded sides with cooking juices. Lift the chicken on top of them. Put the chicken in the oven and take out the hot baking tray. Put the potatoes on the tray in a single layer. Roast both potatoes and chicken for 30–35 minutes, turning and basting the potatoes twice during this time.

5. While the chicken roasts, get a medium-sized saucepan. Add the stock and soy sauce. Bring to the boil and boil to reduce by a quarter. Take the pan off the heat. Put the cornflour into a small bowl. Mix it with the 3 tbsp of water. Whisk this into the reduced stock. Bring to the boil and boil for 10 seconds, stirring constantly. Take it off the heat.

(continued overleaf)

6. Once roasted, get the chicken out of the oven. Baste it. Put the chicken and onions onto your big plate. Leave the wings and wishbone in the tray. Take the potatoes out of the oven. Brush them with 2 tbsp of the chicken fat. Roast the potatoes on the upper middle shelf for 10 minutes longer.

7. If you prefer, drain off the fat from the gravy (I like to leave it in), but be careful not to lose the juices beneath. Add the reduced stock to the tray. Bring to the boil. Scrape and stir to get the bits from the bottom of the tray. Boil for 30 seconds. Tip the gravy into a saucepan. Simmer for 2–3 minutes, no longer. Take the gravy off the heat. Lift out the wings and wishbone and put them with the roast chicken. You'll have about 400ml of gravy.

8. Carve the chicken into 6 portions (see right). Or to carve it into 4 portions, follow the technique for roast duck (page 279). Add any juices from the resting plate and carving board to the gravy. Serve with the roast potatoes.

Cook extra
Roast 2 chickens at the same time with the oven at 220°C/Gas 7. Let the extra chicken cool, then store in portions with the onions and gravy in your fridge for 2 days, or in the freezer, to make the subsidiary recipes.

Variations
For any of these, the butter will need to be softer and you'll need to push it into the breast with a spoon. You can flavour the butter with citrus zest or your favourite herb or curry powder, sweet or smoked paprika, or garlic.

Preparing a chicken for roasting
This is optional but makes carving easier and the breast more succulent.

 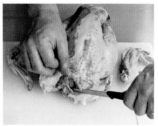 

1. Pull out the wings and slice through the middle joint closest to the breast. You should be left with one little winglet on each side.
2. Turn the chicken around. Lift the skin over the breasts. Find the wishbone between the breasts with your fingers. Run the tip of a small knife around the top, then down either side of it. Reach in, hook your middle finger through the top of the wishbone and pull it out. This leaves two pockets.
3. Push a stick of butter into each wishbone pocket. Pull the skin back over the breasts and tuck it underneath the chicken.

Carving the chicken

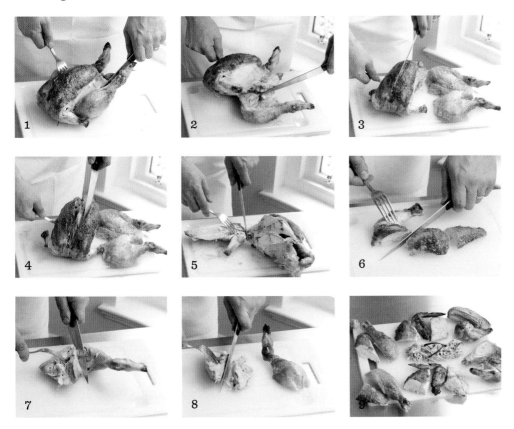

To serve 6, with an extra 110–140g for the recipes on pages 238, 240 and 242:
Take your time. You can keep the chicken pieces warm in the roasting tray
in a low oven as you carve, then freshen it up with a brush of gravy.

1. Hold the chicken firmly with a fork. Slice between the breasts and thighs.
2. Slice downwards and cut through the joint that joins the leg to the carcass.
3. Carefully find the breast bone with the blade of your knife.
4. Cut along either side of the breast bone. Keep your knife close to the bone
    to slice the halves of the breasts closest to you away from the bone.
5. Turn the chicken around. Carve each breast off the carcass and through
    the joint at the top to ensure that the winglet stays attached to the breast.
6. Cut each breast into three: winglet, middle section and boneless tip.
7. Cut each leg through the joint where the thigh and drumstick meet.
8. Follow the line of the bone to cut each thigh in half.
9. Make 6 portions (from left to right in the picture): put each drumstick
    with a boneless breast tip; put each middle section of each breast with half
    a thigh and the wings from the roasting tray; put each wing end of the
    breast with half a thigh. Scrape 110–140g meat off the carcass (centre of the
    picture). Make chicken stock with the carcass (see page 25).

1/ Roast chicken with peas, bacon & chestnuts

This is the peas, butter, bacon and nuts gang that will go with anything from chicken to an egg. It doesn't even matter if you don't have any chicken left so long as you've got roast gravy. A double portion of this buttery bunch alongside fat slices of buttered toast would make a marvellous if slightly mischievous meal. I use a lot of pre-cooked chestnuts and the way I prepare them here is a favourite discovery. The chestnuts are fond of the bacon fat so I fry them until golden on the outside but still chewy, to make a chestnut croûton to toss through salads, onto soups or just nibble as a salty snack.

The crispy goodies make this chicken very appealing to kids and it can be a good way to introduce them to broad beans, either on their own or in a mixture with peas and corn. Take out the bacon and this is good to purée or chop and freeze for babies and toddlers.

SERVES 2

Sides Mashed potato (page 338)

Prep/cooking 30 mins

Active time 30 mins

1 tsp vegetable oil

4 rashers of streaky bacon, cut into 3cm slices

10 cooked chestnuts, cut into 5mm slices

7 tbsp roast chicken gravy (page 229)

3 roast onion halves, (page 229), cut into 2cm slices

20g butter

4 tbsp water

2 portions of roast chicken pieces (page 229)

100g peas, broad beans or sweetcorn

1 tbsp chopped rosemary

Salt and freshly ground black pepper

1. Preheat your oven to 200°C/Gas 6, position upper middle and lower middle shelves. Boil your kettle.

2. Start with the bacon. Get a medium-sized ovenproof frying pan (with a lid). Add the oil and put the pan on a high heat. When it is really hot, add the bacon. Fry for 1 minute. Add the chestnuts. Lower the heat to medium. Fry, turning 2 or 3 times, for 2 minutes until the chestnuts are golden; watch them carefully or they will burn. Spoon the bacon and chestnuts onto a small oven tray. Don't drain the fat from the pan.

3. Add the gravy, onions, butter and the 4 tbsp of water to the pan. Bring to the boil. Add the chicken, skin side down. Bring back to the boil. Put the lid on. Put the pan on the upper middle shelf in the oven for 5 minutes.

4. Take the chicken out of the oven. Take the lid off. Turn the chicken skin side up. Put it back into the oven for 5 minutes. Put the oven tray with the bacon and chestnuts on the lower middle shelf.

5. Get a medium-sized saucepan; fill it with the water from your kettle. Add salt and bring to the boil. Add the peas, beans or sweetcorn. Bring to the boil and boil for 3 minutes or until tender. Drain.

6. Take the chicken, bacon and chestnuts out of the oven. Add the peas or other vegetables and rosemary to the chicken. Grind black pepper over the top. Scatter over the crisp bacon and chestnuts. Serve.

Cook extra
Double the recipe and freeze half.

No roast chicken?
Bake 2 chicken breasts (see page 41). For the gravy, use 2 tbsp of brown sauce mixed with 6 tbsp of chicken stock. Don't add the water in the recipe. Replace the onions with 90g of shop-bought onion marmalade. Serve the chicken breasts with the sauce, beans, bacon and chestnuts.

2/ Sticky chicken with marmalade, fennel & grapefruit

I've cooked with marmalade since I met the Bineau family of marmalade makers during the Menton lemon festival in 2004. I fancy I can still smell the welcome of simmering citrus at the entrance to their workshop. Back in England I discovered that marmalade could be a seasoning as well as a sweetener. The trick is to balance its sweetness, so that the chicken tastes like dinner rather than breakfast. I do this with the roast gravy and the crisp fennel, which could just as easily be baby gem or Romaine lettuce.

This chicken is good for kids – sweet enough to get them interested, but not so sweet that you feel like you're cheating. The first time you give them fennel, don't dress it, serve it as finger food. Leave the chilli out of their sauce, then add it to yours. The chicken but not the fennel can be chopped or puréed and frozen.

SERVES 2

Sides (pages 320–43)
Plain grains. Glazed fennel

Prep ahead Citrus can be segmented and juice reduced, half a day ahead

Prep/cooking 30–35 mins

Active time 25–30 mins

3 tbsp citrus marmalade

5 tbsp roast chicken gravy (page 229)

2 portions of roast chicken (page 229)

200ml orange juice (freshly squeezed or from a carton)

1 red grapefruit, segmented (see page 29)

1 orange, segmented (see page 29)

½ fennel bulb

1 tbsp plus 2 tsp extra virgin olive oil

40g rocket (½ small packet)

½ mild red chilli, deseeded and finely chopped

Salt and sugar

1. Preheat your oven to 200°C/Gas 6, position upper middle shelf.

2. Start with the glaze. Get a medium-sized ovenproof frying pan (with a lid). Add the marmalade and gravy. Bring to the boil over a medium heat, stirring until the marmalade dissolves. Boil for 30 seconds or until the glaze is thick enough to lightly coat the back of a spoon. Take the pan off the heat.

3. Add the chicken pieces, skin side down, to the frying pan. Cover the pan and put it into the oven for 4 minutes. Take the pan out and remove the lid. Turn the chicken skin side up. Brush with the sauce. Put the chicken back in the oven for 6 minutes.

4. While the chicken is in the oven, get a medium-sized saucepan. Add the orange juice, along with any juice from your citrus segments. Bring to the boil and boil until the juice has reduced by two-thirds.

5. Slice the fennel thinly, season with salt and add the 2 tsp of extra virgin olive oil. Put the fennel, rocket and citrus segments onto your plates.

6. Once the chicken is hot, the marmalade and gravy glaze will be very thick and sticky. Brush the glaze over the chicken. Put the chicken next to the salad on your plates.

7. Now make the sauce. Add the reduced orange juice, chilli and remaining 1 tbsp of extra virgin olive oil to the glaze in the frying pan. Bring to the boil and boil for 30 seconds until the olive oil emulsifies with the juice and the sauce is thick enough to coat the back of a spoon. Season to taste. Spoon the sauce over the chicken and salad.

No roast chicken?

Bake 2 chicken breasts (see page 41). Make the glaze using stock instead of gravy. Brush it over the chicken breasts for the last 4 minutes of their cooking time. Make the sauce from the glaze as above.

3/ Roast chicken with apple & black pudding

This is the most charming panful. I was very tempted to add cream (I'm always tempted to add cream) but instead of making it richer, I decided to make it more tart and more intense by adding apple juice. This combination would also work with curry powder instead of smoked paprika.

   If you can, get kids to eat their chicken off the bone – it's good to get them chewing. Younger kids may not like the black pudding, but get them to try a bit with some apple. Meals with apple and juice have always been a success with my kids. Beware of fennel seeds for kids, they can be quite chewy, so you may want to chop them or leave them out. This meal can be puréed or chopped and frozen for babies and toddlers.

SERVES 2

Sides (pages 320–43)
Chickpea purée or soft polenta or olive oil mashed potato

Prep ahead Apple sauce, a day ahead

Prep/cooking 30–35 mins

Active time 25–30 mins

2 portions of roast chicken (page 229)

1 tbsp plus 1 tsp extra virgin olive oil

1 Cox, or Granny Smith apple, halved, each half cut into 6 wedges

150ml apple juice

8 tbsp roast chicken gravy (page 229)

4 roast onion halves (page 229), cut into 1cm slices

½ tsp fennel seeds, finely chopped or ground

60g black pudding, cut into 6 slices

Salt and smoked paprika

1. Preheat your oven to 200°C/Gas 6, position upper middle shelf.

2. Start with the chicken. Put it in a bowl. Sprinkle ¼ tsp of smoked paprika over the chicken and brush it over the skin and flesh so they're well coated.

3. Next, prepare the apple and sauce. Heat a medium-sized ovenproof frying pan with the 1 tsp of extra virgin olive oil. Add the apple wedges. Sauté over a medium heat for 1 minute. Add the apple juice. Bring to the boil and boil to reduce by just over half until it becomes slightly sticky. Add the gravy, onions and fennel seeds. Bring to the boil.

4. Add the cooked chicken, skin side down, to the pan. Bring back to the boil. Cover and put into the oven for 5 minutes. Take out the pan and remove the lid. Turn the chicken skin side up. Put the black pudding in the pan. Put the pan back into the oven for 5 minutes.

5. Take the pan out of the oven. Brush the remaining 1 tbsp of extra virgin olive oil over everything. Serve straight from the pan.

Cook extra
Make twice the recipe and freeze half.

No roast chicken?
Season 2 chicken breasts with smoked paprika and bake them (see page 41). For the gravy, use 2 tbsp of brown or hoisin sauce mixed with 6 tbsp of chicken stock. Replace the onions with 90g of shop-bought onion marmalade or sticky onions (page 161). Add the black pudding to the sauce at the end of step 3 and boil it for an extra minute.

4/ Baked tomatoes with chicken, couscous, dried figs & ginger

Stuffed tomatoes are a possibility for every 'hero' recipe in this chapter. They ended up here because I love the taste of roast chicken gravy with tomatoes slightly more than I love it with lentils or lamb. I get completely carried away with excitement when I get an extra meal out of a bird, and I use the juicy scraps that I scrape off the carcass for this one.

For a bowl of hedonistic comfort, cook the couscous in the roast chicken gravy, stir in lashings of butter and grated cheese, then eat yourself to sleep with a trashy novel. Best eaten with a spoon from a warm plate resting on your grateful tummy.

This was a triumph with my kids. Pull the skin off the baked tomatoes for younger kids. The meal is no good to purée but can be finely chopped and frozen.

SERVES 2

Sides None needed. For bulk, extra couscous on the side

Prep ahead Up to 2 days ahead. Reheat, covered, in a low oven or the microwave

Prep/cooking 45–50 mins

Active time 15–20 mins

200ml roast chicken gravy (page 229) or 100ml gravy and 100ml chicken stock

6 tbsp water

1 garlic clove, peeled and sliced

3 tsp grated ginger

2 tbsp plus 2 tsp extra virgin olive oil

70g couscous

4 medium-large tomatoes

4 roast onion halves (page 229), cut into 1cm slices

4 large dried figs, cut into 5mm dice

110–140g boneless roast chicken (page 229), chopped

2 tbsp pine nuts (optional)

Salt, sugar and ras-el-hanout

1. Preheat your oven to 200°C/Gas 6, position upper middle shelf.

2. Start with the couscous. Get a small pan. Add 125ml gravy, the 6 tbsp of water, garlic, 2 tsp of the ginger, ½ tsp of ras-el-hanout and 1 tbsp of the extra virgin olive oil. Bring to the boil. Add the couscous and bring back to the boil. Turn off the heat, cover and leave to sit for 5 minutes.

3. While the couscous sits, prepare the tomatoes. Cut a tiny slice off their bottoms so they sit flat. Cut a 1.5cm slice off the top of each tomato and keep these for the lids; I leave the stalks on because I like the way they look. Use a teaspoon to scoop the seeds and pulp out onto your chopping board, leaving the tomato shells intact. Chop the seeds and pulp. Scrape these and the juice from your board into a 20cm baking dish or ovenproof frying pan. Add the remaining gravy, the onions, remaining 1 tsp of grated ginger, half the diced figs, ½ tsp of ras-el-hanout, a pinch of salt and a pinch of sugar to the dish.

4. Once the couscous has sat, add the chicken, the rest of the figs, and the pine nuts if you're using them. Mix together with a fork. Season to taste with salt and ras-el-hanout. Stuff this mixture into the tomatoes. It will come above the top of the tomato; this is intended. Press the lids on top.

5. Sit the tomatoes in the sauce. Cover the dish with foil. Bake for 10 minutes. Remove the foil and bake for another 20 minutes. Serve straight from the baking dish.

Cook extra
Double the recipe and freeze half.

No roast chicken?
You can replace the roast chicken with roast pork, lamb, turkey or braised lentils. The roast gravy or lentil braising juices are the key, so you need to have these as well.

Roast chicken, sweetcorn & kidney bean tortilla cake

This is just the thing when you fancy something really yummy and jolly to make. It comes out of the oven as an irresistible melted-cheese-topped tasty treat – the avocado, chilli and lime perking it up into a meal that wakes you up. I use the chilli as a seasoning rather than a spice to make the dish hot. If you like more, then feel free to blow your head off.

For younger kids, make individual less spicy cakes and leave the chilli out of the salsa.

SERVES 2

Sides (pages 320–43)
None needed. A crisp green salad would be good

Prep ahead Sauce mixture can be cooked a day ahead

Prep/cooking 30–35 mins

Active time 15 mins

3 roast onion halves (page 229), cut into 1cm slices

2 garlic cloves, peeled and finely chopped

4 tbsp roast chicken gravy (page 229)

400g tin chopped tomatoes

½ x 410g tin kidney beans, drained and rinsed

200g tin sweetcorn, drained

¼ tsp medium-hot chilli powder, or to taste

110–140g boneless roast chicken (page 229), cut into 2cm slices

3 tortillas, 17–22cm in diameter

80g Cheddar, grated

1 ripe avocado

Zested or grated zest and juice of ½ lime

½ mild red chilli, deseeded and finely chopped

1 tbsp extra virgin olive oil

4 tbsp soured cream

Salt and sugar

1. Preheat your oven to 200°C/Gas 6, position upper middle shelf.

2. Get a medium-sized saucepan. Add the onions, garlic, gravy, tinned tomatoes, kidney beans, sweetcorn and chilli powder. Stir to mix it all together. Bring to the boil over a high heat. Boil for 6–7 minutes until the mixture is thick and very little liquid remains (about a quarter of the amount you started with). Stir in the chicken. Take the pan off the heat.

3. Get an ovenproof dish or pan large enough for the tortilla. Put 1 tortilla on the base. Spoon one-third of the chicken mixture and one-third of the Cheddar on top. Repeat twice to make 3 layers. Bake for 15 minutes or until the Cheddar is melted and golden.

4. While the tortilla is in the oven, make the salsa. Cut the avocado in half and remove the stone and skin. Chop the avocado flesh into 1cm dice. Put it into a small bowl. Mix in the lime zest, lime juice, fresh chilli and extra virgin olive oil. Season to taste with salt and sugar.

5. Transfer the tortilla cake to a board. Cut it a quarter at a time so that it stays hot while you eat. Serve the avocado salsa and soured cream on the side.

Cook extra

Double the bean mixture, with or without the chicken. Roll it into tortillas with crisp lettuce and avocado for lunch or dinner the next day.

No roast chicken?

You can make this with any cooked meat, or just leave out the meat altogether and add the rest of the tin of beans. Replace the onions with 90g of shop-bought onion marmalade or sticky onions (page 161). It's a good one to keep in mind for leftover turkey or ham at Christmas.

6/ Roast chicken in a potato pancake with fried egg

I am as sure as I can be that putting things inside potato pancakes before they cook is my idea. I started making them fifteen years ago at Raymond Blanc's Cookery School with lots of Cheddar. I use a floury potato and don't wash it after I grate it. Before you start, practise turning the pan onto the baking sheet to get the position of your wrists right so that you don't end up doing a dangerous move with a hot pan of potatoes.

I call these surprise potato pancakes for my kids. Crisp grated potato is usually a hit and easy for younger kids to eat. I don't alter the stuffing. Chop it more finely if necessary and substitute Cheddar for Parmesan. No good to purée or freeze.

SERVES 2

Sides None needed
Prep ahead Potato pancake, up to 4 hours ahead. Reheat in a hot oven for 5–7 mins
Prep/cooking 30–35 mins
Active time 15 mins

110–140g boneless roast chicken or carcass trimmings (page 229), cut into 2cm slices
2 roast onion halves (page 229), cut into 1cm slices
8 sun-dried or sunblush tomatoes in oil, drained and cut into 1cm dice
½ mozzarella ball (about 60g), cut into 5mm dice
14 black olives, pitted and halved
6 tbsp grated Parmesan
2 large floury potatoes (650–750g), such as King Edward
2 tbsp vegetable oil
40g butter
2 large eggs
4 tbsp roast chicken gravy (page 229)
Salt and freshly ground black pepper

1. Preheat your oven to 200°C/Gas 6, position upper middle shelf.

2. Get a medium bowl. Add the chicken, onion, tomatoes, mozzarella, olives and half the Parmesan. Mix together. Season to taste with salt and pepper.

3. Peel the potatoes and wash them. Lay a tea towel on your chopping board. Grate the potatoes onto the tea towel. Enclose the grated potato in the tea towel to form a bag. Twist the ends of the bag to squeeze as much water as you can out of the grated potato.

4. Get a 20cm ovenproof non-stick frying pan. (This will not work in a pan that is not non-stick). Add the oil and get it really hot. Put a baking sheet next to your cooker.

5. Season the grated potato. Use a fish slice to spread half of it over the base of the pan and press it down firmly. Spoon the chicken mixture over the top, to about 2cm from the edge. Cover with the rest of the potato, spreading it to the edge of the pan. Press down well. Dot half the butter around the edge. Fry over a medium-high heat for 2 minutes until golden; lift the pancake to check the colour.

6. Now, be confident, hold the pan handle in two hands. Flip the pancake onto the baking sheet in one quick movement. Slide the pancake back into the pan. Tidy the pancake around the edges with your fish slice if necessary. Fry over a medium heat for 2 minutes. Add the remaining butter in little knobs around the edges.

7. Put the pan in the oven. Bake the pancake for 15 minutes or until the potato is cooked through and the outside is dark golden. Remove from the oven. Slide the pancake onto the baking sheet. Keep it warm in the oven.

8. Return the frying pan to a medium heat. Add 2 eggs and fry until the whites are set. Once they are nearly ready, add the gravy to the pan. Sprinkle the remaining Parmesan over the egg whites. Cover and leave to sit for 30 seconds. Cut the pancake in half and serve each half with an egg and the gravy.

BRAISED LAMB SHOULDER

This recipe captures the irresistible flavour of a roast in the melting richness of a slow braise. Lamb shoulder is cheaper than leg, but in no way inferior – it just needs different treatment. First, you roast the shoulder at a high heat to get the glorious taste of the roasted skin. Next, you seal this taste in the tray so the roast goodness has nowhere to go except into the lamb, vegetables and gravy. Finally, you glaze it to a mouth-watering sheen.

Kids love this braise. For younger kids, the little bit at the end of the shank is the most tender and perfect. Can be chopped or puréed and frozen for babies and toddlers.

SERVES 6
WITH SOME LEFT OVER

Sides (pages 320–43)
None needed. Bread and
a salad would be good

Prep ahead The whole dish,
up to 45 minutes ahead;
keep warm in a low oven

Prep/cooking 4¼–4¾ hours
Active time 40–50 mins

1 tbsp vegetable oil
2kg shoulder of lamb
750g smallish waxy
    potatoes (at least 9),
    such as Anya or
    Charlotte, halved
12 small onions (about
    1kg), peeled and halved
4 large carrots, peeled,
    halved widthways, each
    half cut in 3 lengthways
650ml lamb or chicken
    stock
1½ tbsp dark soy sauce
1 heaped tbsp tomato purée
2 large garlic heads, cloves
    separated and peeled
    (see page 22), optional
2 tsp cornflour
2 tbsp water
Salt and freshly ground
    black pepper

1. Preheat your oven to 220°C/Gas 7, position upper middle shelf. Get a wide roll of strong foil.

2. Get a deep roasting tray. Add the oil. Put the tray in the oven for 5 minutes. Rub the lamb shoulder with salt. Put it fat side up into the hot tray. Roast for 45 minutes. Take the tray out. Turn the oven down to 160°C/Gas 3. Transfer the lamb to a plate.

3. Scatter the potatoes, onions and carrots in the roasting tray. Season with salt and pepper. Turn the vegetables with a spoon until they're coated in the lamb fat. Put the lamb shoulder on top of the vegetables. Cover the tin tightly with foil, sealing it well. (If it's not well sealed or there is a hole in the foil, the heat will escape and the lamb will take longer and won't cook properly.) Put the roasting tray back in the oven. Braise for 3–3½ hours until the lamb is so tender that you can push a spoon right through it.

4. While the lamb braises, get a medium-sized saucepan. Add the stock, soy sauce and tomato purée. Bring to the boil and boil to reduce by half. Add the garlic cloves. Turn the heat to low. Simmer for 5 minutes or until the garlic is tender. Turn off the heat. Transfer the garlic cloves to a plate. Dissolve the cornflour in the 2 tbsp of water. Put both next to your cooker.

5. Once the lamb is cooked, take it out of the oven. Turn the oven up to 230°C/Gas 8. Lift off the foil. Transfer the lamb shoulder to a plate. Loosely re-cover with the foil. Put the lamb to rest at the back of your cooker.

6. Put a sieve over the pan of reduced stock to catch any of the vegetables that drop. Drain three-quarters of the braising juices into the stock; this is what gives your gravy the roast lamb flavour. You'll have about 500ml.

7. Add the simmered garlic to the vegetables in the roasting tray. Turn the vegetables cut side up; be careful as you do because they will be soft. Brush everything with the braising juices. Put the tray back in the oven and roast for 15–20 minutes, until the vegetables and garlic have soaked up the remaining pan juices and are lightly roasted, turning them once; be careful because they will be soft.

(continued overleaf)

8. Bring the reduced stock and lamb juices to the boil. Whisk the cornflour into the stock. Bring back to the boil. Boil, whisking constantly, for 15 seconds or until the gravy has thickened enough to lightly coat the back of a spoon. If you like your gravy thicker, add more cornflour.

9. Take the vegetables out of the oven; put the lamb back on top. Brush with the gravy; put it back in the oven for 5 minutes to glaze the top.

10. Take the lamb out of the oven. Brush it and the vegetables all over with gravy. If you're going to eat it all, you can put the shoulder on the table and tear off bits with tongs or a fork and spoon. If you want even-sized portions to keep for the subsidiary recipes, carve the shoulder as I show you (on the right).

Cook extra

If you have 2 trays, braise 2 lamb shoulders. Allow an extra 45 minutes to 1 hour, checking from time to time. (Or if you're eating alone, halve the recipe and use a half lamb shoulder; this will give you a few meals during the week.) Let the extra lamb cool, then store it in portions with the onions and gravy in your fridge for 2 days, or in the freezer, to make the subsidiary recipes. The lamb defrosts and reheats well in the microwave.

Variations

Soy and ginger lamb In a small bowl, mix 3 tbsp of soy sauce, 3 tbsp of honey and 1 heaped tbsp of grated ginger together. Brush the lamb with half of this mixture before you cover it with foil. Add the rest to the gravy. This combination doesn't go well with potatoes, so leave them out, double the carrots, and serve with rice.

Ras-el-hanout lamb with apricots and olives Season both the lamb and vegetables with ras-el-hanout. Add 12 quartered dried apricots and 15 pitted and halved olives to the sauce after you thicken it. Season the sauce with ras-el-hanout instead of pepper.

No braised lamb, gravy or onions?

You'll find specific suggestions in some of the subsidiary recipes where it is possible to make them with something instead of braised lamb. The dishes won't be quite the same, but you can replace the gravy with brown or hoisin sauce mixed with chicken stock. Replace each braised onion half with 30g of soft, sweet, sticky onions (page 161) or shop-bought onion marmalade. Don't worry about the garlic, or add a little chopped fresh garlic if you want a strong garlic flavour.

Carving the lamb

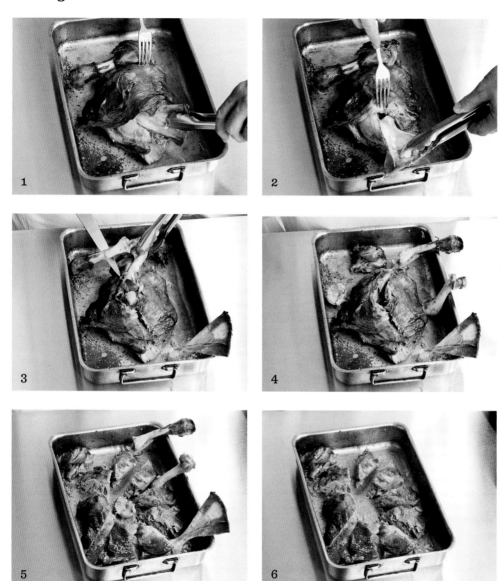

To carve the lamb shoulder into 9 portions:

1. Hold the lamb shoulder firmly with a fork. Grab the top of the shoulder blade with tongs. Twist it away from you.
2. Pull the skin away from the top with your fork. Pull the shoulder blade out.
3. Slice down the line of the bone. Lift the bone out with tongs.
4. You are now left with the boneless shoulder.
5. Cut the lamb, like a cake, into 8 portions, and your ninth is the bit that came off the bottom end of the bone in step 3.
6. Discard the bones and you are left with 9 pieces of lamb.

1/ Melting lamb, pepper, lentil & artichoke tian

A tian. I taste the word (*tee an*) and immediately I want to be in Provence and for now the quickest route runs through my kitchen. The name tian comes from the gratin dish the ingredients are baked and then served in. It is a glowing emblem of Provençal food and friendship, one that resonates with this chapter as tians were once baked in communal ovens in the same way as lamb shoulders would be braised.

For younger kids, leave out the cayenne. Or, so you can have the spice, get your kids to help you make little individual tians in ramekins. Then once you've made theirs, add the extra cayenne to yours. Good to purée or chop and freeze for babies and toddlers.

SERVES 2

Sides (pages 320–43)
Salad with the remaining artichokes
Prep ahead The tian can be made a day ahead
Prep/cooking 35–40 mins
Active time 20–25 mins

1 large red pepper, deseeded and cut into 1cm dice
4 tbsp extra virgin olive oil
2 tbsp water
400g tin chopped tomatoes
2 portions of braised lamb shoulder (page 245), cut into 1cm slices
4 braised onion halves (page 245), cut into 1cm slices
8 tbsp lamb gravy (page 245)
2 anchovies, very finely chopped (optional)
250g cooked Puy lentils (a drained 400g tin or 250g pouch)
2 braised garlic cloves (page 245)
8 tbsp sliced basil
4 artichoke hearts (from a jar or tin)
5 tbsp grated Parmesan
Salt, sugar, cayenne pepper

1. Preheat your oven to 200°C/Gas 6, position upper middle shelf.

2. First make the sauce. Get a medium-sized saucepan. Add the red pepper, 2 tbsp of the extra virgin olive oil, the 2 tbsp of water, a pinch of salt and a pinch of sugar. Cover and sweat over a medium heat for 12 minutes, stirring occasionally, until the pepper is soft. Add the tinned tomatoes. Turn the heat up to high. Bring to the boil and boil for 4–5 minutes until the sauce is very thick and almost all the liquid has evaporated. Take the pan off the heat. Season with salt, sugar and enough cayenne to make it gently spicy.

3. Next, prepare the lamb mixture. Get a medium bowl. Add the braised lamb, onions, gravy and half of the anchovies if you're using them. Stir together. Season to taste. Transfer the mixture to a medium baking dish (22 x 16cm or thereabouts) or a 20cm ovenproof pan and spread evenly.

4. Tip the lentils into the empty bowl. Add the remaining 2 tbsp of extra virgin olive oil, the garlic, 2 tbsp of the basil and the rest of the chopped anchovies if you're using them. Stir together well. Season to taste.

5. Spread the pepper and tomato sauce evenly over the lamb. Spread the lentils in an even layer over the sauce. Cut each artichoke heart into 3 slices. Lay the artichoke slices on top of the lentils and press them in lightly.

6. Using a mini chopper/processor, blend the Parmesan and remaining 6 tbsp of basil together. Sprinkle the mixture over the lentils. Bake for 15 minutes until the cheese has set in a delicate crust on top.

No braised lamb?
Replace the lamb with roast or braised chicken, duck, pork or beef. Replace the gravy with 6 tbsp chicken stock mixed with 2 tbsp of brown or hoisin sauce. Replace the onions and garlic with 120g of sticky onions (page 161) or shop-bought onion marmalade.

2/ Quick navarin of lamb with spring vegetables

What a happy coincidence that lamb and spring vegetables share our affection at the same time of year; few things are prettier or more delicious than a light stew of the two. The name comes from *navet*, the French for turnips, and I love these young, tender and bittersweet beauties in a navarin. Keep the turnips in so that the stew doesn't have an identity crisis, but feel free to change the other vegetables, or just use one. Mangetout, asparagus and pea shoots are all good in this navarin. The vegetables can be simmered in the light lamb gravy, but I prefer to boil them separately and quickly. They then join the lamb at the last minute and each flavour sings its own version of springtime.

For younger kids, cook the vegetables until tender and remove strings from sugar snaps, mangetout or beans; these all make excellent finger food. Take out sugar snaps and mangetout and the rest is good to purée or chop and freeze for babies and toddlers.

SERVES 2

Sides (pages 320–43)
None needed. For bulk, simmered new potatoes
Prep/cooking 15–20 mins
Active time 15 mins

200ml lamb gravy
   (page 245)
2 portions of braised lamb
   shoulder (page 245)
30g butter
100g small Chantenay
   carrots, halved
   lengthways, or 1 large
   carrot, peeled and cut
   into 1cm slices
2 small turnips (150g),
   peeled and cut into
   6 wedges
4 spring onions, trimmed,
   each cut into 3 lengths
50g podded peas
   (frozen are fine)
50g soya or broad beans
50g sugar snap peas
Salt and freshly ground
   black pepper

1. Boil your kettle. Get a large pot. Fill it two-thirds full with boiling water. Add salt, cover and bring to the boil. Put a colander in your sink.

2. Get a medium-sized shallow pan. Add the lamb gravy. Put it over a high heat and bring to the boil. Add the braised lamb and 20g of the butter. Bring back to the boil. Cover the pan and take it off the heat.

3. Next, cook the vegetables. Add the carrots to the boiling water. Cover, bring back to the boil and boil for 3 minutes. Add the turnips and boil for a further 2 minutes. Bring back to a rolling boil. Add all of the green vegetables. Cover and bring back to the boil. Take the lid off and boil for 3 minutes or until the vegetables are tender.

4. Drain the vegetables in the colander. Put them back into the pan. Add the remaining 10g butter. Put the pan over a medium heat for 30 seconds to dry the vegetables and glaze them with the butter.

5. Add the vegetables to the pan with the lamb. Put it back on a high heat. As soon as it comes to the boil, brush the lamb all over with the gravy. Season to taste with salt and pepper. Put the lamb into deep plates. Spoon the gravy and vegetables over the top.

3/ Quick lamb 'cassoulet'

Cassoulet is a dear old friend that I turn to for comfort. Having cooked it so often, I have simplified the classic recipe, but I always include lamb. This, however, is the first time I've made a variation solely with lamb, and pre-cooked lamb at that. The best morsel to use for this is the meat from the shank or the fattier parts of the shoulder.

For younger kids, cut some of the lamb into little chunks then set aside in smaller dishes so they can have their own mini cassoulet. Cut the rosemary as tiny as you can. For an even quicker version, mix the lamb with some low-salt baked beans, tinned corn and peas. Breadcrumbs are a good way of introducing wholemeal bread and you can add cheese to them if you like. Good to purée or chop and freeze for babies and toddlers. Use the pulse button rather than leave the motor running or the purée will be gluey.

SERVES 2

Sides None needed

Prep ahead Up to a day ahead, ready to bake. If heated from cold, bake for an extra 7 minutes

Prep/cooking 35 mins

Active time 15 mins

2 braised onion halves
   (page 245), sliced
4 braised garlic cloves
   (page 245), sliced
8 tbsp lamb gravy
   (page 245) or stock
300–400g tin cannellini,
   haricot or flageolet beans
½ x 400g tinned chopped
   tomatoes
40g butter
2 tbsp chopped rosemary
2 portions of braised lamb
   shoulder (page 245), cut
   into 2–3cm pieces
75g dry bread, cut into
   chunks (or prepared
   coarse, crisp crumbs)
3 tbsp extra virgin olive oil
Salt and cayenne pepper

1. Preheat your oven to 200°C/Gas 6, position upper middle shelf.

2. Get a medium-sized shallow pan (ovenproof if possible). Add the onion, garlic, gravy, beans and their liquid, tinned tomatoes, butter and half of the rosemary.

3. Put the pan over a high heat. Bring the mixture to the boil. Take the pan off the heat. Spread the lamb evenly over the top. Put the lid on.

4. Get your food processor. Put the bread and the remaining rosemary into it. Blend, using the pulse button, to coarse breadcrumbs. Add the extra virgin olive oil. Season to taste with salt and cayenne.

5. If your pan is ovenproof, you can just sprinkle the breadcrumbs over the lamb and beans. If not, spread the lamb and beans into a baking dish or small roasting tray, about 24 x 18cm, then scatter the breadcrumbs over the top. Bake for 15–20 minutes until crunchy and golden.

Cook extra

Make double and freeze half.

No braised lamb?

Replace the lamb with roast or braised chicken, duck or pork. Replace the gravy with 6 tbsp of chicken stock mixed with 2 tbsp of brown or hoisin sauce. Replace the onions and garlic with 60g of sticky onions (page 161) or shop-bought onion marmalade.

4/ Lamb salad with walnuts, shallots, beans & bacon

This rich, contrasting and powerful combination of flavours has the feel of southwest France. I often lust after tart salad dressings with a lick of fatty roast gravy, two apparent opposites that make a mouth-watering couple. Feel free to use just one or the other of French or flageolet beans; you could also use runners or cannellini beans. To get the best possible flavour, the French beans need to be very well drained and tossed with the dressing when they are hot so they absorb the dressing and take on its flavours.

For younger kids, make the dressing first with only a quarter of the mustard and vinegar, mix the salad, separate theirs, then add more seasoning to yours. Cook French beans until tender and offer as finger food. Good to purée or chop and freeze for babies and toddlers.

SERVES 2

Sides Warm bread

Prep ahead Dressing, except bacon, a day ahead

Prep/cooking 25–30 mins

Active time 20–25 mins

2 braised garlic cloves
    (page 245)
1 heaped tsp Dijon mustard
2 tsp red wine vinegar
2 tbsp plus 1 tsp vegetable
    oil
40g walnuts, roughly
    chopped
2 small shallots, peeled and
    thinly sliced
6 rashers of streaky bacon,
    cut into 2cm chunks
100g French beans
4 tbsp sliced flat-leaf
    parsley
½ x 400g tin flageolet or
    cannellini beans, drained
2 portions of braised lamb
    shoulder (page 245), cut
    into 6 chunks
6 tbsp lamb gravy (page 245)
Salt, freshly ground black
    pepper and sugar

1. Preheat your oven to 200°C/Gas 6, position upper middle shelf. Boil your kettle.

2. Start with the dressing. Get a large bowl. Add the braised garlic. Mash it to a purée with the back of a fork. Stir in the Dijon mustard, wine vinegar and the 2 tbsp of oil. Season to taste with salt, black pepper and sugar. Stir in the walnuts and shallots.

3. Heat a medium-sized frying pan with the remaining 1 tsp of oil. Add the bacon. Fry for 2 minutes until it is crisp but not hard. Add the bacon and fat from the pan to the dressing.

4. Get a large pot. Fill it with boiling water from your kettle. Add salt, cover and bring back to the boil. Put a colander in your sink. Cut off the tops but not the pointy ends of the French beans. Cut the beans in half diagonally. Add them to the boiling water, cover and bring back to the boil. Take the lid off and boil for 3–4 minutes or until the beans are tender. Drain them in your colander. Return the French beans to the pan for 20–30 seconds over a medium heat. Now add them to the dressing. Toss with two-thirds of the parsley.

5. Get a shallow plastic bowl (that can go in the microwave). Add the tinned beans. Put the lamb on top. Pour over the gravy. Cover with cling film. Heat in the microwave on low/medium for 5 minutes or until well heated through. Stir in the remaining parsley.

6. Scatter the French bean salad over your plates. Put the lamb on top. Spoon the flageolets and gravy over everything. Finish with a grind of pepper.

No braised lamb?
Make the French bean salad as explained above. Heat the flageolet beans for 2 minutes in your microwave and fold them into the salad. Serve with the lamb shoulder chops (see page 134) and their pan juices in place of the gravy.

5/ Sweet potato shepherd's pie

Sometimes food is just fun: fun to prepare, fun to cook and fun to eat. Actually, for me it is fun most of the time, but this recipe is not only joyful but outlandishly tasty. It is worth searching out the Mauritius masala spice blend as it's a magical mixture. Sweet potatoes cook brilliantly in the microwave and they are ready in a flash.

    This is a great recipe to introduce kids to new vegetables. Carrots, peas, corn, beans, broccoli and cauliflower can be tossed through the lamb, and you could mix parsnips, potatoes or pumpkin with the sweet potatoes. Good to purée or chop and freeze for babies and toddlers.

SERVES 2

Sides (pages 320–43)
Broccoli or Brussels sprouts or cabbage

Prep ahead To end of step 5, a day ahead. If heated from cold, bake for an extra 5 minutes

Prep/cooking 35–40 mins

Active time 25–30 mins

2 medium sweet potatoes, about 200g each
4 braised onion halves (page 245), sliced
4 braised garlic cloves (page 245), sliced
2 small portions of braised lamb shoulder, about 140g each (page 245), cut into 1–2cm slices
8 tbsp lamb gravy (page 245)
50g soft butter, plus 2 tsp to top the potatoes
Salt and ground cinnamon or (better still) Mauritius masala spice blend

1. Preheat your oven to 200°C/Gas 6, position upper middle shelf.

2. Start with the sweet potatoes. Put them on a plate that can go in your microwave. Prick them on one side with a fork. Season with salt and a pinch of cinnamon or Mauritius masala spice blend. Cover with cling film. Microwave on high for 10–12 minutes or until the sweet potatoes are soft. If you bake them in the oven they'll need 45 minutes.

3. While the sweet potatoes cook, get a medium bowl that can go in the microwave. Add the onions, garlic, lamb, 4 tbsp of the gravy, ¼ tsp of cinnamon or masala spice blend and one-third of the butter. Set aside.

4. Once the sweet potatoes are cool enough to handle, use a serrated knife to cut them in half. Get a shallow bowl. Carefully scoop most, but not all, of the sweet potato flesh out of the skins and into the bowl, using a teaspoon. Try not to break through the skins; you need fairly robust shells so that the gravy won't seep out. Get a baking tray and lay the sweet potato shells on it. Season them with salt and Mauritius masala spice blend. Mash the scooped-out flesh with the remaining butter and season to taste.

5. Heat the lamb mixture on medium in the microwave for 2 minutes or until it is hot. Stir together well and season to taste with salt. Fill the sweet potato shells with the lamb mixture. Spoon the sweet potato mash on top.

6. Put a ½ tsp-sized knob of butter on top of each stuffed potato half. Bake for 15 minutes. Heat the remaining 4 tbsp of gravy. Brush the sweet potato tops with gravy. Serve the stuffed sweet potatoes with the rest of the gravy and broccoli.

No braised lamb?

Replace the lamb with roast or braised chicken or duck. Replace the gravy with 6 tbsp of chicken stock mixed with 2 tbsp of brown or hoisin sauce. Replace the onions and garlic with 130g of sticky onions (page 161) or shop-bought onion marmalade.

6/ Warm lamb 'tagine'

You won't need the beautiful spire-shaped vessel that gives the traditional dish its name.
My 'tagine' is quick, saucy and warm with a soft scent of Morocco and it looks like a
handful of jewels has been scattered over the top. It tastes warm and exotic but feels
light and delightful. Ras-el-hanout is a mix of many spices and has the most astonishing
flavour; if you don't have any to hand, try using ginger, cardamom or a mixture of the two.

My kids enjoy the sweet combination of dried apricots, raisins and cherry tomatoes.
I use it with chicken and beef, I stir it into couscous and lentils, I add chopped vegetables
to it and I serve it with aubergines. Ras-el-hanout is one of my magical spice mixtures for
kids. Go gently with the olives, or leave them out. This dish is good to purée or chop and
freeze for babies and toddlers.

SERVES 2

Sides Couscous (page 340)

Prep/cooking 15–20 mins

Active time 15–20 mins

200ml lamb gravy (page
   245), or lamb or chicken
   stock, or half and half
2 braised onion halves
   (page 245), sliced
4 braised garlic cloves
   (page 245), sliced
50g ready-to-eat dried
   apricots, chopped
50g plump raisins
2 portions of braised lamb
   shoulder (page 245), cut
   into 2cm slices
125g baby plum tomatoes
   (½ punnet), halved
   lengthways
2 tbsp extra virgin olive oil
12 black olives, pitted
2 heaped tbsp sliced mint
Salt and ras-el-hanout

1. Get a medium-sized sauté pan or saucepan with a tight-fitting lid. Add the gravy, onion, garlic, 1 tsp of ras-el-hanout, the dried apricots and raisins. Bring to the boil. Turn the heat to low. Season to taste with salt.

2. Put the sliced lamb and tomatoes on top of the onion mixture. Spoon the extra virgin olive oil over the top. Cover and bring to the boil. Take the pan off the heat. Leave to sit for 5 minutes to warm the lamb through. If you heat it slowly like this the lamb will be soft and moist.

3. Put the pan back on the heat. Scatter the olives and mint over the top. Bring to the boil. Take the pan off the heat. Season to taste with salt and ras-el-hanout. Serve straight from the pan.

No braised lamb?

Make the 'tagine' mixture using chicken or lamb stock rather than gravy. Replace the onions with 60g of sticky onions (page 161) or shop-bought onion marmalade. Replace the braised garlic with ½ garlic clove, very finely chopped. Pan-fry 2 lamb shoulder chops (cooked as for the recipe on page 134) and their pan juices. Rest the chops, slice them thickly, then add to the tagine.

ROAST BELLY PORK

Crunchy crackling. Soft, tasty fat. Succulent, pleasantly chewy meat. I love it all. I like to serve roast pork medium. I'm not talking about rare, but a pink rosy blush, moist and smooth rather than dry and rough. The interior temperature at its thickest point needs to be 63°C; use a probe thermometer to check (see page 35).

If you can, buy belly pork from your butcher and ask him or her to take off the bones, to add to the roasting tray to get more flavour into your sauce (and eat as spare ribs). Take all the packaging off the pork when you get home, pat the skin dry and store the pork uncovered in the fridge. This dries out the skin and helps make the crackling crunchier.

When you introduce roast pork to younger kids, slice it thinly at first, and then move slowly towards chopping it into chunks. This applies to all of the subsidiary recipes. The pork is better finely chopped than puréed. It can be frozen.

SERVES 4

WITH SOME LEFT OVER

Sides (pages 320–43) Grains or mashed potatoes and roast vegetables and/or a leaf salad

Prep ahead Pork can be scored and the juice and stock reduced a day ahead

Prep/cooking 1¼ hours

Active time 45 mins

1kg boneless belly pork

1½ tbsp vegetable oil

6 medium red onions, peeled and halved

500ml pomegranate juice

1 tbsp dark soy sauce

500ml chicken stock

2 tsp cornflour

2 tbsp water

8 dried apricots, finely chopped

1 heaped tbsp chopped rosemary

20g butter

½ pomegranate, seeds extracted (optional)

Salt, freshly ground black pepper and sugar

1. Preheat your oven to 160°C/Gas 3, position upper middle shelf.

2. Get a Stanley knife. Score the pork and rub it all over with salt (see overleaf).

3. Get a thick-bottomed roasting tray or ovenproof frying pan large enough to comfortably fit the pork. Add the oil. Put the pan onto your largest burner on a high heat. Get the oil really hot. Add the pork, skin side down. Turn down the heat and fry over a medium heat for 12–15 minutes. Listen for a steady sizzle like the sound of bacon frying. Raise the heat if this sound subsides. Lower the heat if the oil in the pan begins to smoke heavily. Move the pan if one side of the pork gets hotter than the other. Lift the pork up to check the colour frequently; it may need a little longer. The crackling should be golden and look ready to eat before it goes in the oven.

4. When the crackling is ready, put the onions around the outside of the pork, rounded side down. Roast in the oven for 10 minutes. Take the pork out of the oven. Turn the onions so that they are flat side down. Turn the pork, skin side up, on top of the onions. Roast for 25 minutes.

5. While the pork roasts, make the sauce. Get a medium-sized pan. Add the pomegranate juice, soy sauce and chicken stock. Bring to the boil and boil until the liquid is reduced by two-thirds; this takes about 25 minutes. Put the cornflour into a small bowl. Mix it with the 2 tbsp water. Whisk this into the sauce. Bring to the boil, stirring constantly. Turn off the heat.

6. Once the pork is roasted to 63–66°C (check with your probe or press the pork flesh – it should feel as firm as the end of your nose), put it onto an ovenproof plate. Leave to rest for at least 10 minutes. Turn the oven up to 200°C/Gas 6. While the pork rests, put the onions back in the oven for 10 minutes or until they are soft.

(continued overleaf)

7. Turn the oven off. Put the onions with the pork. Put them in the oven and leave the door slightly open until you are ready to carve.

8. Drain the fat from the roasting tray. Add the pomegranate sauce and bring it to the boil, stirring and scraping the roasted bits from the bottom of the pan. Simmer for 1 minute. Pour the sauce back into the saucepan. Add the dried apricots and rosemary. Stir in the butter. Season to taste. For a pretty finish and a fresh touch, add the fresh pomegranate seeds.

9. Carve the pork along the scored lines. Serve with the roasted onion halves and pomegranate sauce.

Cook extra
Roast double the amount to use for the subsidiary recipes and packed lunches. If the pork has enough room in the tray and you have crisped the crackling on the hob, the extra weight doesn't change the cooking time. Strain the extra gravy, as the rosemary and apricots won't reheat well. Let the extra pork cool and then store it in portions with the onions and gravy in your fridge for up to 2 days, or in the freezer.

Variations
For the sauce, the pomegranate juice boils down to an excellent flavour and good acidity to balance the rich pork. Here are a few variations you can make by simply replacing the pomegranate juice and seeds:

Cranberry sauce Use cranberry juice and dried cranberries.

Apple sauce Use apple juice and put 2 large apple quarters per person around the pork when you turn it over. Add chopped dried apples to the sauce. You can do exactly the same with pear.

Orange sauce Use orange juice and serve the roast with fluffy couscous and a fennel and orange salad.

Plain pork gravy Put 4–6 pork bones around the outside of your pork. Replace the juice with more chicken stock. At the point when you add the reduced and thickened stock to the roasting tray, boil it for 1 minute, then transfer the gravy to the pan. Simmer it for 5 minutes with the bones in.

No roast pork, sauce or onions?
You'll find specific suggestions in some of the subsidiary recipes where it is possible to make them with something instead of roast pork. The dishes won't be quite the same but you can replace the sauce with brown or hoisin sauce mixed with chicken stock. Replace each roast onion half with 30g of soft, sweet, sticky onions (page 161) or shop-bought onion marmalade.

Scoring the pork skin

It's best to score the pork in lines as thick as the slices you want to carve, and it is much easier to do this if the skin is dry. Your crackling will separate easily along these lines and each slice gets its share. A heavy Stanley knife with a new blade makes scoring the skin much easier than it is if you use a light plastic cutter or a knife. The hard pork skin is easier to cut through if your blade only has to move a small distance, which is why I start from the middle and cut to the edge then turn it around to complete each line. If you can, ask your butcher to do this for you.

1. Start with the blade of your Stanley knife in the middle of the pork belly on one side. Score the pork skin, starting from the middle and cutting to the edge, all the way through the skin and halfway through the fat, widthways, 11 times at even intervals, to give you 12 slices.
2. Turn the pork around. Start at the point you cut from in the centre and cut through to the other edge. Repeat to extend all the cuts to the other edge.
3. The pork should now be evenly scored from end to end.
4. Rub salt all over the pork.

1/ Belly pork with carrots, dried apricots, olives & lemon

I was nineteen when I arrived in Besançon. I'd caught the wrong train and was fined for having the wrong ticket. At the hotel, I was paying for a day what I thought I'd be paying for a week. Too scared to come out of my hotel room, I read about food in Elizabeth David's *French Provincial Cooking*. I read about the carrot salad so many times I could almost taste it. After 2 days I left the hotel and found a language course that was starting soon. The college arranged a room with a local family. It had an electric ring and a fridge and I had my own knives. The family took me shopping. I bought carrots, lemons and Provençal olive oil that smelt like flowers. I still remember the taste of that salad. It felt like a victory. I've added dried apricots and olives to help the combination spark the pork into life, but this meal has its roots in that hotel room and Elizabeth David's words.

This is an excellent meal for younger kids, as it is sweet and gentle. Good to chop for toddlers; take out the pork and you can purée it for babies. Both can be frozen.

SERVES 2

Sides (pages 320–43)
Plain grains or olive oil mashed potato and/or green vegetable or salad

Prep ahead Carrots can be cooked a day ahead

Prep/cooking 30 mins

Active time 20–25 mins

2 large carrots (250–300g), peeled

1 large garlic clove, peeled and sliced

250ml water

3 roast onion halves (page 261), cut into 1.5cm slices

6 dried apricots, cut into 5mm slices

6 tbsp pork sauce (page 261)

12 black olives, pitted

Zested or grated zest and juice of ½ lemon (1 tbsp)

2 tbsp extra virgin olive oil

200g roast pork (page 261), in 1 piece

2 tbsp sliced basil

Salt and sugar

1. Preheat your oven to 200°C/Gas 6, position upper middle shelf.

2. Start with the carrots. Cut them in half lengthways, then cut each half into 1cm slices. Get a medium-sized ovenproof frying pan (with a lid). Add the carrots, garlic and the 250ml water. Cover, bring to the boil and boil for 10–12 minutes until the carrots are soft. By this time the liquid should have reduced by about half. If there is a lot more liquid, take the lid off the pan and boil to evaporate more of it. Take the pan off the heat.

3. Add the onions, dried apricots, pork sauce, olives, lemon zest, lemon juice and extra virgin olive oil to the carrots. Stir. Put the pork in the centre and turn it in the sauce to coat it all over. Make sure the pork is fat side up. Put the pan on a high heat and bring to the boil. Cover and put the pan in the oven for 5 minutes.

4. Take the lid off. Leave the pan in the oven for a further 5 minutes. Take the pan out of the oven. Carve the pork into 8 slices. Put it onto your plates. Stir the basil into the carrots. Season to taste with salt and sugar. Spoon the carrot mixture onto the pork.

Cook extra
Chop the pork into lardon-sized chunks. Mix it into the carrot mixture and sauce with plain or tasty grains. Season with extra lemon.

No roast pork?
Use pork belly slices (grilled as for the recipe on page 222) or a pan-fried pork chop (see page 83). Rest for 2 minutes in the carrot mixture once you have added all the ingredients in step 3. Put the pork onto plates, heat the carrot mixture, add the basil and spoon it over the pork. Replace the onions with 90g of sticky onions (page 161) or shop-bought onion marmalade. For the sauce, use 4 tbsp of chicken stock mixed with 2 tbsp of hoisin sauce.

2/ Fried belly pork with sweet potato & red pepper relish

This little belly shows Slow Cook Sorcery off perfectly. The meat becomes barbecued, sticky and almost burnt on the outside while the colours are a Halloween display. It looks particularly beautiful served in a black pan. I played with the idea of softening the red pepper but the textures were better in layers, from the crisp to chewy to the soft surrender of the sweet potatoes.

For younger kids, the pork may be a little too chewy, but slice it thinly and get them to give it a go. Don't sprinkle cayenne on their portions. The combination of sweet potatoes, peppers and raisins should be irresistible. This meal can be finely chopped for toddlers.

SERVES 2

Sides (pages 320–43) None needed. A crisp salad is nice
Prep ahead Sweet potatoes can be simmered a day ahead
Prep/cooking 25 mins
Active time 25 mins

400g sweet potatoes
   (2 small or 1 large),
   scrubbed, halved if large
   and cut into 1cm slices
½ red pepper, deseeded
   and cut into 1cm dice
Zested or grated zest of
   ½ lime and 1 tbsp juice
2 tbsp extra virgin olive oil
4 tbsp raisins
4 tbsp chopped coriander
6 tbsp pork sauce
   (page 261)
1 tbsp plus 1 tsp vegetable
   oil
200g roast pork (page 261),
   cut into 6 slices
20g butter
4 spring onions, trimmed
   and thinly sliced
Salt and cayenne pepper

1. Preheat your oven to 200°C/Gas 6, position upper middle shelf. Boil your kettle.

2. Start with the sweet potatoes. Get a medium-sized pan. Fill it with boiling water from your kettle. Add salt, cover and bring to the boil. Put a colander in your sink. Add the sweet potato slices to the boiling water. Turn the heat to medium and simmer for 5–7 minutes or until they are just tender. Drain the sweet potato slices in the colander.

3. While the sweet potatoes simmer, make the red pepper relish. Get a small bowl. Add the red pepper, lime zest, lime juice, extra virgin olive oil, raisins and chopped coriander. Season to taste with salt and cayenne.

4. While the sweet potatoes drain, start the pork. Put 2 tbsp of the pork sauce into a small bowl. Get a large frying pan. Add the 1 tsp of oil and get it really hot. Add the pork and fry for 1 minute. Turn. Fry for 30 seconds. Brush each slice generously with the pork sauce. Fry for 30 seconds each side. Put the pork slices onto a plate. Wipe out the pan with kitchen paper.

5. Put the pan back on a high heat. Add the remaining 1 tbsp of oil. Once the pan is very hot, add the sweet potato slices in a single layer. Fry over a medium-high heat for 2 minutes. Turn the slices. Add the butter. Fry for 30 seconds more or until the butter bubbles, but doesn't quite start to brown. Add the spring onions. Toss them with the sweet potatoes for 30 seconds until they soften slightly.

6. Put the pork on top of the sweet potatoes. Pour the remaining 4 tbsp of pork sauce into the side of the pan rather than over the potatoes, so that it soaks into the potatoes a little but leave the tops nice and crisp. Turn off the heat. Scatter the red pepper relish over the top. Serve straight from the pan.

No roast pork?
Use grilled belly pork slices (grilled as for the recipe on page 222). Replace the sauce with 4 tbsp of chicken stock mixed with 2 tbsp of hoisin sauce.

3/ Hot pork, leek & potato salad with fried egg

When I worked for Jean Bardet in Tours, there was a day of the year he called La Saint Cochon. On that day, the pig that he'd been rearing all year would be killed and bits of the walking meal would be splattered through the kitchen into *rillettes*, black pudding and these marvellous *rillons* – salted belly cubes that are first roasted to taste like good gravy, slowly braised in pork fat, then fried and served with a salad. I've used the roast belly pork to go for the same taste here; the potatoes and egg make it into a generous meal.

For younger kids, leave the vinegar out of their dressing. No good to purée or freeze.

SERVES 2

Sides None needed

Prep ahead Potato salad, without yoghurt, a day ahead

Prep/cooking 25–30 mins

Active time 25–30 mins

350g waxy potatoes, such as Charlotte or Anya (about 10), halved

2 small leeks (240g), trimmed and cut into 2cm slices

½ medium red onion, peeled and thinly sliced

1½ tbsp red wine vinegar

1 tsp Dijon mustard

4 small gherkins, cut into 3mm slices

2 tsp capers (optional)

3 tbsp pork sauce (page 261)

2 tbsp plain yoghurt

1 tbsp vegetable oil

200g roast pork (page 261), cut into 4cm x 3cm chunks

100g cooked chestnuts, cut into 5mm slices

4 tbsp sliced parsley

2 eggs

40–50g mixed salad leaves

Salt, sugar and freshly ground black pepper

1. Start with the potatoes. Boil your kettle. Put a colander in your sink. Get a medium-sized pan. Fill it with the boiling water. Add salt and bring back to the boil. Add the potatoes and bring back to the boil. Lower the heat to medium and simmer for 8 minutes. Add the sliced leeks. Bring back to the boil. Simmer for 6 minutes or until the leeks and potatoes are tender.

2. While the potatoes and leeks simmer, make the dressing. Put the red onion into a shallow dish. Add a generous pinch each of salt, sugar and pepper. Stir in the wine vinegar, mustard, gherkins and capers if you're using them.

3. Drain the potatoes and leeks in the colander. Shake them well to make sure that they are as dry as possible. Add them to the dressing with the pork sauce. Toss gently but well. Stir in the yoghurt. Season to taste.

4. Get a medium-sized frying pan. Add the oil and get it really hot. Add the pork. Fry for 1 minute; be careful as it may spit a little. Add the chestnuts. Fry for 1 minute or until the chestnuts are hot and the pork is golden. Turn off the heat. Add the parsley and turn the pork and chestnuts until they are well coated in parsley (I use a fish slice for this). Add the pork and chestnuts, but not the frying fat, to the salad.

5. Put the pan back on a medium heat. Break the eggs into the fat. Cover the pan and fry over a low heat for 1½–2 minutes until the whites are just set.

6. Toss the salad leaves with the potato salad and divide between your plates. Put the fried eggs on top. Sprinkle salt onto the eggs.

No roast pork?

Replace the pork with 150g of bacon lardons or rashers – a little less than the pork as the full quantity would be overpowering. Replace the pork sauce with 2 tbsp of chicken stock mixed with 1 tbsp of brown sauce.

4/ Roast belly pork with vegetables & noodles

Toss them, twirl them, suck them up – noodles are an irresistible way to turn roast pork into a playful plateful. These noodles are based on chow mein, but I'm not trying to give you a traditional version, just one that I like to eat. I cut the vegetables into long strips where possible so they can get into a tasty tangle with the noodles. I must have my bean sprouts, but I'm happy to vary the other vegetables – try cabbage, radishes, mangetout, sugar snaps and broccoli or cauliflower stalks and florets.

Noodles are enormous fun for kids and a good way to introduce new vegetables. Make carrots, parsnips and courgettes into ribbons using a vegetable peeler. Dice any vegetables that you can't cut into ribbons. No good to purée.

SERVES 2

Sides None needed

Prep/cooking 25 mins

Active time 25 mins

1 medium carrot, peeled

200g roast pork (page 261), cut into 4cm x 2cm chunks

2 tbsp hoisin sauce

1 heaped tsp Chinese five-spice powder

1 tbsp cornflour

1 tbsp vegetable oil

2 nests of egg noodles

2 tsp sesame oil

1 red onion, peeled and cut into 5mm slices

1 red pepper, deseeded and cut into 5mm slices

3 tsp grated ginger

4 tbsp water

100g bean sprouts

2 small pak choi, halved and each half cut into 3 lengthways

2 tbsp dark soy sauce

2 tbsp pork sauce (page 261)

1. Slice the carrot lengthways into ribbons with a speed peeler. Put on a plate next to your cooker with the rest of your prepared ingredients, a plate to put the pork on and a bowl to drain the fat into. Once you start frying you don't want to have to search for anything. Boil your kettle. Fill a large pan with boiling water. Fill and boil the kettle again. Put a colander in the sink.

2. Next, prepare the pork. Put the pork chunks into a shallow bowl. Add the hoisin sauce and Chinese five-spice powder. Stir until the pork is well coated. Add the cornflour. Stir until it is all stuck to the sides of the pork.

3. Get a large sauté pan or wok. Add the oil and get it really hot. Add the pork and stir-fry for 2–2 ½ minutes until it is dark brown.

4. While the pork stir-fries, add the noodles to the pan of boiling water and boil for 2–3 minutes until cooked but just firm to the bite. Drain them in your colander. Put the colander on top of the pan you cooked the noodles in. Pour the boiled water from your kettle over the top. Put the pan lid over the noodles in the colander. They will finish cooking and stay warm.

5. Put the pork onto a plate. Drain the fat. Don't worry if there are some dark, sticky bits on the bottom of the pan, they will loosen off in the next step.

6. Add 1 tsp of the sesame oil, the red onion, red pepper, 2 tsp of the ginger and 3 tbsp of the water to the pan. Cover and sweat over a high heat for 2 minutes. Take off the lid. Add the bean sprouts, carrot ribbons, pak choi and the remaining 1 tbsp of water. Cover for 10 seconds. Take off the lid. Stir-fry for 30 seconds until the pak choi and carrots wilt.

7. Add the cooked noodles, pork, soy sauce, pork sauce and the remaining 1 tsp of sesame oil and 1 tsp of ginger. Turn rather than stir everything together with a pair of tongs. Serve straight from the pan.

Cook extra

Double the recipe and freeze half. The greens will discolour and won't be as crisp but it will still taste great warmed through in the microwave.

5/ Roast pork 'petit salé' with bacon & parsley butter

Petit salé is a great French stew, a peasant's pot that deserves the sort of universal adulation that dishes like coq au vin enjoy. It is basically boiled bacon with lentils, so a French take on pea and ham soup if you like. I was delighted that my Slow Cook Sorcery version worked so well. To give it a taste of tradition, all I needed to do was fry some bacon and get it to shout saltily into the lentils.

Puy lentils are ideal for kids. Properly cooked or pre-cooked, they are always soft enough and easy to eat. Start with pieces of cooked carrots that they can pick up with a fork and bite, then cut them smaller if you need to. This is a good meal to chop for toddlers. Take out the pork and bacon and you can purée it for babies. Both can be frozen.

SERVES 2

Sides None needed

Prep ahead To end of step 4, at least a day ahead

Prep/cooking 25–30 mins

Active time 15–20 mins

2 medium carrots, peeled, halved lengthways and each piece cut into 3

1 tsp vegetable oil

4 rashers of streaky bacon

250ml chicken stock

250g cooked Puy lentils (a drained 400g tin or 250g pouch)

4 roast onion halves (page 261)

200g roast pork (page 261), cut into 10 chunks

30g butter

1 garlic clove, peeled and finely chopped

3 tbsp chopped parsley

Salt, sugar and freshly ground black pepper

1. Preheat your oven to 200°C/Gas 6, position upper middle shelf.

2. Start with the carrots. Get a medium-sized saucepan. Add the carrots, a pinch of salt and a pinch of sugar. Cover just to the level of the carrots with water. Put the lid on. Bring to the boil and boil for 7–8 minutes until the carrots are tender. Take off the lid. Boil for 3–5 minutes until the water has all evaporated. Turn off the heat.

3. While the carrots boil, start the bacon. Get a medium-sized ovenproof frying pan (with a lid). Add the oil and get it really hot. Add the bacon rashers. Fry for 30 seconds. Turn and fry for 30 seconds on the other side. Lift the bacon out and put it on a plate.

4. Add the chicken stock to the frying pan. Bring to the boil. Add the lentils and bring back to the boil. Lower the heat and simmer for 1 minute. Turn off the heat. Taste and season well with pepper; you'll not need much salt. Put the bacon, carrots, onions and pork on top of the lentils.

5. Get a small bowl. Add the butter, garlic and parsley. Stir them together. Dab the butter over the top of everything in the pan. Cover the pan and put it in the oven for 5 minutes. Take off the lid. Heat in the oven for a further 3–4 minutes until the butter is melted. Brush the melted butter all over everything. Serve straight from the pan.

Cook extra

Make twice the recipe up to the end of step 4. Freeze half.

No roast pork?

Fry 4 pork sausages until they are pale gold and half-cooked, then add them in place of the pork in step 4. Replace the onions with 120g of sticky onions (page 161) or shop-bought onion marmalade.

6/ Sticky pork, soy, ginger & garlic broth

This dish was inspired by plastic food. At Tokyo airport, I was pulled into a restaurant by plates of plastic food illustrating each dish on the menu. I was served a bowl of pork with noodles in 2 minutes and it looked exactly like its plastic sibling in the window. Almost shockingly, it was delicious, hot, revitalising food. To this imitation I've added glazed pork and ginger at the end for a refreshing blast. I serve the lime on the side as I like to start adding it about halfway through eating to freshen the broth as it cools. Serve the broth as hot as you can. Somehow the hotter it is, the more refreshing it is.

Noodles are tremendous for younger kids. Let them make a mess, let them slurp and have fun. Serve theirs before you add the chilli and ginger at the end. Good to chop and freeze, but not to purée.

SERVES 2

Sides None needed

Prep ahead Broth, a day ahead

Prep/cooking 25 mins

Active time 20–25 mins

3 tbsp dark soy sauce

4 tsp grated ginger

2 garlic cloves, peeled and thinly sliced

750ml vegetable stock

2 large mushrooms (120g), cut into 1cm slices

6 spring onions, trimmed and cut into 1cm slices

100g asparagus (4–5 spears), trimmed, each cut into 5 diagonally

2 packets pre-cooked thick ribbon rice noodles

1 tbsp honey

2 tsp vegetable oil

200g roast pork (page 261), cut into 4cm x 2cm chunks

½ mild red chilli, deseeded and finely chopped

4 tbsp sliced coriander

2 lime quarters

1. Start with the broth. Get a medium-sized saucepan. Add 2 tbsp of the soy sauce, 2 tsp of the ginger, the garlic and the vegetable stock. Bring to the boil, lower the heat to medium and simmer for 2 minutes. Add the mushrooms, spring onions and asparagus to the pan. Cover and bring back to the boil. Take off the lid and boil for 1 minute. Add the noodles and bring back to the boil. Turn off the heat.

2. Get a small bowl. Add the remaining 1 tbsp of soy sauce and the honey. Stir together. Put the bowl next to your cooker.

3. Get a small frying pan and put it on a high heat. Add the oil and get it really hot. Add the pork. Fry for 1 minute over a very high heat until it is pale golden. Take the pan off the heat. Drain the fat.

4. Add the soy and honey mixture to the pan and put it back on the heat; watch carefully because this mixture will reduce and burn very quickly. Toss the pork for 1½ minutes until the pork is coated and glazed with the soy and honey.

5. Use tongs to put the noodles and vegetables into bowls. Bring the broth back to the boil. Add the remaining 2 tsp of ginger, the chilli and coriander. Pour the broth into the bowls. Scatter the pork cubes over the top. Serve with the lime quarters.

Cook extra
Double the broth recipe. Before adding the vegetables, pour half of the broth into a container to freeze for another time.

No roast pork?
Replace the pork with any cooked meat or tofu. Or pan-fry a pork chop (see page 83), cut it into cubes and glaze it with soy sauce and honey as per the recipe.

GLAZED ROAST DUCK

This sweet and sour roast duck has powerfully flavoured flesh, scrumptious skin, lots of gravy, and it pretty much looks after itself in the oven. I'm always amazed by how much flavour permeates through a duck's flesh when you put aromatics in the cavity – in this case, ginger peel and Chinese five-spice. Cranberry gives the gravy a vibrant sheen that you would swear came from port, and a sour note to contrast with and enhance the duck's rich flesh.

Give younger kids the softer breast meat and make sure that the ginger is very finely grated or scrape off the glaze. If they are not used to eating spices, halve the quantities and have some plain rice on hand to mellow the flavours. Good to chop or purée and freeze.

SERVES 4–6

Sides (pages 320–43) Rice
Prep/cooking 2¼ hours
Active time 45 mins

1 Gressingham or Barbary duck, about 2kg, with giblets
1½ tsp Chinese five-spice powder
2½ tbsp grated ginger (peelings kept)
1 tbsp vegetable oil
2 medium onions, peeled and cut into 3cm dice
3 garlic cloves, halved
500ml cranberry juice
4 tbsp dark soy sauce
300ml plus 3 tbsp water
4 tbsp soft brown sugar
Grated zest and juice of 1 lime (2 tbsp)
300g cooked beetroot (see page 327), halved
2 small pears, halved and cored
2 small sweet potatoes, washed and halved
1 heaped tsp cornflour
Salt and brown sugar

1. Preheat your oven to 220°C/Gas 7, position middle shelf.

2. Start with the duck. Cut out the wishbone (as for chicken, see page 230). Rub ¼ tsp of salt into the duck's skin. Put ½ tsp of the Chinese five-spice, the ginger peelings and a pinch of salt into its cavity.

3. Get a large roasting tray. Put the duck in the tray. Roast for 45 minutes.

4. While the duck roasts, make the stock for the gravy. Get a medium-sized saucepan. Add the oil and get it hot. Add the onions and giblets. Fry over a medium-high heat, stirring frequently, for 7–10 minutes until they are golden. Add 1 tbsp of the ginger, the garlic, cranberry juice, soy sauce and the 300ml water. Bring to the boil. Lower the heat to medium. Simmer rapidly for 1 hour.

5. Meanwhile, make the glaze. In a small bowl, mix the brown sugar, lime zest, half the lime juice, the remaining 1½ tbsp of ginger and the remaining 1 tsp of Chinese five-spice together. Put the glaze, a pastry brush, a bowl for hot fat and a big plate next to your cooker.

6. When the duck's 45 minutes are up, take it out of the oven. Use a roasting fork to lift it onto the big plate. Tip three-quarters of the fat from the roasting tray into your bowl. Put the duck back into the roasting tray. Put the beetroot, pears and sweet potatoes, cut side down, evenly around the outside of the duck. Brush them with the duck fat. Roast for 45 minutes.

7. Get the roasting tray out of the oven. Turn the oven up to 230°C/Gas 8. Turn the sweet potatoes, beetroot and pears cut side up. Brush them and the duck with the glaze. Roast for 5 minutes or until everything is glazed and golden. Watch carefully during this time; it will burn quickly.

8. Transfer the duck, vegetables and pears to your big plate. Turn the oven to its lowest setting. Put the plate in the oven and leave the door slightly ajar to keep everything warm.

(continued overleaf)

9. Drain half the fat from the roasting tray; be careful not to lose the roasting juices that lie beneath the fat. Strain the giblet stock into the roasting tray. Discard the giblets, vegetables and spices. Keep the saucepan handy. Put the roasting tray on a high heat. Bring the stock to the boil.

10. Mix the cornflour with the 3 tbsp of water. Stir it into the gravy little by little. Bring to the boil, stirring constantly. Simmer for 2 minutes or until the gravy is thick enough to coat the back of a spoon. Pour the gravy into your saucepan. Bring it back to the boil. Season to taste with salt, sugar and the remaining lime juice. You'll have 350–400ml. I like to present the duck in its roasting tray.

11. Carve the duck into 4 portions (see right). Or to carve it into 6 portions, follow the technique for roast chicken (on page 231). Serve half a leg and half a breast with the gravy, beetroot, sweet potatoes and pears.

Variations and tips

To get a golden skin The duck should be as dry as possible, so take the duck out of its packaging the minute you get home and dry it very well. It is best if you can keep the duck uncovered in the fridge to dry it for at least 2 days before you roast it. Wipe it inside and out with kitchen paper if necessary. After this there are no real secrets. If the skin is dry and you roast it for the time I tell you to, it will be thin, glazed and golden. There's no need to slash and score or poke the skin to help release the fat, the heat of the oven will do this for you.

Keep the duck fat Save the duck fat you drain; there are uses for it in the subsidiary recipes and it's great to have on hand to fry potatoes and eggs in.

Plain roast duck and potatoes If you'd like a plain roast duck, simply leave out the ginger, Chinese five-spice and lime, and replace the juice in the gravy with chicken stock. Then cook the potatoes on a separate tray (as for the roast chicken on page 229).

Orange duck Put a halved orange in the cavity. Replace the cranberry juice with orange juice, leave out the Chinese five-spice, replace the lime juice and zest with orange, and the brown sugar with orange marmalade. The sauce will go beautifully with the vegetables in this recipe.

No roast duck, gravy or onions?

You'll find specific suggestions in some of the subsidiary recipes where it is possible to make them with something instead of the roast duck. The dishes won't be quite the same but you can replace the gravy with brown or hoisin sauce mixed with chicken stock. Replace each roast onion half with 30g of sticky onions (page 161) or shop-bought onion marmalade.

Carving the duck

To serve 4 with 110–140g meat from the carcass and some skin extra:

1. Hold the duck firmly with a fork. With your very sharp knife, cut off the top bits of both wings, leaving just the winglets. Cut off the legs.
2. Cut each leg through the joint where the thigh and drumstick meet.
3. Find the breast bone. Slice down either side of it.
4. Carve each breast off the carcass and cut through the joint at the top.
5. Cut each breast in half into winglets and boneless tip.
6. Serve each winglet with a thigh and each drumstick with a boneless breast tip. Scrape the meat off the carcass. Make stock with the carcass (see page 25).

1/ Buttery duck with peppers & garlic toast

Sweet and sour duck and onions on toast: this is a real lip-smacking meal. The rich and saucy duck gets glossy, first with the gravy and then with the butter, and these glorious juices soak into the hot and more buttery toast. You take a messy bite and silence descends. This recipe is good for leftover roast chicken as well.

Give kids breast rather than leg meat as it is softer. Cut the quantity of garlic or chop it and the thyme very finely, as I do. For younger kids, cook the onion and pepper until very soft and chop it finely. Can be chopped or puréed and frozen for babies and toddlers.

SERVES 2

Sides (pages 320–43) Crisp leaf salad. For bulk, sweet potatoes or double the bread
Prep ahead Pepper mixture and garlic butter, up to 2 days ahead
Prep/cooking 30 mins
Active time 20 mins

4 garlic cloves, peeled and cut in half
1 large red pepper, deseeded and thinly sliced
1 medium red onion, peeled and thinly sliced
1 tbsp duck fat or vegetable oil
100ml plus 2 tbsp water
30g butter
2 tbsp thyme leaves
½ baguette
2 portions of roast duck (page 277)
6 tbsp roast duck gravy (page 277)
Salt

1. Preheat your oven to 200°C/Gas 6, position upper middle and lower middle shelves.

2. Get a medium-large ovenproof shallow pan. (If you don't have one, you will need to start in a medium-sized saucepan then transfer everything to a baking dish.) Add the garlic, red pepper, red onion, duck fat, 100ml water and a pinch of salt to the pan. Cover and sweat over a medium-high heat, stirring occasionally, for 15 minutes or until the vegetables are soft and the water has nearly all evaporated. Turn up the heat. Fry for 2–3 minutes until the pepper and onion barely begin to brown around the edges. Take the pan off the heat. Season to taste with salt.

3. Take the lid off. Pick out half the garlic. Chop it finely. Get a small bowl. Add the chopped garlic, butter and thyme. Mix it all together with a fork.

4. Split the half-baguette, then cut each piece in two diagonally. Spread the cut surfaces with half of the garlic butter.

5. Slice the duck thickly, or leave it whole if it's on the bone. Add the gravy and the 2 tbsp of water to the pepper and onion in the pan. Bring to the boil. Put the duck on top. Brush it with the gravy from the pan. Spread the second half of the garlic butter over the top. Cover the pan and put it on the upper middle shelf in the oven. Put the bread on the shelf below. Bake for 8 minutes. Serve straight from the pan with the bread on the side.

No roast duck?

Roast and rest 2 duck breast fillets (as for the recipe on page 186). For the gravy, use 2 tbsp of brown or hoisin sauce mixed with 4 tbsp of chicken stock. Add the gravy and water to the pepper and onion in step 5, bring to the boil, then stir in the garlic butter. Slice the duck breasts and then serve with the pepper, onion and gravy.

2/ Duck with fried mushrooms, bacon, chestnuts & parsley

This is an autumnal treat that you could eat all year round. Alongside the bacon, mushrooms and chestnuts I've used sweet potatoes, as they are easiest to portion, but pumpkin and squash would work well in their place, as would parsnips, carrots and Jerusalem artichokes. If you have some sweet potatoes left from the main roast (page 277) you could use them for this; the beetroot and pear would also be very good. The cooked chestnuts come in vacuum-pack bags and the leftovers can be frozen.

For younger kids I would leave out the bacon – just eat it yourself. The first time you serve it, water down the gravy, and chop the mushrooms, chestnuts and parsley. I leave the skin on the sweet potatoes, but it is easy to take it off. Take out the bacon, then it's good to purée or chop and freeze for babies and toddlers.

SERVES 2

Sides Bread to mop up the gravy
Prep/cooking 30–35 mins
Active time 25–30 mins

2 small sweet potatoes (140–160g each)
6 tbsp roast duck gravy (page 277)
4 tbsp water
2 portions of roast duck (page 277)
2 tsp duck fat or vegetable oil
100g bacon lardons or 4–5 rashers of streaky bacon, cut into slices
100g button mushrooms, trimmed to the size of the chestnuts
10 cooked chestnuts
1 knob of butter (15g)
6 heaped tbsp flat-leaf parsley leaves with stalks
Salt and freshly ground black pepper

1. Preheat your oven to 200°C/Gas 6, position upper middle shelf. Boil your kettle.

2. Start with the sweet potatoes. Fill a medium-sized saucepan with boiling water. Add salt and bring back to the boil. Put a colander in your sink. Cut the sweet potatoes in half lengthways, then cut each half into 1.5cm slices. Add the sweet potato slices to the boiling water. Lower the heat to medium and simmer for 5–7 minutes or until just tender. Drain the sweet potato slices in your colander.

3. While the sweet potatoes simmer, get a medium-sized ovenproof frying pan (with a lid). Add the gravy and the 4 tbsp of water. Bring to the boil. Add the duck pieces, skin side down. Cover the pan and put it into the oven for 5 minutes. Take the lid off. Turn the duck skin side up. Brush it with the gravy. Put the pan back in the oven, uncovered, for 5 minutes. If you're not ready with the rest of the meal, turn the oven off and leave the door slightly ajar; the duck will happily wait for you.

4. Get a large frying pan. Add the duck fat and get it really hot. Add the bacon and fry over a high heat for 1 minute. Add the mushrooms and fry for 2 minutes. Scoop the bacon and mushrooms onto a plate, leaving as much oil in the pan as possible.

5. Add the sweet potato slices to the pan in a single layer. Fry over a high heat for 2 minutes or until golden. Turn them. Fry for 30 seconds. Add the mushrooms, bacon, chestnuts and butter to the pan. Fry for 1 minute more. Add the parsley and toss for 10 seconds until it just begins to wilt. Season to taste.

6. Put the duck on your plates. Spoon the sweet potato, mushroom, chestnut and bacon mixture over the duck. Pour the gravy over everything.

3/ Duck with roast gravy, fried potatoes & chorizo

The gutsy potatoes and chorizo get worked into a frenzy when they jump into the dish with the sweet and sour duck and roast gravy. Eat this when you're a bit chilly or sad and you need a culinary cuddle. Although I sometimes serve it with a salad on the side, it is the sort of meal that seems a little offended by anything except a chunk of bread to mop up the last of its goodies and gravy.

For younger children, use less vinegar in the recipe, 1–2 tsp is plenty. Chop the garlic and rosemary very finely. They may find the chorizo a bit too chewy, but you can just eat that for them or offer some very thinly sliced on the side. Take out the chorizo, leave out the cayenne and the meal is good to purée or chop and freeze for babies and toddlers.

SERVES 2

Sides (pages 320–43) Dark green salad and/or bread to mop up the gravy and dressing

Prep/cooking 30–35 mins

Active time 25 mins

300g (about 8) waxy potatoes, such as Charlotte, washed and halved lengthways
6 tbsp roast duck gravy (page 277)
4 tbsp water
2 portions of roast duck (page 277)
2 tbsp duck fat or vegetable oil
1 small chorizo sausage (50–60g), cut into 5mm slices
2 garlic cloves, peeled and finely chopped
2 tbsp red wine vinegar
4 rosemary stems, needles only (1 tbsp), chopped
Salt and cayenne pepper

1. Preheat your oven to 200°C/Gas 6, position middle shelf. Boil your kettle.

2. Start with the potatoes. Put a colander in your sink. Fill a medium-sized saucepan with boiling water. Add salt and bring back to the boil. Add the potatoes and bring back to the boil. Turn the heat to low and gently simmer for 10 minutes or until tender. Drain in your colander.

3. Get the chorizo, garlic, wine vinegar, rosemary and a bowl for hot fat ready next to your cooker.

4. While the potatoes simmer, get a medium-sized ovenproof frying pan (with a lid). Add the gravy and the 4 tbsp of water. Bring to the boil. Add the duck, skin side down. Put the lid on the pan and put it into the oven for 5 minutes. Take the lid off. Turn the duck so that it is skin side up. Brush it with gravy. Put it back in the oven, uncovered, for 5 minutes. If you're not ready with the rest of the meal, turn the oven off and leave the door slightly ajar; the duck will happily wait for you.

5. Get a large frying pan. Add 1 tbsp of the duck fat and heat. Add the potatoes in a single layer, then turn them so they are all cut side down. Fry over a medium heat, without turning, for 4–5 minutes or until they get a nice thick golden crust. Take the pan off the heat. Spoon the potatoes onto a plate then tip away the fat.

6. Add the chorizo, garlic and wine vinegar to the pan. Standing well back, sauté the chorizo over a medium-high heat as the vinegar bubbles, reduces and coats and glazes it. Turn off the heat. Add the remaining 1 tbsp of duck fat, the potatoes and chopped rosemary. Toss everything together well. Season to taste with salt and cayenne. Serve with the duck and gravy.

No roast duck?

Roast and rest 2 duck breast fillets (as for the recipe on page 186). For the gravy, use 2 tbsp of brown or hoisin sauce mixed with 4 tbsp of chicken stock. Serve the duck breasts with the potatoes and chorizo.

4/ Duck patties with hoisin sauce & stir-fried vegetables

After you've eaten the breasts and legs, there are still juicy morsels that you can pick off the duck carcass, and this patty is their perfect nesting place. The duck mixture is irresistibly rich and you'll have a hard time not eating it all before you've made your patties. The idea for this recipe started as a duck burger because I had a delicious but half-lost memory of eating duck with sweet chewy buns. In the end we ate the duck with supermarket brioche spread with hoisin sauce and it was a feast.

For younger kids, chop rather than slice the onions, cut the stir-fry vegetables into smaller pieces and leave out the sesame seeds. Serve their portions of stir-fry with a tiny touch of the ginger, then add the remaining ginger and chilli to yours. The duck mixture, but not the vegetables, is good to purée or chop and freeze for babies and toddlers.

SERVES 2

Sides Hoisin sauce. For bulk, brioche

Prep ahead Patties can be shaped, ready to bake, a day ahead

Prep/cooking 35–40 mins

Active time 25–30 mins

300g onions (2 medium), peeled and thinly sliced

1 tbsp plus 1 tsp duck fat or vegetable oil

6 tbsp water

1 large carrot, peeled

2 heads of pak choi

4 spring onions, trimmed

110–140g shredded roast duck (from the carcass), plus the skin, cut into 2cm slices (page 277)

4 tbsp raisins

2 tbsp sliced mint

1 tbsp hoisin sauce

2 tbsp sesame seeds

1 tsp grated ginger

½ mild red chilli, deseeded and finely chopped

1 crisp red apple

Salt

1. Preheat your oven to 200°C/Gas 6, position upper middle shelf.

2. Get a medium-sized shallow pan. Add the onions, the 1 tbsp of duck fat, 2 tbsp of the water and ¼ tsp of salt. Cover and sweat the onions over a medium heat for 10 minutes until they are soft. Take off the lid. Turn up the heat. Fry the onions, stirring frequently, for 4–5 minutes, until they are golden brown; don't let them burn. Take the pan off the heat.

3. While the onions sweat, prepare the vegetables. Cut the carrot into ribbons with your speed peeler. Cut the pak choi in half lengthways, then cut each half into 3 wedges. Halve the spring onions lengthways, then cut each half in two.

4. Put the cooked onions into a large bowl. Add the shredded duck, raisins, mint, hoisin sauce and sesame seeds. Mix together well. Season to taste. Get a non-stick tray. Shape the duck mixture on the tray into 2 large patties (as shown on the top plate) or 6 small ones (shown the bottom plate). The mixture is soft and fragile; don't worry, this is how it should be. Put the duck skin on the tray with the patties. Bake for 10 minutes.

5. When you are ready to serve, heat a large frying pan or wok. Add the remaining 1 tsp of duck fat and get it really hot. Add the vegetables, ginger and remaining 4 tbsp of water (which helps to steam the vegetables and stop the ginger burning). Cover and steam over a high heat for 1½ minutes. Take the lid off. Stir-fry for 1 minute. Add the chilli and season to taste with salt. Take the pan off the heat.

6. Cut the apple in half, take out the pips with the tip of a knife and slice it thinly. Mix half the apple slices with the stir-fry steamed vegetables. Divide this mixture between your plates. Use a fish slice to lift the fragile duck patties on top of the vegetables. Scatter the remaining apple slices and the pieces of duck skin over the top. Serve with brioche and hoisin sauce for spreading.

5/ Roast duck, roast peach, walnut & goat's cheese salad

In this robust, summery salad, the duck is delightful with roast peaches, which are softened and set off by the goat's cheese. Peaches become more acidic as they bake, which supplies the twin bursts of fruit and bite that both duck and cheese love. I stir gravy into the dressing so that each leaf and nut is gently caressed and scented with the duck's flavour. This attention to seasoning brings a dish together, allowing each individual element to retain its identity while creating a delicious whole. I used a mild, melting goat's cheese with a rind; a shy blue like torta di dolcelatte would also work well.

Younger kids will have a problem with the salad leaves, so start them just with the baby gem and put chopped duck and peaches inside. The croûtons are mini cheese on toast, so you could top them with chopped duck and peach. No good to purée or freeze.

SERVES 2

Sides For bulk, extra croûtons, or the rest of the baguette

Prep ahead Dressing, a day ahead

Prep/cooking 30–35 mins

Active time 20 mins

1 tbsp honey

1 tbsp red wine vinegar

1½ tbsp walnut oil, plus extra for brushing

2 small peaches, halved and stoned, each half cut into 3 wedges

3 tbsp roast duck gravy (page 277)

10 walnut halves

2 tbsp water

2 portions of roast duck (page 277)

10 slices from a baguette

50–60g soft goat's cheese

1 head of baby gem, leaves separated

40g mixed salad leaves (½ small packet)

Salt and freshly ground black pepper

1. Preheat your oven to 200°C/Gas 6, position upper middle and lower middle shelves. Boil your kettle.

2. Start with the dressing. Get a small bowl. Add the honey, wine vinegar and 1½ tbsp of walnut oil. Mix together. Season to taste with salt and pepper.

3. Get a medium-sized baking tray. Put the peach wedges in a line at the back of the tray, leaving 2–3cm between each one. Brush with the dressing. Put the tray on the upper middle oven shelf. Bake the peaches for 10 minutes.

4. Get a medium-sized ovenproof frying pan. Add the gravy, walnuts and the 2 tbsp of water. Bring to the boil. Take the pan off the heat. Add the duck and brush it with walnut oil. Put the pan in the oven on the lower middle shelf for 5 minutes.

5. Next, brush the baguette slices with walnut oil. Put the blade of a small sharp knife into a mug of boiling water. Slice the goat's cheese in half lengthways, then cut each half into 5 slices. Dip the hot blade between each slice. Put each slice of goat's cheese on top of a baguette slice.

6. Once the peaches have been in the oven for 10 minutes (and the duck for 5 minutes), take the tray with the peaches out of the oven. Put the cheese topped baguette slices at the front of the tray. Put it back in the oven and bake with the peaches and duck for another 5 minutes.

7. Transfer the duck from the gravy to your chopping board. Cut it into 10 chunks. Add the gravy to the walnut dressing and whisk it in.

8. Put the baby gem and salad leaves into a shallow dish. Toss them with two-thirds of the dressing. Put the salad on your plates. Top with the duck, peaches and croûtons. Brush the duck with dressing. Spoon the remaining dressing and the walnuts over everything.

Cook extra
The duck, peaches, goat's cheese and leaves make a great wrap.

6/ Warm duck, beetroot & orange salad with cranberry salsa

Here the dressing and accompaniments flatter the duck all the way from first sight to the final mouthful of mingled juice. Dried cranberries are the chewy jewels over deep purple beetroot and vibrant slices of orange. I was very tempted to fiddle and put something green on the plate but I resisted, even though rocket or watercress would give the duck a peppery climax.

For younger kids, leave most or all of the onion out of the dressing, separate theirs and then add the onion to yours. Chop rather than slice the beetroot and orange, and add a tablespoonful of water to the sauce. Chop or purée and freeze, without the onion, for babies and toddlers.

SERVES 2

Sides (pages 320–43) Dark green salad. For bulk, tasty or plain grains

Prep ahead Salsa, up to 2 hours ahead

Prep/cooking 20–25 mins

Active time 15 mins

4 tbsp roast duck gravy (page 277)

2 tbsp orange or cranberry juice

2 portions of roast duck (page 277)

½ medium red onion, peeled and very finely diced

½ tsp caster sugar

1 tbsp balsamic vinegar

2 tbsp extra virgin olive oil

1 heaped tsp grated ginger

4 tbsp dried cranberries or raisins

300g cooked beetroot (see page 327)

1 orange

Salt, sugar and freshly ground black pepper

1. Preheat your oven to 200°C/Gas 6, position upper middle shelf.

2. Start with the duck. Get a medium-sized ovenproof frying pan (with a lid). Add the gravy and fruit juice. Bring to the boil. Add the duck pieces, skin side down. Cover the pan and put it into the oven for 5 minutes. Take the lid off. Turn the duck skin side up. Brush it with the pan juices. Put it back in the oven, uncovered, for 5 minutes. If you're not ready with the rest of the meal, turn the oven off and leave the door slightly ajar; the duck will happily wait for you.

3. While the duck heats, make the salsa. Get a medium bowl. Add the red onion, sugar, balsamic vinegar, extra virgin olive oil, ginger and dried cranberries. Stir well. Season to taste with salt, sugar and pepper.

4. Slice the beetroot thinly. Spread the slices over your plates. (If you prefer them hot, slice them first then heat them in the microwave.)

5. Get a small bowl and a sharp knife. Zest or grate the orange zest into the salad. Cut the top and bottom off the orange so that it sits flat on your board. Cut away the peel in strips, being sure to remove all of the white pith. Cut the orange in half and then slice each half into 6 slices. Lay the orange slices on the beetroot.

6. Lift the duck out of the gravy and put it on your chopping board. Cut the pieces into 10 chunks (if it's a leg or wing on the bone, leave it whole). Put the duck on top of the beetroot and orange. Spoon over the gravy, then the cranberry salsa.

No roast duck?
Roast and rest 2 duck breast fillets (as for the recipe on page 186). For the gravy, use 2 tbsp of brown or hoisin sauce mixed with 2 tbsp of chicken stock, the fruit juice and the duck resting juices. Slice the duck breasts and serve with the beetroot and orange and the cranberry salsa.

BRAISED MACKEREL

Mackerel is plentiful, full flavoured, firm textured, versatile, cheap and full of healthy goodies. It also happens to be the only fish that I have ever caught on purpose in the UK. Braising is an outstanding way to cook fish. Get your fishmonger to fillet the mackerel for you and remove the little bones. If you prefer to eat the fish without its skin, braise it with the skin on to keep the flesh moist, then remove it. This recipe works well with sardine or herring fillets, but you'll need 2 or 3 times as many to match the weight of the mackerel.

For younger kids, don't season their fillets with cayenne, but still add a little to the sauce. Try introducing new vegetables by adding them to the tomato sauce with the onions and garlic. A brilliant meal to purée or chop and freeze for babies and toddlers.

SERVES 4

Sides (pages 320–43)
Hot baguette or simmered potatoes, pasta or any grains and/or a leaf salad

Prep ahead Once cooked, the mackerel will keep in the fridge for 2 days. It can also be frozen

Prep/cooking 1 hour 50 mins

Active time 25 mins

2 medium onions, peeled and cut into 5mm dice

4 large garlic cloves, peeled and thinly sliced

4 strips of orange zest and juice of 1 orange (5–6 tbsp)

4 tbsp extra virgin olive oil

400g tin chopped tomatoes

2 tsp tomato purée

300ml chicken or vegetable stock

4 large or 8 very small mackerel fillets (at least 110g per portion)

4 tbsp wine vinegar

Salt, cayenne pepper and sugar

1. Preheat your oven to 120°C/Gas ½, position upper middle shelf.

2. Start with the tomato sauce. Get a medium-sized saucepan. Add the onions, garlic, orange zest, extra virgin olive oil and a pinch of salt. Cover and sweat over a medium heat for 7–10 minutes until soft. Add the orange juice. Boil until nearly dry. Add the tinned tomatoes, tomato purée and stock (first rinse out the tomato tin with the stock). Season lightly with salt, cayenne and sugar. Bring to the boil. Boil for 30 seconds. Take off the heat.

3. Get a shallow ovenproof dish or roasting tray large enough to hold the mackerel in a single layer. Pour in the tomato sauce. Season the mackerel fillets with salt and cayenne. Brush them on the flesh side with the wine vinegar. Push them into the sauce, flesh side down, to make sure that they are submerged up to the skin. Brush a thin coating of sauce over the top of each mackerel fillet. Braise for 1 hour, 20 minutes. Baste the mackerel fillets with the sauce. Serve straight from the pan.

Seasoning transformations
Try flavouring the tomato sauce and seasoning the mackerel fillets with freshly cracked black pepper, chilli powder, curry powder, fennel seeds, dill seeds, smoked paprika, cumin, coriander seeds, ginger, lemongrass, grated horseradish or harissa. Or add a little magic by spreading the mackerel with tapenade, pesto, green curry paste or melted garlic butter.

No mackerel, no sauce?
To make any of the subsidiary recipes, if you can't get or don't have the time to braise the mackerel, you can use bought smoked mackerel fillets. For the tomato sauce, either use a good bottled or tinned thick and chunky tomato sauce, or the tomato compote on page 177.

Cook extra
Double the sauce to give you 4 extra portions of sauce that you can eat with pasta. Add olives, capers and anchovies too for a hearty puttanesca sauce. Or double the whole recipe and freeze half.

1/ Creamy mackerel, tomato, potato & onion bake

As you'll see elsewhere, I have a lingering love affair with tartiflette. This old alpine creation is a mountain of bacon, cream, wine, cheese and onions, the most exquisite gluttony. But however much I might like to, I can't put bacon in every recipe, and here I've decided that oily mackerel will be my bacon from the sea. So this meal is a nod to the comfort and fun of tartiflette, eased into a panful of enormous flavour. You can bake it in an ovenproof frying pan or start off in a pan and then transfer it to a baking dish.

This a good recipe to introduce oily fish to kids – try breaking the mackerel up and mixing it through the sauce rather than leaving it in whole pieces. You can make individual bakes, like little pies, so that each kid can have their own portion. For younger kids, finely chop rather than slice the onions. An excellent dish to purée or chop and freeze for babies and toddlers.

SERVES 2

Sides (pages 320–43) Dark green or crisp leaf salad

Prep ahead Let the potatoes go cold once cooked, then the gratin can be assembled a day ahead

Prep/cooking 40 mins

Active time 15–20 mins

450–500g waxy potatoes, such as Charlotte or Maris Peer, peeled and cut into 1cm slices

2 medium onions, peeled and cut into 1cm slices

2 large garlic cloves, peeled and sliced

1 tbsp extra virgin olive oil

8 tbsp tomato sauce from the mackerel (page 293)

150g whipping cream

2 portions of braised mackerel fillets (page 293), each cut into 4–5cm pieces

6 tbsp sliced flat-leaf parsley

60g Cheddar, grated

Salt and cayenne pepper

1. Preheat your oven to 220°C/Gas 7, position upper middle shelf. Boil your kettle. Put a colander in your sink.

2. Start with the potatoes, onions and garlic. Fill a medium-sized saucepan with boiling water from your kettle. Add salt and a big pinch of cayenne. Bring back to the boil. Add the sliced potatoes, onions and garlic. Bring back to the boil. Cover, turn the heat to low and simmer gently for 7–8 minutes or until the potatoes are tender. Drain thoroughly but carefully in your colander, so as not to break the potatoes up.

3. Get a baking dish, about 24 x 18cm, or medium-sized ovenproof frying pan. Brush it with the extra virgin olive oil. Put the potatoes and onions into the dish. Put the dish into the oven for 5 minutes to dry the potatoes. Season to taste with salt and cayenne.

4. Get a medium bowl. Add the tomato sauce and cream and stir them together. Season to taste with salt and cayenne.

5. Take half the potatoes, onions and garlic out of the dish. Spread the remainder out evenly in the dish so the base is completely covered. Cover the potatoes with half the tomato sauce and cream mixture. Put the mackerel and 3 tbsp of the parsley on top.

6. Layer the second half of the potatoes and onions over the mackerel. Finally, spread the remaining tomato sauce and cream mixture over the potatoes and onions. Sprinkle the remaining parsley and the cheese over the top. Bake for 20 minutes or until golden.

2/ Hot mackerel & chickpea pâté with courgettes & basil

I often lust after the traditional potato and salt cod brandade, but this hot, rich, slightly spicy mackerel pâté with a good waft of garlic gives it a run for its money. The final texture can be as rough or smooth as you like. If you just fancy some comfort food and can't be bothered with the greens, feel free to make double the recipe of brandade, some more toast and then forget the rest.

For younger kids, use less cayenne and lemon juice and make the purée as smooth as you can. The toast can also be made with Cheddar cheese. The baby gem leaves make lovely boats or holders for the courgettes or brandade. Without the baby gem, this meal is good to purée or chop and freeze for babies and toddlers.

SERVES 2

Sides None needed

Prep ahead Pâté can be made a day ahead

Prep/cooking 30–35 mins

Active time 25–30 mins

400g tin chickpeas

2 garlic cloves, peeled and finely chopped

4 tbsp extra virgin olive oil, plus extra for brushing

2 tbsp lemon juice

2 portions of braised mackerel fillets (page 293), 1 portion cut into 4, the other skinned

6 tbsp grated Parmesan

2 thick slices of bread (I use pain de campagne)

1 baby gem lettuce, leaves separated

1 medium, firm courgette, halved, then cut into 1cm slices

4 tbsp tomato sauce from the mackerel (page 293)

4 tbsp sliced basil

Salt and cayenne pepper

1. Start with the pâté. Get a small pan. Add half the chickpeas, all of their liquid, the garlic and 2 tbsp of the extra virgin olive oil. Bring to the boil and boil very fast for 2–3 minutes until the liquid has nearly all been absorbed by the chickpeas; only 3–4 tbsp should remain.

2. Get a small food processor. Add the chickpea mixture and 1 tbsp of the lemon juice. Blend for 2 minutes until smooth. Flake the flesh from the skinned portion of mackerel fillet into the blender. Purée for 1 minute until smooth. (It will look like hummus with tiny strands of mackerel.) Season to taste with salt and cayenne. Put the pâté into a small bowl ready to heat in your microwave, or in a small pan to heat on your hob.

3. Get a medium plate. Sprinkle the Parmesan on it. Brush the bread slices on both sides with extra virgin olive oil. Press both sides of each slice into the Parmesan so that the cheese sticks to the bread. Keep the Parmesan that remains on the plate to add to the courgettes.

4. Put the baby gem leaves on your serving plates. Heat the chickpea and mackerel pâté. Get a medium-sized non-stick frying pan. Add 1 tbsp of extra virgin olive oil and get it warm. Add the bread and fry over a low to medium heat for 1 minute on each side or until it is golden. Put the bread on your plates.

5. Add the remaining 1 tbsp of extra virgin olive oil to the pan. Add the courgettes. Sauté over a medium heat for 1 minute. Add the 4 pieces of mackerel fillet and the rest of the chickpeas. Sauté for 1 minute. Add the tomato sauce and sauté for 1 minute. Add the remaining 1 tbsp of lemon juice and the basil. Sprinkle the remaining Parmesan over the top. Season to taste.

6. Spoon the mackerel, courgette and chickpea mixture onto the baby gem leaves – the idea is to warm and dress the leaves. Spoon the hot mackerel pâté onto the side of your plates.

3/ Mackerel with salad cream & boiled eggs

This bold assembly is full of ways to make the ingredients taste more intensely of themselves. The sauce was originally based on one that is made with tuna and olive oil in the Languedoc region of France. I then decided I wanted to keep it in England so it became an elegant salad cream with plenty of bite. I added the olives because I can't resist them with boiled eggs and I love to see their black sparkle next to the yellow yolks. The fennel seeds are optional. I've found that they are either loved or hated. The potatoes will be just as happy with a vigorous grind of pepper.

For younger children, leave out half of the vinegar in the dressing, serve their meals, then add more vinegar to your taste. The fennel seeds may be too chewy, so take them out. Take out the spring onions to purée or chop and freeze the meal for babies and toddlers.

SERVES 2

Sides Bread

Prep/cooking 30–40 mins

Active time 20–25 mins

12 small waxy potatoes (300g), such as Charlotte or Maris Peer, halved lengthways

2 tbsp extra virgin olive oil

1 tsp fennel seeds (optional)

4 tsp red wine vinegar

8 spring onions, trimmed, each cut into 3, top third sliced

3 large tomatoes

2 portions of braised mackerel fillets (page 293), each cut into 4 widthways, tail ends skinned (for the dressing)

2 large eggs

1 tsp mustard

3 tbsp tomato sauce from the mackerel (page 293)

1 tbsp water

4 tbsp crème fraîche

14 black olives, pitted

Salt and freshly ground black pepper

1. Preheat your oven to 200°C/Gas 6, position upper middle shelf. Boil your kettle.

2. Start with the potatoes. Put them into a medium-sized frying pan with their cut side facing up. Cover with enough water to submerge them, no more. Add 1 tbsp of the extra virgin olive oil, the fennel seeds, if using, 2 tsp of the wine vinegar and a pinch of salt. Cover and bring to the boil. Lower the heat to medium. Simmer rapidly for 7–8 minutes until tender. Remove the lid. Turn the potatoes cut side down. Add the white spring onions. Turn up the heat. Boil for 10–12 minutes until the liquid has almost all evaporated and coats the potatoes and onions like a glaze. Turn off the heat. Toss in the middle green spring onions and sliced tops. Season.

3. Halve or quarter the tomatoes lengthways. Put the tomatoes, cut side up, along the back of a non-stick baking tray. Brush them with the remaining 1 tbsp of extra virgin olive oil and a little salt. Bake for 6 minutes. Take the tray out of the oven. Put the 6 mackerel pieces (not the tail ends) in front of the tomatoes. Bake for 4 minutes.

4. Get a small saucepan. Fill it with boiling water. Add the eggs. Simmer for 8½ minutes. Drain. Peel under running water (just so you don't burn your hands, not to cool the eggs). Cut each egg into quarters.

5. While everything cooks, make the dressing. Get a blender or small food processor. Add the skinned mackerel tails, mustard, tomato sauce, the remaining 2 tsp of wine vinegar, the 1 tbsp of water and the crème fraîche. Blend for 1 minute until smooth; add 1–2 tbsp of water if necessary to get the texture of salad cream. Season to taste. If you don't have a small blender, mash it all together with a fork.

6. Spread the dressing over your plates. Put the glazed potatoes, spring onions, tomatoes, mackerel and olives on top. Put the egg quarters around the plates at even intervals.

4/ Mackerel, prawn, chorizo & lentil 'gumbo'

It was a cold day in October and I wanted to bring out the mackerel's warm and cosy side. I craved a stew, but a light one. I thought back to the gumbo Jess and I ate on our honeymoon in New Orleans and I decided this would be a good place to start. By the end, though, the only similarity was that I'd combined seafood, sausage and spice. We sat down to eat and we left the winter to set in outside while we feasted. For a simpler version you can make this recipe without the prawns; just use double the amount of mackerel.

For younger kids, leave out the cayenne. They may also find the chorizo and prawns too chewy, so give them a little to try or just eat them yourself. That apart, this is a great meal for kids, into which you could introduce other cooked vegetables, such as carrots, parsnips and sweet potatoes, finely chopped and cooked with the onions and garlic. Take out the prawns and chorizo to purée or chop and freeze for babies and toddlers.

SERVES 2

Sides Bread
Prep ahead Lentil mixture, except prawns, a day ahead
Prep/cooking 20–30 mins
Active time 15–25 mins

1 heaped tbsp thyme leaves
    or 1 tsp dried thyme
350ml chicken stock
10 tbsp tomato sauce from
    the mackerel (page 293)
1 tbsp tomato purée
250g cooked lentils
    (a drained 400g tin or
    250g pouch)
125g baby plum tomatoes
    (½ punnet), halved
2 portions of braised
    mackerel fillets (page
    293), each cut into 4
60g small chorizo sausage
    (3cm in diameter), cut
    into 5mm slices
8 raw shelled king prawns
75g sugar snap peas,
    de-strung
3 tsp extra virgin olive oil
Salt and cayenne pepper

1. Boil your kettle.

2. Start with the broth. Get a medium-sized shallow pan. Add the thyme, chicken stock, tomato sauce and tomato purée. Bring to the boil. Add the lentils. Stir in ⅛ tsp of cayenne and a pinch of salt. Bring back to the boil. Add the baby plum tomatoes. Bring back to the boil. Lower the heat to medium and simmer for 1 minute.

3. Put the mackerel, chorizo and prawns in a single layer on top of the broth. Gently press them into the liquid. Put the lid on but leave it slightly ajar so that some of the steam can escape. Poach over a low heat for 4 minutes; don't let the liquid even simmer. Turn the prawns halfway through. Check that the prawns are pink, and therefore cooked through. Turn off the heat, cover and leave to sit for 2 minutes.

4. While the mackerel and prawns poach, get a medium-sized saucepan. Fill it with boiling water. Add salt and bring back to the boil. Add the sugar snap peas. Bring back to the boil and boil for 3–4 minutes until they are tender. Drain and return the sugar snaps to the pan. Sauté for 10 seconds. Add 1 tsp of the extra virgin olive oil. Season with salt. Add more cayenne if you like it hot.

5. Add the sugar snap peas to the 'gumbo'. Spoon it into deep plates. Trickle the remaining 2 tsp of extra virgin olive oil over the top.

5/ Mackerel & couscous baked in cabbage with ras-el-hanout

The idea for this dish springs from Provence's playful *petits farcis*. I add freshness and light with a lemon dressing that seasons the cabbage on its way from the oven to the table. Using leaves as a wrapper is a lovely way to make the gutsy couscous elegant, easy to serve and it helps to retain the heat as you eat. I have made similar combinations using lentils or rice in place of the couscous. The cabbage leaves can be replaced with large lettuce leaves or pak choi. You could also bake the mixture inside tomatoes, peppers or courgettes.

For younger kids, it's best to use the very tender inner leaves of the cabbage. The couscous mixture may well be a good way to introduce them to fish – start by flaking it into tiny pieces. This recipe is no good to purée, but the couscous mixture will freeze.

SERVES 2

Sides (pages 320–43)
None needed. A hot cabbage salad is nice
Prep/cooking 30–35 mins
Active time 20–25 mins

100g couscous
1 tsp ras-el-hanout
150ml plus 8 tbsp water
6 large cabbage leaves
Zested or grated zest of
    1 lemon and 2 tbsp juice
4 tbsp plus 2 tsp extra
    virgin olive oil
2 tbsp sliced mint
10 prunes, cut into 1cm
    dice
2 portions of braised
    mackerel fillets
    (page 293)
8 heaped tbsp tomato sauce
    from the mackerel
    (page 293)
4 tbsp orange or tomato
    juice
12 black olives, pitted
1 tbsp tiny capers, rinsed
8 tbsp water
Salt

1. Preheat your oven to 200°C/Gas 6, position upper middle shelf. Boil your kettle.

2. Start with the couscous. Get a large bowl. Add the couscous, a pinch of salt and ½ tsp of ras-el-hanout. Pour 150ml boiling water over the top. Cover with a plate. Leave for 5 minutes.

3. Meanwhile, fill a medium-sized saucepan with boiling water from your kettle. Add salt and bring back to the boil. Put a colander in your sink. Add the cabbage leaves to the pan and boil for 3–4 minutes or until tender. Drain in your colander. Run cold water over the leaves until they are cool enough to handle.

4. Next, make the dressing. Get a small bowl. Add the lemon zest and juice, the 4 tbsp of extra virgin olive oil and the mint. Mix together. Season to taste with salt.

5. Add two-thirds of the dressing to the couscous with the prunes. Add the mackerel, breaking it up; don't worry about scraping the tomato sauce off the skin. Mix well. Season to taste with salt. Cut 5cm off the hard rib at the base of the cabbage leaves. Slice this thinly and mix it into the couscous.

6. Put the cabbage leaves on your worktop with the inside of the leaf facing upwards like a cupped hand. Fill each leaf with one-sixth of the couscous mixture. Close each leaf to make a tight parcel. Turn them over.

7. Get a medium-sized ovenproof shallow pan. (If you don't have one, heat the sauce in a small saucepan then pour it into a baking dish.) Add the tomato sauce, fruit juice, the remaining ½ tsp of ras-el-hanout, the olives, capers and the 8 tbsp of water. Bring to the boil. Turn off the heat.

8. Add the cabbage parcels to the pan. Brush them all over with the remaining 2 tsp of extra virgin olive oil. Cover with a lid or foil and bake for 8 minutes. Uncover and bake for 4 minutes. Brush the remaining dressing over the cabbage parcels. Serve straight from the pan.

6/ Mackerel & 'full English breakfast' pie

Bacon and mackerel are an odd but irresistible couple. Here I've added eggs and beans, then lit them up with a flash of pepper. There are more dominant flavours here than I'd usually combine, but they work together like a group of muscular men happy in each others' company. It's also a slightly fishy excuse to feed my bacon and egg addiction.

I've had huge success with this pie for kids. You can cut the cooked pies, make smaller pies, or even better, get kids to make their own. No good to purée or freeze.

SERVES 2

Sides Hot haricot beans (to use up the rest of the tin) with lots of butter and pepper

Prep ahead The puff pies can be made 20 minutes ahead, no longer or the pastry will go soggy

Prep/cooking 30–35 mins

Active time 15–20 mins

½ x 320–375g pack pre-rolled puff pastry (35 x 23cm)

½ x 300g tin haricot beans or baked beans (100g drained weight)

1½ tsp coarsely ground black pepper (or more if you like it hot)

6 tbsp tomato sauce from the mackerel (page 293)

2 eggs, plus 1 egg yolk

1 tbsp milk

2 portions of braised mackerel fillets (page 293)

3 rashers of streaky bacon, cut in half

Knob of butter (15g)

Salt

1. Preheat your oven to 220°C/Gas 7, position upper middle shelf.

2. Start with the puff pastry. Unroll it carefully and cut into 4 rectangles, about 17 x 13cm. Get a baking tray. Line it with greaseproof or non-stick paper. Put 2 pastry rectangles on it. Put the tray in the coldest part of your fridge; the pastry will be much easier to work with when it is cold. (Freeze the other 2 rectangles for another use.)

3. Get a medium bowl. Add the haricot beans and ½ tsp of pepper. Mash the beans slightly with a fork, so that they will soak up the sauce a little. Add the tomato sauce. Mix together, seasoning with salt.

4. Next make the egg wash. In a small bowl, mix the egg yolk and milk together with a fork. Brush the pastry very lightly all over with the egg wash.

5. Spread the tomato and bean mixture over the centre of the pastry rectangles, on a slight diagonal, to roughly the same size as the mackerel fillet, leaving a 3–4cm clear margin. Put the mackerel fillets on top.

6. Turn the tray so that the mackerel is side on. Break the tail and stick the broken bit underneath if it doesn't quite fit. Pull the top left corner of the pastry on the tail side over the tail and stick it onto the side of the pastry closest to you; this should cover the bottom third of the mackerel with pastry diagonally. Take the bottom right corner of the pastry on the opposite side at the top of the fillet, turn it over the mackerel and stick it down well, stretching the pastry a little if you need to; this should cover the top third of the mackerel. You'll still see the middle of the fillet.

7. Brush the pastry all over with egg wash. Sprinkle ½ tsp of pepper over each pie. Bake for 5 minutes. Put the bacon rashers at the front of the baking tray. Bake for another 7–9 minutes until the pastry is golden.

8. Once the pies are almost ready, heat a small frying pan over a medium heat with the butter. Add the eggs. Fry over a low heat for 1½–2 minutes until the whites are just set. Serve them and the bacon on top of the pies.

RICHLY BRAISED LENTILS

I spend a lot of time with Puy lentils and I've learnt how they can be both glamorous and comforting, and are delicious hot or cold. These lentils grow and absorb their cooking liquor as they braise and swell gently as they rest. Their flavour is forward to the point of being brazen and they taste even better the next day.

For younger kids, you can mix the lentils with mince or tomato sauce to start with, and they are a good way to introduce new, finely chopped, vegetables. The alcohol is cooked out. The lentils can be puréed or chopped and frozen for babies and toddlers.

SERVES 2

Sides (pages 320–43)
Pasta, plain grains, potatoes or couscous

Prep ahead Up to 2 days ahead. The braised lentils can also be frozen

Prep/cooking 1 hour 20 mins

Active time 20 mins

2 medium onions, peeled and cut into 5mm dice
4 garlic cloves, peeled and finely sliced
2 tbsp extra virgin olive oil
700ml plus 2 tbsp water
3 tbsp tomato purée
375ml gutsy red wine, such as Cabernet Sauvignon
250g Puy lentils
400g tin chopped tomatoes
2 bay leaves
Salt, sugar and freshly ground black pepper

1. Preheat your oven to 170°C/Gas 3.

2. Start with the onions. Get a large ovenproof pan. Add the onions, garlic, extra virgin olive oil and the 2 tbsp of water. Cover the pan and put it on a medium heat. Sweat for 7–10 minutes until the onions and garlic are soft, adding an extra 2 tbsp of water if they start to dry out. Take the lid off.

3. Add the tomato purée. Turn the heat to high. Fry, stirring constantly, for 2 minutes, watching carefully, until the tomato purée is lightly browned. When it smells like sun-dried tomatoes, it's ready.

4. Add the red wine and lentils. Bring to the boil and boil until the wine has reduced by half. Add the tinned tomatoes, bay leaves and the 700ml water. Boil for 5 minutes.

5. Cover the pan and put it into the oven. Braise the lentils for 30 minutes. Take off the lid. Braise for a further 30 minutes, stirring twice, or until the lentils are tender but still holding their shape.

6. When the lentils are cooked, the liquid should be thick and be just at the level of the lentils. If there is too much liquid, boil for 1–2 minutes. Season to taste with salt, sugar and pepper. Cover the pan tightly and leave to sit for 10 minutes to allow the lentils to soak up the seasonings.

Storage

Store the lentils in the quantities you intend to use in plastic containers. If you're freezing some to make fritters, drain these lentils, then add the liquid to the remaining lentils, which will make them much more saucy. Store in the fridge for up to 2 days, or in the freezer for up to 3 months.

Seasoning transformations

Try seasoning with orange zest and fennel seeds; smoked paprika, harissa or ras-el-hanout; lemon zest and finely chopped dried apricots; thyme, rosemary or sage; cinnamon and nutmeg; garlic butter, pesto or tapenade.

Cook extra

Double the recipe and freeze half. The lentils freeze brilliantly.

1/ Stuffed mushrooms in puff pastry, creamy porcini & lentils

Whoever said life is too short to stuff a mushroom wants to taste this and think again.

Mushrooms are a hard sell for kids, mainly because of their texture, but you can bake the lentil pies in ramekins or ovenproof cups; just make sure you seal the pasty well on the rim. Without the pastry this can be puréed or chopped and frozen for babies and toddlers.

SERVES 2

Sides (pages 320–43)
None needed. For bulk, bread. Broccoli or cabbage would be good

Prep ahead The pies can be made, ready to bake, up to 2 hours ahead

Prep/cooking 30–35 mins

Active time 20–25 mins

½ x 320–375g pack
   pre-rolled puff pastry
   (35 x 23cm)
4 large mushrooms (about
   250g), each 8–10cm in
   diameter
300g braised lentils
   (page 307)
5 tbsp sliced flat-leaf
   parsley
8 tbsp crème fraîche
   (full or half fat)
1 egg yolk
1 tsp milk
10–12g dried porcini
   (½ small pack), soaked
   in 150ml boiling water
   for 5 minutes
Salt and freshly ground
   black pepper

1. Preheat your oven to 220°C/Gas 7, position upper middle shelf. Boil your kettle.

2. Start with the puff pastry. Unroll it carefully and cut into 4 rectangles, about 17 x 13cm. Get a baking tray. Lay 2 pastry rectangles on it and put in the coldest part of your fridge; the pastry will be much easier to work with when it is cold. (Freeze the other 2 rectangles for another time.)

3. Next, prepare the mushrooms. Get a baking tray and a large bowl. Put the mushrooms, rounded side down on the tray. Pull out their stalks. Chop the stalks into lentil-sized pieces. Put them in the bowl. Add 200g of the lentils and 3 tbsp of the parsley. Season to taste with salt and pepper.

4. Season the mushrooms. Put 1 tbsp of crème fraîche into the cup of each one. Put a quarter of the lentil mixture on top of the crème fraîche in each mushroom and squash them down. Turn one mushroom on top of the other quickly so the lentils don't fall out, to make 2 sandwiches.

5. Next, prepare the egg wash. Get a small bowl. Add the egg yolk and milk. Mix together with a fork.

6. Brush the puff pastry rectangles with egg wash. With the egg-washed side facing down, lay the pastry rectangles over the top of the mushrooms. Cup your hands over the top and mould the pastry around the sides of each mushroom sandwich, making sure you seal the join where the 2 mushrooms meet; you may need to stretch the pastry slightly on the narrower side of the rectangles. Brush the pastry generously all over with egg wash. Bake for 18–20 minutes or until the pastry is golden.

7. While the mushrooms bake, make the porcini and lentil sauce. Lift the porcini out of their soaking water onto a board. Carefully pour the water into a small saucepan, leaving behind any grit at the bottom; throw this away. Chop the porcini into lentil-size pieces. Add the chopped porcini to the pan. Add the remaining 100g lentils. Put the pan over a high heat. Bring to the boil, turn the heat down and simmer for 1 minute to heat the lentils through. Take the pan off the heat.

8. When the pies are ready, stir the remaining 4 tbsp of crème fraîche and 2 tbsp of parsley into the lentil sauce. Warm the sauce through. Season to taste. Serve with the mushrooms.

2/ Lentil chilli with roast squash & sweet & sour marmalade

No drab chilli and rice here. Instead I've gone for an all-out, no-holds-barred glamour show. The bright, spicy and oh-so-tasty lentils contrast beautifully with the golden slices of tender squash – roasted to intensify their colour and flavour. Crowning this bounty and dressing the watercress is the extravaganza of the savoury marmalade. Squash vary in size, so take what you need for the recipe and roast the rest at the same time. It will be lovely with mozzarella or ricotta, wrapped in bacon or Parma ham, or on pasta or risotto.

For younger kids you'll need to leave the chilli off their squash before you roast it, but be sure to season yours. Leave the chilli out of their lentils and marmalade, serve theirs, then add it to yours. Good to purée or chop and freeze for babies and toddlers.

SERVES 2

Sides None needed
Prep ahead Marmalade, up to 2 days ahead, keep in fridge
Prep/cooking 45 mins
Active time 30 mins

½ medium butternut
   squash (450–500g)
2 tsp vegetable oil
3 tbsp extra virgin olive oil
4 dried apricots, very
   finely sliced
2 tbsp pumpkin seeds
200g tin sweetcorn,
   drained (or 1 boiled cob,
   kernels removed, see
   pages 329–30)
2 tbsp honey
⅓ red chilli, deseeded and
   finely chopped
Grated zest of ½ lemon and
   2 tbsp juice
125g baby plum tomatoes
   (½ punnet), quartered
400g braised lentils
   (page 307)
4 tbsp plain yoghurt
40g watercress
Salt, sugar and chilli powder

1. Preheat your oven to 220°C/Gas 7, position upper middle shelf.

2. Start with the squash. Peel it with a speed peeler. Scoop out and discard the seeds. Cut a 5cm piece off the top; this should weigh about 60g. Cut the rest of the squash into quarters lengthways.

3. Get a baking tray. Lay the squash pieces on one side of the tray and brush generously with the vegetable oil. Season with salt and chilli powder. Roast for 15 minutes, basting once. Turn the squash onto its other side. Roast for a further 15 minutes, basting once again, or until the flesh is golden on the outside and feels soft within.

4. While the squash roasts, make the marmalade. Get a medium-sized sauté pan or frying pan. Using your coarse grater, grate the 5cm piece of squash into it. Add 2 tbsp of the extra virgin olive oil, the dried apricots and pumpkin seeds. Cover the pan and put it on a medium heat. Sweat for 5 minutes or until the squash is soft but still holding its shape; the texture will be slightly chewy. Add the sweetcorn, honey, chilli, lemon zest, lemon juice and tomatoes. Bring to the boil and boil for 20–30 seconds until the mixture is glazed and looks a bit like marmalade. Season to taste with salt, sugar and chilli powder; use as much chilli as you like, but remember, it gets stronger as it sits.

5. Get a medium saucepan. Add the lentils and the remaining 1 tbsp of extra virgin olive oil. Season with salt and as much chilli as you'd like. I intended this to be spicy, but it's up to you. Once the squash is roasted, heat the lentils for about 2 minutes.

6. Spoon the lentils onto your plates. Put the roast squash on top. Spoon the marmalade and yoghurt over everything. Scatter the watercress on top. Serve any extra watercress on the side.

Cook extra
Drain the lentils, make a wrap with cheese and eat grilled or cold.

3/ Lentil 'moussaka'

I've always thought moussaka would quite fancy reinventing itself as a vegetable dish, and this one is so tasty that even the staunchest meat eater won't miss the mince. These are not strictly individual portions but the fact that they are slightly separate makes them easier to serve. Don't worry if they collapse a little or the lentils spill out the sides. In a way it suits them – it makes them look a little rakish.

For younger kids, leave the chilli out and peel the aubergine. Once you've made theirs, then add the chilli to the lentils for yours. The 'moussaka' can be puréed or chopped for babies and toddlers, but the sauce is no good to freeze.

SERVES 2

Sides (pages 320–43)
Bread and/or green salad, beans or peas

Prep ahead Ready to bake, up to a day ahead

Prep/cooking 40 mins

Active time 15 mins

1 large, firm aubergine, green tip cut off
2 tbsp extra virgin olive oil
2 tsp wine vinegar
Zested or grated zest of ½ orange and 2 tbsp juice
⅓ mild red chilli, deseeded and finely chopped
2 tbsp sliced coriander
350g braised lentils (page 307)
125g mascarpone
60g Cheddar, grated
Salt, freshly ground black pepper and nutmeg

1. Preheat your oven to 230°C/Gas 8, position upper middle shelf.

2. Start with the aubergine. Cut it in half lengthways. Lay the halves cut side down on your chopping board. Cut each half lengthways in two, to give you 4 thinner slices. Get a baking tray and line it with a non-stick mat. Lay the 4 aubergine slices on the tray in a single layer. Brush the extra virgin olive oil and wine vinegar evenly over both sides of the aubergine slices. Season with salt, pepper and nutmeg. The pepper is there for a bit of heat and the nutmeg for fragrance; be careful with the nutmeg as it can easily overpower the other flavours; I like to be just aware that it is there. Bake the aubergines for 12–15 minutes or until the flesh is soft.

3. While the aubergine bakes, get a small bowl. Add the orange zest, chilli and coriander. Mix together.

4. Get a medium bowl. Add the lentils, half the orange zest mixture and the orange juice. Toss together and season to taste.

5. Next make the 'cheese sauce'. Get a medium bowl. Add the mascarpone and Cheddar. Mix together and season to taste.

6. Put the 2 aubergine slices with their skin on, skin side down and side by side, in an ovenproof dish. Spoon half the lentils evenly across each slice; don't worry if some fall over the edge. Top each with a second aubergine slice. Using a knife dipped in boiling water, cover the top of the aubergines with the cheese sauce (the hot knife blade will make it easier to spread). Bake for 18–20 minutes, or until the top is golden.

7. Once the 'moussaka' is ready, sprinkle the rest of the orange zest mixture over the top. Put it back into the oven for 1 minute, then take the dish to your table.

4/ Mackay's lentil pie

If I was a meal, a pie I would be – rough and ready, a bit coarse and satisfying when you're in the mood. It's comforting to eat a soft mash-topped pie, but sometimes an extra texture adds a frisson of excitement. Here filo pastry acts like a savoury version of hard sugar on a crème brûlée – a crunch through to the soft purée and saucy lentils. This pie can change to suit you: black pepper or curry powder instead of smoked paprika; mashed potato or sweet potato instead of chickpea purée. If you don't have individual dishes, make the pie in a single ovenproof dish or 20cm frying pan.

Make smaller pies for younger kids. Even better, get them to make their own in little ramekins. Without the pastry this is brilliant to purée for babies and can be given to toddlers as it is. Both can be frozen.

SERVES 2

Sides (pages 320–43)
Green salad, French beans
or broccoli

Prep ahead Pies, ready to
bake, a day ahead. Put the filo
on top just before baking;
allow 5 minutes extra

Prep/cooking 30–35 mins

Active time 15–20 mins

400g tin chickpeas
4 tinned or bottled cooked
    peppers (about 160g),
    cut into 5mm slices
2 garlic cloves, peeled and
    thinly sliced
3 tbsp extra virgin olive oil,
    plus extra for brushing
4 tbsp full-fat milk, heated,
    plus a little extra,
    if needed
300g braised lentils
    (page 307)
4 tbsp vegetable stock
3 tbsp raisins
4 sheets of filo pasty
    (see page 22)
Salt and smoked paprika

1. Preheat your oven to 200°C/Gas 6, position upper middle shelf.

2. Start with the chickpea purée. Get a small saucepan. Add the chickpeas with their liquid, half the peppers, the garlic and 2 tbsp of the extra virgin olive oil. Put the pan on a high heat. Bring to the boil and boil until only about 6 tbsp of the liquid remains. Add the milk and bring back to the boil. Tip the contents of the pan into your food processor. Blend for 4–5 minutes until you have a smooth purée, the texture of hummus. If it is too thick, add more hot milk, 1 tbsp at a time, until you get the right texture.

3. Get a small pan. Add the lentils, vegetable stock, raisins, the remaining peppers, ¼ tsp of smoked paprika and the remaining 1 tbsp of extra virgin olive oil. Put the pan on a medium heat. Warm the lentils slightly for 1 minute. Stir in 2 tbsp of the chickpea purée; this thickens the mixture and makes it creamy. Season to taste with salt.

4. Spoon the lentils into 2 small ovenproof dishes and spread them out evenly. Spoon the chickpea purée into the centre of each, then use a spatula to smooth it to the edges. Don't push too hard, but don't worry if the purée sinks into the lentils a little.

5. Put 2 sheets of filo pastry on your worktop. Sprinkle them with smoked paprika. Brush the pastry all over with extra virgin olive oil. Scrunch the filo sheets up to the size of your dishes. I scrunch it to try and keep as much of the pastry as possible off the surface of the chickpea purée because the moisture will make it go soft. Sprinkle another 2 filo sheets with smoked paprika and brush them with oil. Put a second sheet of filo on top of each pie. Bake for 12–15 minutes or until the pies are golden reddish brown on top.

Cook extra
Make double the lentil mixture and chickpea purée and freeze half.

5/ Pasta & vegetables with lentil 'bolognaise'

The lentils give this meal the guts to rival any pasta bolognaise, the vegetable ribbons are edible eye candy and I've used tagliatelle because it is a similar shape. Fresh or dried pappardelle or spaghetti are also good; adjust the cooking time accordingly.

The vegetable 'pasta' gets kids excited about vegetables and the lentils are a great way to introduce a new pulse. I have also had huge success with the lentils as a pasta sauce on their own. Good to purée or chop and freeze for babies and toddlers.

SERVES 2

Sides None needed

Prep ahead Vegetables and tomatoes, at least 3 hours ahead

Prep/cooking 25–30 mins

Active time 25–30 mins

2 large ripe, ideally plum
  tomatoes (100g each)
1 tsp tomato purée
2 tbsp grated Parmesan,
  plus extra to shave
3 heaped tbsp sliced basil
½ leek (100–150g),
  trimmed
1 medium, firm courgette
  (150g), topped and tailed
1 large carrot (150g),
  peeled, topped and tailed
80g runner beans
300g braised lentils
  (page 307)
2 tbsp extra virgin olive oil
200g fresh tagliatelle or
  pappardelle
2 garlic cloves, peeled and
  finely chopped
⅓ mild red chilli, deseeded
  and finely chopped
Salt, sugar and cayenne
  pepper

1. Start with the tomatoes. Get a medium bowl. Chop the tomatoes into 1.5cm dice. Put them into the bowl with all their juice. Add the tomato purée, grated Parmesan and basil. Season to taste with salt and sugar.

2. Next, prepare the vegetables. Cut the leek in half lengthways and cut each half widthways in half. Open the leeks out to separate the layers within into ribbons; these will be 2–3cm wide. Use a speed peeler to cut the courgette and carrot into long ribbons. If this gets too difficult as you get near the thin ends, then just cut the remainder widthways with a knife. Slice the runner beans very thinly lengthways.

3. Boil your kettle. Fill a large pot with boiling water. Add salt and bring back to the boil. Put a colander in your sink.

4. Get a medium bowl or small pan. Add the lentils and 1 tbsp of the extra virgin olive oil. Heat through for 2 minutes on medium in the microwave or in your pan over a medium heat. Add the tomato and Parmesan mixture. Season to taste with salt and cayenne; I like to add enough cayenne to get a little bite at the back of my mouth.

5. Once the water is boiling, add the pasta. Cover and bring back to the boil. Take off the lid and boil for 1 minute. Add the leek and runner beans and boil for 1 minute. Add the courgette and carrot. Boil for 30 seconds or until everything is just cooked. Scoop out a mug of the cooking water. Drain the pasta in your colander.

6. Put the remaining 1 tbsp of extra virgin olive oil, the garlic and chilli into the pasta pan. Sweat for 20 seconds. Take the pan off the heat. Add the pasta, 2 tbsp of the pasta water and the vegetables. Gently toss the pasta so that everything is well coated. Add some more of the pasta water if it's too dry. Season to taste. Divide the pasta and vegetables between your plates and top with the hot lentil mixture. Serve with Parmesan to shave or grate over the top.

6/ Lentil fritters with roast beetroot & hot Camembert cream

You may have noticed that I like food that oozes. These fritters ooze inside and out, while the lentils give them great guts and tons of taste. I first made the Camembert cream when I worked in Delia's Restaurant at Norwich City Football Club. She served it with a delightful watercress, apple and croûton salad. I never cut the rind off the Camembert; it adds more taste and turns into hot, chewy and cheesy treats.

I am increasingly convinced by fritters as an excellent way to introduce pulses, vegetables and cheeses to kids. The meal can be puréed or chopped and frozen for babies and toddlers.

SERVES 2

Sides None needed

Prep ahead Chop the cheese and prepare the fritter mixture, 3–4 hours ahead

Prep/cooking 20–25 mins

Active time 20–25 mins

200g cooked beetroot
(see page 327)

2 small apples
(90–100g each)

1 tbsp wine vinegar

15g butter

2 tbsp hazelnuts, roughly
chopped (optional)

1 egg

4 tbsp self-raising flour

½ Camembert (125g),
cut into 1.5cm dice

300g braised lentils
(page 307)

3 tbsp crème fraîche

3 tbsp apple juice

2 tbsp vegetable oil

40g watercress (½ small
packet/bunch)

Salt, freshly ground black
pepper and cinnamon

1. Preheat your oven to 220°C/Gas 7, position upper middle shelf.

2. Start with the beetroot. Cut them into 1.5cm wedges. Cut 1 apple into 10 wedges. Get a small baking tray. Add the beetroot, apple wedges and wine vinegar. Dot the butter on top. Season with salt, pepper and cinnamon. Toss everything together. Roast in the oven for 8 minutes. Use a fish slice to turn the beetroot and apple. Sprinkle the hazelnuts onto the tray. Roast for 7 minutes or until the apple wedges are very soft and golden around their edges. Turn off the oven and leave the tray inside with the door slightly ajar to keep everything hot until you need it.

3. While the beetroot and apple wedges roast, make the fritter mixture. Get a large bowl. Add the egg and flour. Whisk them together until there are no lumps. Add half of the diced Camembert. Put a sieve over the top of another bowl. Put the braised lentils into the sieve and shake them until most of their liquid is drained off (keep it for other recipes). Weigh 250g lentils and add to the egg and flour. Grate the other apple. Weigh 60g grated apple and add it to the bowl. Stir everything together. Season to taste.

4. Next, make the Camembert cream. Get a small saucepan. Add the rest of the diced Camembert, the crème fraîche and apple juice. Melt over a low heat for 3–4 minutes. It needs to be hot, but don't let it boil or it will separate. Season to taste. Remove from the heat.

5. Get a large non-stick frying pan. Add the oil and get it really hot. Add the lentil mixture in 4 large spoonfuls; flatten each to a fritter, about 8cm in diameter. If your pan isn't big enough, cook them in 2 batches. Fry the fritters over a medium heat for 1½ minutes. Turn them and fry for 1½ minutes on the other side until golden but still a little soft in the centre.

6. Put 2 lentil fritters on each of your plates. Spoon the beetroot, apple wedges and hazelnuts alongside. Add the watercress sprigs. Warm the Camembert cream and pour it over everything on your plates at the table.

SIDE DISHES

Making your everyday side dishes taste as good as they can is mostly about learning to make them taste intensely of themselves. I'd be delighted if you could shop for the freshest seasonal vegetables every day, but I know that's not practical for everybody. I think it's wonderful to ask for a hand from a packet, a tin or the freezer, especially when the help from the freezer can be home-cooked.

I've deliberately kept my sides plain so that they can be served with as many recipes as possible. Don't serve too many for one meal; it's better to concentrate on one excellent side dish. Bread to soak up a sauce or a pre-mixed salad with your own made-in-bulk dressing can be the only accompaniment you need.

Throughout this book, if I think there's a perfect partner for a main recipe, I've said so, otherwise I've given you the widest choice I can from this chapter; if broccoli is ideal, another brassica, such as Brussels sprouts, cabbage or cauliflower will do fine. If it suits a recipe, I've suggested a salad, a vegetable or a carbohydrate, to give you a choice depending on whether you fancy something fresh, crunchy or comfy. Check the main recipe's cooking times before you start to see where your side dish fits in, but don't worry too much, all of the hot sides can either be kept warm for a short while or reheated.

If you can shop only once a week, or you cook only for one or two, I can help you. As very little is sold loose or in the exact size you need, it's easy to end up with half tins, packets and bunches of vegetables. Just don't let them become leftovers. Serve half your mangetout boiled and half in a salad, or fry half a tin of chickpeas and purée the rest. Cook the whole broccoli, bag of runner beans, box of lentils or almost anything else to heat up the next day or use in a salad, or freeze them if you're not sure when you'll need them.

I won't offer you alternative seasonings here, just techniques that go beyond single recipes. Once you're comfortable cooking a vegetable, pulse or grain, you can treat it like a 'hero' from Adventures with Ingredients (pages 36–123) and season it with a spice or something else instead of pepper, flavour it with a saucy standby from The Magic Fridge (pages 124–223), or make some mash to eat with leftover gravy from Slow Cook Sorcery (pages 224–319). Your side dishes will be heroes in their own right.

HOW I COOK VEGETABLES

I'll take you through the various cooking methods I use in detail, then I'll give you specific preparation and cooking times for each vegetable. I won't suggest every cooking option for every vegetable on earth, just the ones that are easy to find and I use regularly. The cooking times given are for each vegetable to be tender to my taste. Before you drain them, taste your vegetables to make sure they're cooked to your liking.

The Mackay boil, drain and dry

Use this technique and your vegetables will stay greener, taste better, stay hotter and be more evenly seasoned than if you just boil and drain them. The best way to boil green vegetables is in a large pot of fast-boiling salted water. Because there is a lot of water, the vegetables come back to the boil quickly and cook quickly, keeping their colour bright and their flavour fresh. The size of pot is relative to the quantity of vegetables you are cooking, because the more you add, the more you lower the temperature of the water.

For an average portion for 1–2 people, a 20cm pot is fine, but a 24cm pot is best for up to 6 people. Very large amounts need to be boiled in batches. The times I give for green vegetables are as they cook in these pots, two-thirds to three-quarters filled with water, boiling furiously on the highest heat on my biggest burner. But taste, check and taste, and find what works best for you.

The basic method The quickest way to get a large pot of water to the boil is this. First boil your kettle. Fill your pot one-third full with water from the tap and bring to the boil. Once the kettle boils, top the pan up until it is just over two-thirds full. Salt well. When the water is boiling furiously, add the vegetables. Cover and bring back to the boil. Take the lid off. Start your timer and use my cooking times as a guide. The exact time will depend on your hob and how you like your vegetables cooked. I like mine to be tender, by which I mean firm but completely cooked through. Have a small bowl of cold water ready. To check if your vegetables are cooked as you like them, lift one out with tongs, dip it in the cold water and then taste it.

After you drain your vegetables, put them back into the empty pot. Put the pot back over a medium-high heat. Sauté for 10–30 seconds to evaporate the water left in the vegetables, no longer than necessary or they will stick; shake rather than stir them so that they don't break up. Add butter or olive oil if you want to. Season the vegetables to taste once they are dry. Drying vegetables in this way maximises their taste, as it is not diluted by water. They will also be hotter, and any butter or oil will cling to and coat them more fully. If vegetables aren't well drained, water from them will dilute your gravy, sauce or dressing. I use butter to moisten vegetables if the main meal has butter, and olive oil if it has olive oil. But you don't have to add either.

Cook extra If you have more French beans, mangetout or sugar snaps in a packet than you need, or your broccoli, cauliflower or cabbage is too big for a single meal, you can prepare, boil and drain all of it.

Put the vegetables you don't need into a large bowl of cold water to refresh (stop them cooking), just long enough to cool completely – 30 seconds to 1 minute should do it. Drain the cooled vegetables in your colander and leave them until you've finished your meal. Then store the vegetables on kitchen paper to absorb their excess water.

These pre-cooked vegetables can also be used to make salads or quick stir-fries. If you're unlikely to use your cooked vegetables within the next 2 days, freeze them.

To stir-fry steam vegetables

I use this technique to quickly wilt spinach, pak choi, rocket, watercress and beetroot leaves. The idea is to cook the leaves in almost no water, very quickly, so they keep as much flavour as possible and don't get waterlogged. You can also do this in your microwave – simply put the vegetables in a bowl.

The basic method Heat 1–2 tbsp of water (plus 1 tbsp of butter or olive oil if you like) in a large pan over the highest possible heat until it boils. Add the leaves and put the lid on. After 30 seconds or so when the leaves start to wilt, stir for 10–20 seconds until the leaves are all wilted. Season to taste.

To glaze vegetables

This technique intensifies a vegetable's flavour and makes it look glossy and glorious. To maximise its flavour, season the vegetable lightly at the start, then season it to taste at the end. I cook carrots, radishes, leeks, spring onions, swede and turnips this way.

Note that through this book, I also refer to boiled vegetables that I make shiny with butter, olive oil, gravy or dressing as glazed vegetables.

The basic method For 2 portions, cut 200–250g of your chosen vegetable (see ABC of Everyday Vegetables, page 326) into even-sized pieces, usually 1–2cm slices. Put the vegetable into a medium saucepan, sauté or frying pan. Add just enough water to barely cover it and 15g butter or 1 tbsp of extra virgin olive oil. Season lightly with salt. Cover and simmer for 6–10 minutes until the vegetable is just tender; taste a piece to check – the vegetable needs to be tender before you reduce the liquid down. Take the lid off. Boil rapidly for 3–5 minutes until all of the liquid has evaporated and the vegetable is glazed in a moist, shiny coating of the butter, oil and their juices. Watch for the last 2 minutes, as the vegetable will burn quickly once the liquid has gone. The reduction will take less time in a shallow pan.

To roast vegetables

I roast vegetables to intensify their flavour and give them an irresistible sticky and caramelised surface. I'd like to reassure you before you begin that even if they are perfectly cooked, golden and glorious, most roast vegetables will not become crisp, simply because they contain too much moisture. If you get rid of this moisture completely the vegetables will be dry. Parsnips can be the exception to this.

It is vital to toss the vegetables with oil and preheat your roasting tray before you add the vegetables to it; if you don't they will stick. It is important to spread the vegetables out in a single layer on the tray, or they will steam rather than roast. It is more important to baste vegetables than most meat, because vegetables don't have their own fat. I do this with a heatproof brush.

Different vegetables call for different treatment. I pre-cook beetroot (or buy it pre-cooked), carrots, fennel and parsnips until they are barely tender to ensure that they have a soft interior before I roast them. Pumpkin, squash, sweet potatoes and Jerusalem artichokes don't need to be pre-cooked, so I roast them from raw. Oddly, they all roast for roughly the same time, so you can roast them together. If you want roast vegetables for two, the easiest way is to do them in a frying pan, as in the recipe on page 104.

Per person, allow 150–200g unpeeled weight of beetroot, carrots, parsnips, sweet potatoes or Jerusalem artichokes, ½ large fennel bulb or 200–250g squash or pumpkin.

The basic method Cut the vegetables into even-sized pieces. (For size, see the individual entries in the ABC of Everyday Vegetables, page 326.) You can cut them smaller or larger than I suggest; the sizes I give are those I prefer for a mixture of roast outside and soft inside.

If necessary, simmer the vegetables until they are barely tender. (For times, see individual entries.) To check if the vegetables are ready, dip an end of one piece in cold water, cut off a bit and taste; it should be slightly undercooked. Drain your vegetables thoroughly in a colander, then on kitchen paper, preferably a couple of hours or even a day before you roast them to give their surfaces plenty of time to dry. Keep them uncovered in the fridge.

When you are ready to roast your vegetables, preheat your oven to 220°C/Gas 7, position upper middle shelf. Get a roasting tray or baking tray just large enough to hold the vegetables in a single layer. Heat the tray in your oven for 5 minutes. Toss the vegetables with salt, pepper and 1 tsp of vegetable oil per 100g of vegetables. Spread the vegetables out on the tray in a single layer, then quickly put them back into the oven. After 10 minutes, turn and baste the vegetables. Roast for 10 minutes more. Add 5g of butter per 100g of vegetables. Turn the vegetables to coat them in the butter, then roast them for another 5–10 minutes or until they are caramelised on the outside.

Vegetable purée

This smooth, mousse-like vegetable purée makes an elegant accompaniment. To give a delightful contrast of textures I like to make the purée with part of a vegetable and then roast or make a salad with the remainder to serve on the same plate.

It is hard to make the purée in smaller quantities than this, but feel free to cook more; it will keep in the fridge for 2 days and can be frozen. Reheat the vegetable purée over a low heat or in the microwave on a low setting; it will look like it is separating, but it will come back together once you stir it.

To get the weight of each vegetable that I suggest in the recipe, add roughly 25 per cent before you start peeling and trimming; 30 per cent for squash and pumpkin. To make a purée with cauliflower or broccoli, see the recipe that I serve with the pork chop on page 92.

These purées are an excellent base for baby food – just leave out the seasoning. A lot of the meals in this book are strongly flavoured so it's a good and economical idea to mix the meat or fish and sauce purée for babies with a vegetable purée. As your baby gets older, you can pulse instead of purée the vegetables to get him or her more used to textured food. We would often make a large batch of this purée, serve some for our meal, then freeze the remainder in flexible ice-cube trays. Once the purée is frozen, you can easily transfer it from the trays to plastic containers, seal them tightly and store them in the freezer.

Serves 4

400g prepared weight of parsnip, carrot, butternut squash,
    Jerusalem artichoke, pumpkin or swede, cut into 3cm dice
100ml whipping cream
30g butter
Salt and freshly ground pepper

Boil your kettle. Fill a medium pan with boiling water. Add salt, cover and bring back to the boil. Add the vegetable and bring back to the boil. Take the lid off. Lower the heat and simmer for 12–15 minutes or until the vegetable is completely cooked through, almost to the point of breaking up. Put a colander in your sink.

Tip the vegetable into your colander. Press with the back of a ladle to remove as much excess moisture as possible. Put the cream and butter into the empty pan. Bring to the boil. Put everything in your blender. Blend for 3–4 minutes, scraping the mixture off the sides occasionally until the purée is totally smooth. The longer you blend the purée, the lighter the texture, the paler the colour and the smoother it will become. Season to taste with salt and pepper.

ABC OF EVERYDAY VEGETABLES

A few notes:

- **Portion size** As a rough guide, allow 80–100g of a green vegetable (ie enough to cover about a third of an average-sized plate) per person if you're serving just one, and 40–50g if you are serving 2 green vegetables alongside a carbohydrate (enough to cover about a quarter of a plate). Add 20 per cent more for a leafy vegetable. Pack sizes may mean you end up with a little more or less, which is fine.
- **Cooking time** The times I have given are a guide. Start tasting after the shortest time I've suggested.
- **Cooked salad** This refers to boiled, refreshed, thoroughly drained and dried vegetables to be served at room temperature. Take the cooked vegetables out of the fridge 30 minutes or so before serving, or warm them slightly in your microwave. You can also serve these as freshly cooked hot salads. A hot salad needs less dressing than one at room temperature because the flavours dull as they cool.
- **Raw salad** Any green vegetable that you add lemon juice to will discolour quickly, so mix it in just before serving.
- **Dressing quantity** When you dress your vegetables, start with 1 tsp of the dressing per 50g of vegetable, then taste. Add more to taste, little by little.

Asparagus

Asparagus is a bit of a luxury. I like the fat spears best. To prepare them, break the hard bottom off the stalk at the point where it snaps naturally. If I boil asparagus whole, I peel the thicker bottom half of the stalks from 6–7cm below the tip with a vegetable peeler; this skin can be thick and stringy. If not, I cut each stalk in half; the tender tip cooks more quickly than the rest. You don't need to peel or cut very thin asparagus, just snap off the woody bottoms.

Boil Allow 3–6 minutes for whole peeled asparagus spears. For average spears (the size of a man's index finger), cut them in half widthways, boil the bottom halves for 2 minutes, then add the tips and boil for 2–3 minutes more.

Cooked salad Dress well-drained boiled whole spears with a little lemon dressing (page 336) and sprinkle with salt flakes just before you serve them.

Raw salad Dress thinly sliced asparagus with a little lemon dressing (page 336) and sprinkle with salt flakes just before you serve them.

Beans, Broad

These have a short season so I use frozen broad beans more often than fresh ones. Unless the broad beans are very small (no more than 1.5cm long) and tender, I boil and refresh them, then take off their tough, bitter outer skins.

Boil Allow 2–3 minutes. Refresh in cold water. To peel, nip the skin at the top of the bean with your thumbnail and gently squeeze out the bright green bean. Reheat very quickly with 1–2 tbsp of water and a little butter or olive oil.

Raw salad If you are lucky enough to get hold of tiny, very fresh broad beans, they make an excellent sunshine salad. As their flavour is very delicate, dress them with a tiny amount of lemon dressing (page 336).

Beans, French

I don't take the pointy ends off French beans (also called green beans), just the hard tops. Keep them in a line or bundle and push the tops of the beans against your hand to get the ends to the same point so you can cut them off all at once.
Boil Allow 3–4 minutes for average 1cm-thick beans.
Cooked salad Dress with a mustard dressing (page 336).

Beans, Runner

Take the strings off with a peeler or knife. Cut the beans into 4–5cm lengths, or halve them widthways, then slice each half lengthways into ribbons.
Boil Allow 3–4 minutes.
Cooked salad Dress with a mustard dressing (page 336).
Raw salad Thinly slice and dress with lemon dressing (page 336).

Beetroot

I usually use the tasty and convenient pre-cooked beetroot sold in vacuum packs (usually 300g, sometimes 250g or 400g). The beetroot vary in size so it's easiest to go by weight for my recipes, but feel free to add more to use up your pack, or fresh beetroot. If you get the chance to cook your own, you'll be rewarded with the most intense flavour when you bake the beetroot in foil. If they come with leaves and stalks, stir-fry steam these (see page 323).
Bake Preheat your oven to 200°C/Gas 6, position upper middle shelf. Wash 4 medium beetroot, halfway between golf and tennis ball size (about 150g). Put a 60cm length of foil across a baking tray. Put the beetroot on one half. Toss with 2 tbsp of extra virgin olive oil, 1 tbsp of wine vinegar and 3 tbsp of water. Season with salt and pepper. Fold the foil over the top and seal the edges tightly. Bake for 1 hour. Open the package. The beetroot should be firm but easy to pierce with a knife. Peel them once they are cool enough to handle.
Cooked salad Toss slices, cubes or wedges of beetroot with vinaigrette (page 336) while they are still warm and they will absorb the dressing better.
Raw salad Peel, grate and toss the beetroot in lemon dressing or vinaigrette (page 336).

Broccoli

I use broccoli stalks as well as the florets. Sometimes I cut off the stalks from the base of the head, peel off the skin, then cut them into thin strips for salads and stir-fries, or chunks to boil. Alternatively, I divide the head into florets with long sections of the stalks attached.

Boil Allow 3–4 minutes. Once the broccoli is cooked to your taste, transfer the florets tenderly from the water to your colander, using a wire skimmer or they may break up. When you put the florets back into the pan to dry them out, again treat them gently. Alternatively, you can drain the florets into a metal colander then put them in the oven to dry for 2–3 minutes. Broccoli is also good to stir-fry steam (see page 323).

Purée This is particularly delicious. Follow the recipe for the cauliflower purée on page 92.

Cooked salad Keep the florets whole and thickly slice the stalks. Dress with a mustard dressing (page 336).

Raw salad Slice the florets and stalks thinly. Dress with lemon dressing (page 336) or the dressing used for the cauliflower salad on page 92.

Broccoli, Purple sprouting

This is as special as asparagus in the spring. If the stalks are thick, I peel them. If they are very thick I cut them off, peel and cook them for 2–3 minutes before I add the tender flowers. Purple sprouting broccoli is delicate. Once it's cooked, transfer it tenderly from the water to your colander with a wire skimmer. I always eat this vegetable boiled with butter, salt and pepper.

Boil Allow 2–3 minutes.

Brussels sprouts

Trim off any brown leaves but not the delicious dark green ones. I don't cross their bottoms. I cut Brussels sprouts in half as they cook more quickly, stay greener and the salt in the water gets into them more fully. If you have some left over, they are good in stir-fries. At Christmas you can boil, refresh and store your Brussels sprouts a day ahead (see Cook extra, page 323).

Boil Allow 3–5 minutes, depending on size.

Cabbage, Green, Savoy, Tenderheart, White

I slice the cabbage leaves about 1cm thick and cut the crisp core into slices about 5mm thick.

Boil Allow 2–4 minutes. The boiling time varies according to the type and age of the cabbage and how thickly you slice it. The tough outer leaves take longer to cook than the tender inner ones. Either boil the outer leaves first for 2–3 minutes, then add the inner ones or use the two for separate meals.

Cooked salad Drain the sliced cabbage thoroughly. Mix it with a mustard or lemon dressing (page 336).

Raw salad Use the pale inner leaves and the core only and cut them into 5mm–1cm thick slices. Toss with a lemon or mustard dressing (page 336). The longer you leave the cabbage in the dressing, the less crisp it becomes; after 2–3 hours it will have the texture of coleslaw.

Carrots

Glazed carrots taste more strongly of carrot than boiled ones. I often glaze whole or halved Chantenay carrots because they are pretty and don't need to be peeled. Alternatively, I peel the same weight of large carrots and slice them 1.5cm thick, diagonally because I like the way it looks.

Glaze Simmer, covered, for 10 minutes or until tender. Take the lid off. Boil for 4–5 minutes to glaze (see page 323).

Roast Halve the carrots lengthways, then cut them into 6cm (or even-sized) lengths. Simmer rapidly for 7–8 minutes. Drain and dry, then roast at 220°C/Gas 7 for 25–30 minutes (see page 324).

Raw salad Grate the carrots very finely, almost to a purée. Mix with lemon dressing (page 336). I also like to cut carrots into strips with a speed peeler for salads (see page 222).

Cauliflower

I use the stalks, leaves and ribs, as well as the cauliflower florets. Peel the outer skin from the stalk and ribs. Cut the stalk into 5mm strips for salads or stir-fries. Cut the ribs and leaves into 2–3cm thick slices to boil. Slice both thinly for salads.

Boil Allow 4–5 minutes. Once the cauliflower is cooked to your taste, transfer the florets tenderly from the water to your colander, using a wire skimmer or they may break up. When you put the florets back into the pan to dry them out, again treat them gently. You can also drain the florets into a metal colander, then put them in the oven to dry for 2–3 minutes.

Cooked salad Dress with a mustard dressing (page 336).

Raw salad Slice very thinly and dress with lemon dressing (page 336), or the dressing used for the cauliflower salad on page 92.

Chard, Swiss

I love this vegetable. The leaves and stalks need to be treated individually as they have different cooking times. Cut the stalks from the leaves. Cut both into 2–3cm thick slices but keep them apart.

Boil Cook the chard stalks for 3–4 minutes or until they are tender. Add the leaves, bring back to the boil, then drain and dry.

Cooked salad Drain the chard and dry it very well. Dress with lemon dressing or vinaigrette (page 336).

Corn

Freshly cooked corn-on-the-cob in season is one of life's great pleasures, and I like tinned sweetcorn too. If you want to use the kernels from fresh corn rather than eat it from the cob, one average cob yields roughly the same amount of kernels as a 200g tin.

Boil Cook corn-on-the-cob in salted water, allowing 8–10 minutes, then eat it from the cob or cut off the kernels. If you cut off the kernels before you boil the corn, the flavour won't be as good.

Courgettes

These are excellent sautéed, but no good to boil because they get waterlogged. Choose firm, small to medium courgettes as their texture is much better and they have fewer seeds. Allow 1 medium courgette per person.

Sauté Cut 2 medium courgettes into 1cm thick slices. Heat 1 tsp of vegetable oil in a large frying pan. Add the courgettes and sauté over a medium heat for 2 minutes or until they soften slightly and just begin to brown. Add 2 tsp of extra virgin olive oil, toss and season to taste with salt and pepper.

Fennel

Fennel has a pronounced anise flavour and is very good either raw or cooked (but not half-cooked, when it is stringy). Allow ½ large fennel bulb per person. Trim and discard any dry-looking bits on the top and peel the outer skin.

Glaze Cut into quarters and simmer, covered, for 8–10 minutes until tender. Take the lid off. Boil for 3–5 minutes to glaze (see page 323).

Roast Trim and quarter lengthways. Simmer rapidly for 8–10 minutes. Drain and dry, then roast at 220°C/Gas 7 (see page 324).

Raw salad Cut into 5mm slices and dress with lemon dressing (page 336).

Greens, Spring

Discard the tough very outer leaves. I slice the leaves 1.5cm thick and the stalks 5mm thick, so they cook in roughly the same time.

Boil Allow 4–6 minutes for outer leaves, 2–4 minutes for inner leaves.

Jerusalem artichokes

Peel the artichokes, but don't put them into water, especially not with lemon. It doesn't matter if they discolour. They are odd shapes, so I can't give you a size. Just cut them as evenly as you can so that they cook in the same time. They are delicious roasted or made into a purée (see page 325).

Roast Simmer very gently for 5–6 minutes or until just tender. Drain and dry, then roast at 220°C/Gas 7 (see page 324).

Leeks

These can be boiled, but they are best glazed. Allow 230–250g leek per person. Trim off the base and the tough green part of the leaves. Cut the leek into 2cm slices. Wash the slices in plenty of water.

Glaze Simmer, covered, for 6 minutes or until just tender. Take the lid off. Boil for 3–5 minutes to glaze (see page 323).

Cooked salad Slice as above, wash and boil for 6–7 minutes until soft. Drain in a colander. Press dry. Toss the leeks with mustard dressing (page 336) while they are still hot so that they absorb it more fully.

Lettuce

This is nice stir-fry steamed (see page 323) and excellent braised with onions (see page 132). I buy Romaine lettuce to boil, or I braise the dark outer lettuce leaves that aren't crisp enough for a salad to serve as a side dish for one meal, and then use the crisp, sweet centre as a salad for another.

Boil Allow 2–3 minutes.

Pak choi

I like the stalks to stay crunchy. Cut small pak choi into quarters lengthways and large ones into eighths, or cut them widthways into 2cm slices.

Stir-fry steam See page 323. Double the water and the cooking time.

Parsnips

These are delicious roasted or made into a purée (see page 325).

Roast Peel and halve lengthways or quarter if very fat, then cut in half widthways or into 6cm lengths. Simmer rapidly for 4–5 minutes. Drain and dry, then roast at 220°C/Gas 7 (see page 324).

Peas

Because of their short season, I use frozen peas much more often than fresh.

Boil Allow 3–4 minutes from frozen. Very fresh young peas will cook in 1–2 minutes; older ones take longer; keep tasting.

Cooked salad Dress with lemon dressing (page 336) at the last minute.

Raw Freshly picked young, small peas eaten as you pick them from the pods are a real treat.

Peas, Mangetout

Check these for strings (even 'stringless' packs) and remove as necessary.

Boil Allow 2–3 minutes.

Cooked salad Drain very well and toss with lemon dressing, mustard dressing or vinaigrette (page 336) at the last minute.

Raw salad Thinly slice and dress with lemon dressing (page 336) at the last minute.

Peas, Sugar snap

Check these for strings (even 'stringless' packs) and remove as necessary.

Boil Allow 3–4 minutes.

Cooked salad Dress with lemon dressing (page 336) at the last minute.

Pumpkin

Peel with a Y-shaped speed peeler, deseed and cut into 4cm chunks.
Roast or purée (see page 325).
Roast Roast at 220°C/Gas 7 (see page 324).

Radishes

Excellent as a slightly spicy vegetable, glazed with olive oil rather than butter.
Glaze Cut the radishes in half. Simmer, covered, for 3–4 minutes or until just tender. Take the lid off. Boil for 3–5 minutes to glaze (see page 323).
Raw salad Slice and toss with lemon dressing (page 336). Or cut each radish in half, spread with butter and sprinkle with salt flakes.

Spinach

This is best stir-fry steamed. Wash the leaves only if you need to.
Don't remove the stalks; they have an excellent texture.
Stir-fry steam See page 323.

Spring onions/Salad onions

Trim the roots off the spring onions. Cut each onion into 3 lengthways.
Glaze Boil, uncovered, for 4–5 minutes or until just tender. Boil for 3–5 minutes to glaze (see page 323).

Squash

Peel with a Y-shaped speed peeler, deseed and cut into 4cm chunks.
Roast or purée (see page 325).
Roast Roast at 220°C/Gas 7 (see page 324).

Swede

Peel and cut into 2cm chunks. Roast or purée (see page 325).
Glaze Simmer, covered, for 8–9 minutes or until just tender. Take the lid off. Boil for 3–5 minutes to glaze (see page 323).
Raw salad Peel, grate and toss with mustard or lemon dressing (page 336).

Sweet potato

Wash, then cut into 3cm thick slices. Halve lengthways if they are fat.
Roast Roast at 220°C/Gas 7 (see page 324).

Turnips

I like small turnips, halfway between golf and tennis ball size (about 150g).
Glaze Peel the turnips and cut them into 2cm wedges or chunks.
Simmer, covered, for 7–8 minutes or until just tender. Take the lid off.
Boil for 3–5 minutes to glaze (see page 323).

SALADS & DRESSINGS

I serve a salad as a side dish, to be a crisp contrast, a great way to soak up a sauce, or both. When you dress salad, use a big shallow bowl, a deep oven dish or oven tray, so that you can coat the leaves in dressing without crushing them. Salads want to be seasoned, so don't forget the salt and pepper. The seasoning in the dressing seasons only the dressing, not the salad. Dress a leafy salad just before you're going to eat it so that it doesn't wilt, and don't overdo the dressing; you can always add a little more, but you can't take it away. One advantage of a salad over a hot vegetable accompaniment is that both the salad and dressing can be put on the table before you even start cooking.

Balance is everything to a salad dressing. I add a tiny amount of water to help balance the oil and vinegar so that the result is neither too oily nor too acidic. Sugar helps balance the acidity, then you have to taste, adjust the seasoning and taste again until you're happy with the mixture. A baby gem leaf makes an ideal tasting spoon.

Every time I make a vinegar-based dressing (vinaigrette), I prepare a couple of weeks' worth and store it in a bottle or jar with a screw-top lid. Don't fill the jar more than two-thirds full, as you will need space to shake it and emulsify the oil and vinegar before each use.

Wipe the rim of your jar with kitchen paper before you put it away every time. Often it is just the dressing at the top that goes rancid, but as you pour your dressing through the top it all tastes bad. The dressing will keep for weeks in a cool dark place if you don't add any fresh ingredients like herbs or garlic; these are best added directly to the leaves anyway.

Leaf salads

There is a huge variety of salad leaves available. These are the ones I like best:

Crisp leaves Baby gem, Romaine, Chinese cabbage, pak choi, escarole, iceberg, chicory. Pak choi and baby gem are ideal for 1–2 people, because you'll use the whole thing; Chinese cabbage and Romaine lettuce are a more useful size if you are serving 3–6.
Peppery/spicy leaves Rocket, watercress and, to a lesser extent, mizuna.
Pleasantly bitter and firm leaves Radicchio, curly endive (frisée).
Sweet and delicate leaves Baby chard, baby spinach, lamb's lettuce, butterhead (round lettuce), pea shoots.

Choosing salad leaves The most important consideration is that the leaves are kept as fresh as possible, and the best mixture is the one you like the most. I love the taste of rocket, but I like to mix it with something crisp like baby gem, Romaine, radicchio, curly endive (frisée) or chicory, which all give the salad some body. I love a combination of watercress, spinach and rocket tossed in lemon dressing, and sometimes I'll add cooked peas or beans if

I've got some left over. This is a great accompaniment for smoked food, salmon and lentil recipes. I must have salad with a roast, and I like to have watercress to soften into the roast gravy, and crisp baby gem or Romaine leaves to catch and contrast with the gravy.

Preparing salad leaves If you need to wash your leaves, cut or tear as much as you'll use. Fill your sink with cold water, then add the leaves and turn them gently, rather than run water over the top, which will bruise them. Dry salads in a salad spinner, filling it no more than halfway to avoid battering the leaves. Check that salad leaves are well dried after washing, to ensure the dressing will coat them rather than slide off. Put the salad on the table with a double sheet of damp kitchen paper over the top to keep it fresh until you're ready to dress and serve it. This is also a good way to keep prepared salads in the fridge.

Tomato salad

Try to buy tomatoes that are as ripe as possible. Don't put tomatoes in the fridge, keep them in your fruit bowl; they have no flavour when they're cold.

For a simple tomato salad, slice 1 large tomato per person into 1cm thick slices, or cut them in half and then cut each half in 3 wedges. Put the tomato slices or wedges onto a plate. Sprinkle them evenly with salt and a tiny pinch of sugar. Leave to sit for 10 minutes or so. This intensifies their flavour and colour. I brush my tomatoes with extra virgin olive oil and sprinkle them with salt flakes and basil before serving. I prefer not to add vinegar or lemon juice.

The tomatoes I use most often as part of my recipes are baby plum tomatoes because I find that their flavour is consistently good. They are also good for a side salad, on their own or mixed with larger tomatoes.

Cucumber salad

Allow one-sixth of a cucumber per person. Cut it in half lengthways. Use a teaspoon to scoop out and discard the seeds; these are mainly water and they will dilute your dressing. Cut the cucumber into 1cm slices diagonally. Toss with vinaigrette or lemon dressing, allowing 1 tsp per portion. Season to taste with salt and pepper.

Raw onions in salads

I tend to use red onions in salads, for their looks and also because they are more delicate. I use the following technique to make onions less aggressive and overpowering any time I want to use sliced or diced raw onion in a recipe.

Peel and slice or dice 1 small onion. Spread the onion out on a plate. Toss with a generous pinch each of salt and sugar, and 1 tsp of wine vinegar. Leave to sit for at least 10 minutes to soften. The onion gets sweetened and slightly cooked by the vinegar.

Avocado in salads

To make avocados easier to peel and to stop them discolouring, bring a medium saucepan of water to the boil and have a bowl of cold water to hand. Gently add the avocados to the boiling water. Boil for 1 minute. Immediately transfer to the cold water to cool quickly. Cut the avocados in half lengthways and twist to separate the two halves. Push a fork into the stone and twist it out. Scoop out the avocado halves from the skin with a large spoon. Slice or dice. Dress with lemon dressing (page 336). If you need to wait, cover the avocado's surface with cling film directly touching it to stop it discolouring.

Pulses and grains in salads

Tinned, home-cooked or pouches of pulses make excellent salads. Warm them up before you mix them with a mustard, yoghurt, lemon or vinaigrette dressing so that they absorb it more fully. Start with 2 tsp of dressing per 125g portion, then add more to taste, little by little. Season and taste again.

Potato salad

The two most important things are to cut the potatoes and to get them into the dressing while they are still hot so they can suck up the seasoning. Serve the potato salad hot, warm or at room temperature but never straight from the fridge.

Serves 2

400g small waxy potatoes (Charlotte, Anya, Maris Peer), washed
1 tsp Dijon or English mustard
1½ tbsp white wine vinegar, plus extra to taste
4–6 tsp extra virgin olive oil, or 2 heaped tbsp crème fraîche
   or mayonnaise
Salt, sugar and freshly ground black pepper

Boil your kettle. Cut the potatoes into 1.5cm slices. Fill a medium saucepan with boiling water. Add salt and bring to the boil. Add the potatoes. Cover and bring back to the boil. Simmer for 12–15 minutes or until tender; taste one to check. Drain and shake dry.

Get a shallow dish that will fit the potatoes in a single layer. Add the mustard and vinegar. Season with salt, sugar and pepper. Add the potatoes and turn them gently in the dressing; it seems like too much at this stage, but don't worry, the potatoes will absorb it. Cover with cling film and leave the potatoes for 5 minutes to absorb the dressing and seasonings. If you're adding oil, add it now; if you're using cream or mayonnaise, let the potatoes cool to pleasantly warm first. Season the salad to taste just before you serve it.

Vinaigrette

I've made this with wine vinegar, but it can just as easily be made with cider vinegar, sherry vinegar or balsamic (if you want a little black dressing and the specific taste). The olive oil can be replaced by vegetable or rapeseed. For a walnut or hazelnut dressing (lovely with cheese), use half nut oil to half vegetable oil, rather than all nut oil, which is overpowering. This quantity is enough to dress about 15 side portions of leaf salad.

Makes 260ml

1 tbsp water
4 tbsp red or white wine vinegar
180ml (12 tbsp) extra virgin olive oil
Salt, freshly ground black pepper and sugar

Get a large bowl. Add the water and vinegar. Whisk in the oil. Season to taste with salt, pepper and sugar. Taste, adjust and taste again. Pour the dressing into a jar, filling it no more than two-thirds full. Store in a cool, dark place. Shake the dressing each time you use it.

Variations

Mustard dressing Add 1 tsp of Dijon, English or grain mustard to 3 tbsp of vinaigrette. Taste and add more mustard if you like it stronger.
Yoghurt or cream dressing Whisk 1 tbsp of yoghurt or crème fraîche into 3 tbsp of vinaigrette.
Oil-free dressing Substitute apple, tomato or orange juice for the oil and use a delicate, slightly sweet dark or white balsamic vinegar or spiced black rice vinegar. Use 3 tbsp of tomato or orange juice to 1 tbsp of vinegar. Add 1 tsp of mustard if you like. Season to taste with salt, pepper and sugar.

Lemon dressing

When you take the time to taste and season this carefully, it can be the most wonderful dressing. The sugar is vital to balance and enhance the lemon. This quantity is more than enough to dress 2 portions of any of the salads I suggest it with. Feel free to make a couple of days' worth.

Makes 40ml

Finely grated zest of ¼ lemon
2 tsp lemon juice
2 tbsp extra virgin olive oil
Salt, freshly ground black pepper and sugar

Get a medium bowl. Add the lemon zest, lemon juice and extra virgin olive oil. Whisk together. Season to taste with salt, pepper and sugar. Taste, adjust and taste again. This dressing keeps for 2–3 days in the fridge.

POTATOES, GRAINS, PULSES & PASTA

Some recipes call for a simple carbohydrate side to balance the meal, bulk it up or soak up the sauce. When I suggest 'plain grains' as a side dish, I'm talking about rice and couscous. The 'tasty grains' (which have a more pronounced taste) are red rice, quinoa and wholewheat couscous.

Potatoes

Use the right potato for the right preparation, cook it the right way and the taste and texture of your potato accompaniment will be better. A waxy potato will make gluey mash and a floury potato is more likely to break up when you simmer it. The size of potatoes varies so much that I'll always give you their weight in my recipes: 150–200g as a main accompaniment; 250g for roast potatoes because they're a treat.

Waxy or floury? Waxy potatoes stay firm and keep their shape when you cook them. They are low in starch and high in water content. Use waxy potatoes for salads, simmered potatoes, glazed potatoes, sautéed potatoes and roast potatoes (thin-crusted wedges with a more chewy exterior). Charlotte and Maris Peer are easy-to-find waxy varieties; others I've used successfully are Amandine, Anya, Ratte and Jersey Royal.

Floury potatoes are high in starch and low in water content. This makes their flesh drier and means it becomes fluffy when you cook them. Use floury potatoes for roast potatoes (wedges with a fluffy interior and crunchier skins), baked potatoes and mashed potatoes. Desirée, King Edward and Maris Piper are easy-to-find floury varieties. Confusingly, these varieties are often labelled 'all rounders', which must be why I've always found all rounders to be better for floury potato jobs. The best idea is to keep a bag each of waxy and floury.

New or old? New potatoes are traditionally harvested in late spring and summer, but they are now available most of the year. Most new potatoes are waxy varieties, often called salad potatoes when their skins are shiny and firm, rather than dirty and flaky like a freshly dug potato. Old or maincrop potatoes are left in the ground to grow bigger and are harvested in the autumn. They can also be stored for longer. Because the seasons are increasingly blurred, the best advice I can give you is to choose by the variety rather than 'new or old'. Enjoy the English new potatoes when they are freshly dug and seek out new varieties that do the job you need them to.

Simmered potatoes (not boiled potatoes)

Boiling is too fast for potatoes. Potatoes cooked in water need to be simmered gently so that the heat and salt goes evenly into their flesh, they don't break up and they don't get waterlogged. It's always worth cooking extra, to have some to dress while they're still warm to make a salad or to sauté the next day.

Peel or wash and cut up your potatoes (Charlotte, Maris Peer). Put them into a pan of boiling salted water. Bring back to the boil. Turn the heat to low and simmer gently with the lid on, but slightly ajar so that the steam can escape. The simmering time will vary, depending on your variety, how long they've been stored and how they are cut. Allow between 10 and 20 minutes and don't be tempted to turn up the heat. Drain them as soon as they are tender. Put them back into the pan for 20 seconds and gently heat them to evaporate any excess water. Take the pan off the heat and cover it if you need to keep them warm.

Mashed potato

Potatoes for mash should be simmered rather than boiled so as not to waterlog them. Make sure they are totally cooked through; undercooked potatoes are hard to mash and will go gluey. Mash your potatoes immediately; if they sit, their surface hardens, which will make your mash lumpy. You can use a masher or ricer, but I push mine through a sieve to get a really smooth mash; it's easier and quicker to do this in 4 or 5 batches. Mashed potato can be frozen.

Serves 2
400g floury potatoes (Estima, King Edward, Maris Piper, Desirée)
4 tbsp full-cream milk
40g butter, or 2 tbsp butter and 2 tsp extra virgin olive oil (or more for a treat)
Salt

Peel and chop your potatoes to the same size, roughly 4cm pieces, so that they will cook evenly. Boil your kettle. Put a colander in your sink. Get a medium saucepan. Fill it two-thirds full with boiling water. Add salt, cover and bring to the boil. Add the potatoes and bring back to the boil. Take the lid off the pan. Lower the heat and simmer for 15 minutes or until the potatoes are completely cooked through. Don't worry if they break up. In the meantime, heat your milk (in the microwave will do).

Drain the potatoes in your colander. Shake out as much water as possible. Wipe out the saucepan. Put a large, sturdy sieve over the top. Put a quarter of the potatoes in your sieve. Use the back of your ladle or a big spoon to push them through. Repeat with the rest of the potatoes. Fold in the milk and butter immediately with a heatproof spatula; don't stir the mash too much now as this makes it gluey. Season to taste with salt.

Roast potatoes

I most often use King Edwards. It's important to put the potatoes onto a hot tray with hot fat so they don't stick. Make sure they are all coated with fat first and baste them once or twice as they roast. As for timing, the best guide is the roast chicken recipe on page 229. The roast potatoes are timed to be ready after the roast so that they don't have to sit for long while the chicken rests.

Glazed potatoes

I eat these more often than boiled, or rather simmered, potatoes. There is no need to peel them.

Serves 2

12 small, waxy potatoes, about 400g (Maris Peer, Charlotte),
   halved and washed
20g butter, or 1 tbsp butter plus 1 tsp extra virgin olive oil
Salt and freshly ground black pepper

Put the potatoes into a medium sauté or frying pan. Add just enough water to cover them, the butter (or butter and olive oil) and a tiny pinch of salt. Put the pan on a high heat and bring to the boil. Turn the heat to medium. Cover but leave the lid slightly ajar to let the steam escape. Simmer for 10–12 minutes or until the potatoes are just soft.

Turn the potatoes so they're all cut side down. Turn up the heat and boil for 5 minutes or until almost all of the liquid has evaporated and the potatoes are glazed in a buttery sheen. Take the pan off the heat. Season to taste with salt and pepper. Cut off a piece of potato and taste to check that it is cooked.

Sautéed potatoes

Simmered potatoes will sauté better if they are very dry, as they're less likely to stick to the pan and will get a thicker crust.

Serves 2

300–400g small waxy potatoes (Maris Peer, Charlotte),
   halved and washed
1 tbsp vegetable oil
10g butter
Salt and freshly ground black pepper

Boil your kettle. Put a colander in your sink. Fill a medium saucepan with boiling water. Add salt. Now add the potatoes and bring to the boil. Lower the heat and simmer for 12 minutes or until the potatoes are just soft. Drain the potatoes, then leave them to sit for at least 5 minutes to allow the surface to dry a little. (They will fry better if you do this.)

Get a large frying pan. Place over a high heat and add the oil. When it is very hot, add the potatoes, cut side down. Lower the heat to medium and fry for 5 minutes or until the potatoes are golden. Meanwhile, put a bowl next to your stove (to drain the fat into). Drain the fat.

Add the butter to the frying pan. Toss the potatoes over the heat for 20–30 seconds until they are coated in the butter and start to smell nutty. Turn off the heat. Season to taste with salt and pepper. Cut off a piece of potato and taste to check that it is cooked.

Rice

I use the absorption method to cook rice, which results in fluffy, separate grains. The rice will keep warm for 10 minutes once it's cooked if you cover it with a clean tea towel or leave the lid very slightly ajar.

The basic technique For 2 portions, put 125g long-grain white, basmati or red rice into a sieve. Rinse very well under cold running water, ideally until the water that comes out is no longer murky. Shake it very dry.

Measure 375ml water for white rice, 350ml for basmati, or 500ml for red rice. Get a small saucepan. Add the water, rice and ¼ tsp salt. Bring to the boil. Cover and simmer over your lowest heat. Allow 15 minutes for white rice, 12 minutes for basmati, 35–40 minutes for red rice. (Don't take the lid off or stir.) Turn off the heat. Check that the rice has absorbed all of the water and taste; it may seem very slightly chalky in the centre, that's ok. Put the lid back on. It needs to sit now to let the heat get evenly through to the centre of the rice grains. After 5 minutes, uncover and fluff the rice with a fork.

Quick polenta

Since I was introduced to 1-minute polenta I've turned to it for a side dish every time I want mash but don't have time. Polenta is just ground corn.

The basic technique For 2 portions, put 450ml water, milk or stock into a medium saucepan. Bring to the boil. Take the pan off the heat and add 80g 1-minute polenta in a slow, steady stream. Whisk nonstop until there are no lumps. Return to the heat and bring to the boil. Stir for 1 minute. Be careful as it will boil volcanically. Take the pan off the heat. Stir in 25g grated Cheddar and 25g butter or olive oil. The polenta will be quite soupy, like very soft porridge, but it will thicken as it cools. If it gets firmer than you'd like before you're ready to serve, add 2–3 tbsp of boiling water. Season to taste with salt and pepper.

Polenta chips Use 110g polenta and 400ml stock. Cook as above, then spread the polenta to a 3cm thickness in an oiled tray or container. Leave it in the fridge for an hour to set, or for up to 2 days. Cut the hard polenta into chips. Heat a non-stick frying pan. When it's very hot, shallow-fry the polenta chips with vegetable oil over a medium heat for 2–3 minutes until golden.

Couscous

I put normal white couscous into a heatproof bowl, pour boiling water over it, cover and leave it for 5 minutes to cook in the residual heat. Cooking times can vary, so follow the packet instructions. Once it is cooked, I fork through the couscous to separate the grains. Plain giant couscous needs to be boiled for 6–8 minutes, wholewheat giant couscous for 8–10 minutes.

Quinoa

Quinoa is a wonderful, nutty grain that is great for soaking up gravy and for salads. Once cooked, it'll keep for 2 days in the fridge and freezes well.

The basic technique For 2 portions, bring 360ml water to the boil with 1 tbsp of extra virgin olive oil and a large pinch of salt. Add 120g quinoa. Cover and simmer gently for 15 minutes or until tender. Taste. Turn off the heat. Leave to sit for 5 minutes. Fluff up with a fork. Season to taste. (You can also buy it pre-cooked.)

Pulses

I use Puy lentils, chickpeas and cannellini, flageolet, haricot and red kidney beans in the recipes in this book. More often than not I use tins or pouches. If you prefer to soak and cook your own pulses, 250g dried pulses will yield about 750g once cooked; 125g of cooked beans or lentils is a good portion. Cooking times vary greatly according to the type of pulse, length of storage and the hardness of your water. Puy lentils don't need to be soaked; they cook in 45 minutes, longer if braised.

The basic technique Soak dried pulses (except Puy lentils, see above) for 12 hours in roughly 10 times their volume of water. Or, to speed up, put into a large saucepan, bring to the boil and simmer for 4 minutes. Take off the heat, then leave to soak for 1 hour. Red kidney beans must be boiled for 10 minutes and the water discarded before soaking.

Drain the pulse and rinse thoroughly. Put it into a large pot. Cover with water. Bring to the boil and boil for 2 minutes. Turn the heat down. Cover, but leave the lid slightly ajar. Simmer gently for 1½–3 hours (it varies so much) until tender. Season to taste, then take off the heat. Cover the pan fully, then leave the pulse to sit in its cooking liquid for 10–15 minutes to absorb the seasoning and finish cooking. Drain if you don't need the liquid.

Freeze what you don't use in 250g quantities to give the same drained weight as the tins used in the recipes (ie two portions).

Chickpea (and other pulse) purées

Chickpea purée is familiar as hummus, but it's good hot too. Where I've used half a tin of chickpeas in a main recipe, I suggest making a purée with the rest. You can also do this with tinned lentils. (Cannellini, flageolet and haricot beans go gluey and are better mashed.) You can season the purée with salt and whatever spice or citrus you're using in your recipe, or leave it plain.

The basic technique Tip a 400g tin of chickpeas with its liquid into a small saucepan (or 240g home-cooked chickpeas plus 160ml cooking liquid). Add a pinch of salt. Bring to the boil and boil rapidly for 2–3 minutes until the liquid has reduced by about two-thirds. Tip into a blender, add 2 tbsp of extra virgin olive oil and process for 3–4 minutes to a smooth purée. Season to taste with salt and pepper. Add hot water if it's too thick.

Pasta

Most dried pasta cooks in 11–13 minutes, most fresh pasta in 3–4 minutes, but different brands and varieties of pasta vary, so please look at the packet instructions. I like to eat pasta when it's just cooked through but certainly not 'al dente'. Simply cook your pasta as much or as little as you prefer. 100g of dried pasta makes a good portion for a main course with sauce, 50g is about right for a side dish. Weigh your pasta, because if you use more than the recipe says, it will change the balance of pasta and sauce, so it won't taste as good. A 500g packet will yield 5 main course or 10 side dish portions.

Cooking Use your biggest pan, three-quarters full of salted water. There's no need to add oil – it will not stop your pasta sticking together, lots of furiously boiling water on your highest heat will. The pasta needs space to roll around for it to cook evenly and its starch to disperse into the water. If the pan is too small or there's not enough water, the starch boils back into the pasta, then when you drain it, the starch acts like glue and sticks the pasta together.

When the water boils furiously, add the pasta, put the lid on and bring back to the boil. Now, take the lid off and cook at a rolling boil. Taste your pasta after boiling it for a few minutes less than the packet tells you to. If you like it, it's ready; if you don't, boil it for a few minutes longer, then taste it again. Before you drain your pasta, take the pan off the heat and fill a mug with some of the cooking water to keep for your aftercare. A few spoonfuls of this water help to keep the drained pasta slippery because it's starchy and clings to the pasta.

Draining and aftercare Boil your kettle. Drain the cooked pasta in your colander. Pour boiling water from your kettle over the top. Shake off all the water; more water than you want in your pasta will leak into and dilute your sauce. Next, vitally, return your pasta to the hot empty pan. Put it on a very low heat. Stir in 1–2 tbsp per portion of olive oil, butter or the pasta's cooking water (or a mixture of the cooking water and oil or butter). Turn off the heat. Toss the pasta with tongs for 10 seconds until it is slippery, evenly coated and glossy. Add more pasta water, 1 tbsp at a time, if you need to. Season to taste. This aftercare makes your pasta hotter, better seasoned and better textured.

Keeping pasta warm If your drained pasta is ready before you are, leave it in your colander and toss it with 1–2 tbsp of olive oil. Fill the cooking pot one-quarter full with hot water. Put the colander on top, then put the pan lid on top of the colander. Put the pan over a low heat and you'll have an extra 5 minutes. When ready to serve, discard the water in the pan, return the pasta to the pan, and continue with the aftercare as above, only adding more oil as you need to.

EGGS & EXTRAS

Keep some eggs handy for an almost instant meal, a burst of saucy yolk or to bulk out more expensive protein.

Boiled eggs

Boil your kettle. Get a medium pan. Fill it with boiling water. Bring to the boil. Add 2 large eggs. Simmer for 4½ minutes for soft-boiled eggs for dipping; 7½ minutes for soft-boiled eggs for peeling; 8½ minutes for medium-boiled eggs; and 9½ minutes for hard-boiled eggs. For eggs that you will peel to eat cold, drain them and put them into a very large bowl of cold water or run them under cold water until they are completely cold. (If there is any warmth left in the egg you'll get a green ring around the yolk.)

Fried eggs

If your oven is hot this is a great way to fry eggs. Have your oven at 200°C/ Gas 6. Melt a knob of butter in a non-stick ovenproof pan. When it sizzles, but before it starts to go brown, break your eggs into the pan. Put the pan in the oven for 1½–2 minutes or until the egg whites are just set – they cook very evenly rather than just on the bottom. If your oven isn't on, start the same way, over a gentle heat, then put a lid on top for 2–3 minutes.

Quick sides

This is a list of bits and bobs that I love because it's much easier to cook a fresh meal when part of it is prepared for you. It's ok to ask a bag of frozen peas or a packet of polenta for a hand and it's great to serve vegetables, grains or pulses you've intentionally cooked more than you needed another time and frozen, then reheated for your side dish. You could serve hot buttered popcorn on the side with some gravy, or tortilla chips with a main course salad. Make sure you always have half-baked baguettes in your freezer. A freshly baked baguette is a great way to cheer yourself up, and you don't need both bread and another carbohydrate; bread and a vegetable will do. Make croûtons if you want a bit of crunch: rub a bit of bread with garlic, toast it in the toaster, then brush it lightly with olive oil and cut into cubes.

Cupboard Tinned chickpeas, lentils and beans; pre-cooked lentils and grains in pouches; 1-minute polenta; medium egg noodles; straight-to-wok noodles. Bottled or tinned pre-cooked peppers in oil or brine; tins or jars of artichoke hearts; tinned corn. Popcorn, tortilla chips and prawn crackers.

Freezer Grains and rice that you've cooked ahead and then frozen. Frozen peas, broad beans and soya beans. Vegetables that you've cooked twice as much as you need of and then frozen. Oven chips. Pita, naan and bread with lots of seeds and grains.

Fridge Beetroot in vacuum packs. Sunblush tomatoes in oil.

ACKNOWLEDGEMENTS

Dedicated to Diana and Peter Knab with love. Thank you for being there when I needed it most. I think about you and thank you every day.

This book was a glorious collaboration. Thanks to my amazing agent Ben Mason who taught me how to structure and write my proposal, then forged my link with Bloomsbury. The brilliant and magical Richard Atkinson, my commissioning editor, without whose vision the book literally wouldn't have been what it is, guided and inspired me with great intelligence and kindness. The hugely talented senior editor Natalie Hunt ('General Nat'), an amazing woman who led and conducted us all beautifully and made every part of this book better. The wonderful project editor Janet Illsley, who improved the text with endless skill, patience and attention to detail. The lovely Xa Shaw Stewart, proofreader Sally Somers and indexer Hilary Bird for their valuable contributions.

Gigantic thanks to Peter Knab, the most brilliant photographer and mate a cook could ever hope for; nearly half of the pages in this book are Pete's, and his beautiful work makes the food leap off each one. Xenia Van Oswald, the fantastic home economist, made the hard shoots easier. Thanks also too the lovely people at China and Co for their props.

Huge thanks to Peter Dawson and Louise Evans at Grade Design. Their work is so wonderful that each time I saw a new one of their original designs that light up this book, from the magnificent cover onwards, I would shriek with delight. At Bloomsbury, thanks to Penny Edwards and Polly Napper in production, to Jude Drake, Amanda Shipp, Inez Munsch, Sam Fanaken and Kathleen Farrar and her team at Bloomsbury Australia. Thanks to Sarah Randell and Sue Robinson for commissioning versions of Sorcery, and to Casilda Grigg for commissioning a Magic Fridge article. You all encouraged me to keep going.

Thanks to three geniuses who inspire me endlessly: Raymond Blanc, Delia Smith and Justin North. To earlier inspirations: Martin Bosley, Don Alfonso Iaccarino and my family Marian, Dylan, Penn, Dad, Anna, Tomo and Mum-in-Law Cecilie. My mate Colin Ring who physically delivered my manuscript. Simon Atkinson. Fiona Hamilton-Fairley at thekidscookeryschool.co.uk charity. Thanks to Mary O'Hare, you were there too. Thanks to Clive Moxham, Terence Faulkner, Chris Waters, Martin Macklin, Mark Leatham and Olivier Leatham at Merchant Gourmet for their support and their wonderful ingredients that I cook so often.

Thanks to my sons Jake and James and my goddaughter Casey who make me the happiest man alive. And now to superwoman. Along with working, looking after our two most glorious collaborations Jake and James, and doing everything in the house, Jess did all the shopping, tested, tasted, washed every dish, found lots of props, drove me to shoots, read every word from first scribble to final proof and helped me enormously with everything.

I love you Jess, thank you, this is as much your book as it is mine.

INDEX

Bloomsbury Publishing Plc
50 Bedford Square
London WC1B 3DP
Bloomsbury Publishing, London, New York, Berlin and Sydney

A CIP catalogue record for this book is available from the British Library

ISBN 978 1 4088 1093 4

10 9 8 7 6 5 4 3 2 1

Project editor: Janet Illsley
Designer: Peter Dawson with Louise Evans, www.gradedesign.com
Photographer: Peter Knab
Indexer: Hilary Bird

Printed in China by C & C Offset Printing Co Ltd

www.bloomsbury.com/alexmackay
www.alexmackay.com